# SIXTIES PEOPLE

# SIXTIES PEOPLE

## Jane and Michael Stern

Alfred A. Knopf   New York   1990

THIS IS A BORZOI BOOK
PUBLISHED BY ALFRED A. KNOPF, INC.

Library of Congress Cataloging-in-Publication Data
Stern, Jane.
    Sixties people/Jane and Michael Stern.
       p.   cm.
    ISBN 0-394-57050-2
      1. United States—History—1961–1969.   2. United States—Social
conditions—1960–1980.   3. United States—Popular culture—
History—20th century.   I. Stern, Michael, [*date*]   II. Title.
III. Title: 60s people.
E841.S74   1990
973.92—dc19      89-30871
                           CIP

Manufactured in the United States of America
First Edition

TO JOHN, JOHANNA, SUSAN, AND MARK ROBOHM

# CONTENTS

# ACKNOWLEDGMENTS

WE THANK our intrepid editor, Martha Kaplan, who valiantly stuck by us as we relived the sixties. Thanks to Iris Weinstein for the groovy design of this book; Carol Janeway for the inspiration; and Mary Maguire—our favorite perky girl—for always being there to help. Thanks also to Brenda McCallum for guiding us through the Library of Popular Culture at Bowling Green University; Richelle Frabotta and Sara Palmer for their proficiency as researchers; Maggie Berkvist for her unerring eye in the search for photos; and Sally Barker-Benfield, proprietor of Die Laughing, for sharing her mod library. And, as always, we thank Bob Gottlieb for his editorial advice.

# SIXTIES
# PEOPLE

# INTRODUCTION

WE ARE sixties people. In 1960, we were wide-eyed fourteen-year-olds, twisting like mad to Chubby Checker's hit record. By the end of the decade, we had met at college during a student strike, married, and after graduation lived with a group of long-haired friends, spending our days baking loaves of lumpy seven-grain bread and walking our dog, who sported a hippie-style bandanna around his neck.

Now that we are in our sober middle years, it is embarrassing and startling to look back on the number

*Jane Stern, 1966*

of changes we went through during the decade. Our attic tells a story of many incarnations. Its trunks contain love beads and a Nehru jacket, hootenanny song books, an empty beer keg with a fraternity emblem, a Beatle wig, a disposable paper dress, go-go boots, an "American Bandstand" souvenir book, a first edition of *Sex and the Single Girl*, a wig done up in a flip like Mary Tyler Moore's, a poster that says KILL THE PIGS, and a 45-rpm record of Sergeant Barry Sadler singing "The Ballad of the Green Beret."

*Michael Stern, 1966*

Sometimes we look at this patchwork quilt of discarded identities and wonder: Who were we? In fact, we probably weren't much different than many sixties people who fell in love with the cavalcade of new identities that swept through that prodigious decade. The sixties were a time when, like so many in our generation, we craved to ally ourselves with something bigger and more momentous than our single selves: the newest cause, the latest fad, the hippest beat. It felt important to let the world know where we stood and who we were.

It is customary to remember the sixties as a pageant of big events, great speeches, and tumultuous social unrest. They were all these things, but most people (like us) were not at the front lines of the war, or hobnobbing with the jet set, or burning down the dean's office. The decade's significant moments touched us in that public way which made the sixties feel like a group event. If the seventies were to become the Me Decade, the sixties were the We Decade. It was not a time for alienation. Big news felt like a family affair. When reports of John Kennedy's assassination came over the PA systems in our high schools in 1963, classmates cried in each other's arms. When we watched the Beatles perform on "Ed Sullivan" in 1964, we knew there were millions of teenagers like us, squealing with joy every time John, Paul, George, or Ringo shook his hair.

To capture the essence of sixties people for this book, we have tried to look beyond front-page events. Our interest is in the shapes and sounds and smells of life as real people lived it: in shared attitudes and fashion statements, in hit records, dance crazes, sideburns, hemlines, recipes, popular colognes, and college yearbooks. History's dustbin, like our attic, can be a fascinating cache of details. It is out of details that lifestyles are built, and through them that people signify their ideals.

These kinds of details show how people see themselves, and what image they want to parade down the street. As children of the sixties ourselves, we experienced the big events and important people of the time through such details. For us, the drama of the Black Panthers was their style; the flashy malevolence of their berets and bandoliers and the dauntless tone of their rhetoric meant far more than their ten-point party platform. We thought peace and love were good ideas in 1967; but to be honest, what we really liked was the way we looked in flowing hippie caftans with wildflowers stuck in our long hair. During the mod years, it was easy to believe that if we ordered hip-hugger slacks from Sears's "Carnaby Corner" catalog, somebody might mistake us for a real live Brit; before that, we half-imagined that by playing "Railroad Bill" on the guitar in high-school assembly, our friends just might be convinced that we had known our share of ramblin' and gamblin'.

We wanted to be as sensational as the Beatles, as perky as Marlo Thomas, as cool as James Bond, as hip as Ken Kesey, as tan as a surfer, and as tough as a Hell's Angel. And that is the lesson we learned from the contents of our attic trunk: the sixties were a moonstruck time when people were smitten with new identities, then insouciantly discarded them in search of the next one, always looking for the true light and the real meaning of life.

Original lifestyles blossomed because the sixties were obsessed by the idea that the time had come to start fresh. The decade arrived like a shaken-up bottle of champagne: full of fizz and ready to gush as soon as someone popped the cork. "The torch has been passed to a new generation of Americans," John F. Kennedy said in his inaugural address; and we took him at his word. The world was becoming ours; it was a privilege and a duty—and it was fun —to feel part of a pioneering generation.

Tom Wolfe described the sixties as the "decade when manners and morals, styles of living, attitudes towards the world changed the country more crucially than any political event." We add that it was also a time when it was possible to walk down any street and tell just by looking at someone where he or she stood politically, sexually, and philosophically. Sixties people wore their lifestyles as proudly as the slogan buttons they pinned to their shirts.

Each of the sixties people we describe in this book had a distinct idea of what a better world would be. Some wanted to save it; others wanted to blow it up; a few just wanted to find a pair of fun pantyhose.

In retrospect the sixties were as laughable as they were profound; but it would be hard to imagine a more thrilling time to grow up. The sixties put an indelible mark on all of us who lived through them. To this day, when we hear Chubby Checker yell out, "Come on, baby, let's do the twist," we are up on our feet swiveling our aging pelvises like fourteen-year-olds with ten bright years ahead.

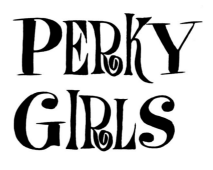

# PERKY GIRLS

SHE'S A PIXIE, a Peter Pan type with a daybreaking smile and mischief in her eyes, and she's finding it hard to believe that she is living in a real world, what with one fabulous thing after another happening to her!"

The enchanted pixie described by *Teen* in May 1963 was Cindy Carol, who was walking on air because she had just been chosen to play "the most enviable role in cinema history"—Gidget in *Gidget Goes to Rome. Teen* showed pictures of Cindy in New York on her way to fabulous Rome—jumping for joy in Times Square, craning her neck to look at tall buildings, and peering through the "magic heart-shaped window" display at Tiffany's—and enumerated these reasons why she was perfect for the role:

She loves life.

She lives joyously.

She thinks positively.

She has a long flip with a left part and full bangs brushed to the right.

She is a great kidder and shakes you up unexpectedly with some devastating remark just when you think she's curled up to do a little quiet thinking.

Cindy Carol was, in other words, the consummate perky girl. She embodied all the qualities of an all-new, uptempo, happy-go-lucky sixties person who peppermint-twisted her way onto center stage as the curtain rose on a decade that promised to be fun. When asked to describe herself, Cindy said, "I'm hysterically happy." The perky girl was a living exclamation point.

Perky girls personify that giddy time after Eisenhower when the world seemed to bubble over with endless expectations of good things to come. "As much as you like; to your heart's content; galore": that is how the *Random House Dictionary of the English Language* describes a phrase that originated in the early years of the sixties—"à go-go."

Life was spectacular—men were getting shot into space! It was a supremely presumptuous moment in history, when the prevailing attitude was one of self-amazement. We were so *modern*, so *capable!* (The world's got problems? We will solve them! We will form a Peace Corps; we will end colonialism; we will go on a Freedom Ride. Anything was possible.) The good

life that had been promised since the end of World War II was *here, now!* The sixties were flying high when they began. The perky girl's favorite expression was "Wheeee!"

Oh, what joy to be fresh, young, and female in 1960! To live in a world of lollipops, shaggy sheep dogs, outrageous bean-bag easy chairs, and wacky homegrown avocado plants! To skip through life's garden of daisies in a thigh-high skirt, polka-dot stretch-knit hose, and poor-boy sweater—spread pep, turn heads, make the world laugh wherever you go! A perky girl believed in sunshine.

She seems so frivolous now, when most people think of the sixties as a time of civil-rights protests and Vietnam anguish and LSD hallucinations. Unless you catch a television rerun of Marlo Thomas in "That Girl" or pick up a mid-sixties issue of *Cosmopolitan*, it is easy to forget how much her flibbertigibbet disposition defined an ideal of young womanhood back then. But the perky girl's influence on history cannot be dismissed. Although she quickly seemed obsolete in a decade that yearned for *issues*, her vigor got things off to a running start. The perky girl was proof that a new decade had begun.

Today she gets none of the respect customarily tendered more "serious" sixties people like folkniks or protesters. Nevertheless, her indestructible panache was a foundation on which the decade was built. Her insistence on being happy—*now!*—was the first glimmer of a whole generation bent on finding total joy. She discovered the good-times thing long before hippies based a lifestyle on getting high.

The perky girl's nonstop, heels-in-the-air image was everywhere. Suddenly there were hordes of TV sit-com bachelorettes living fantasy lives in kicky apartments all over town. Models in magazines looked girlish instead of womanly, and their poses required the elastic spine of Gumby.

It was more than a physical image. For illustrator Jon Whitcomb, who drew perky girls in national magazines, it was a matter of *spirit*. Whitcomb was to the early sixties what Charles Dana Gibson had been to the turn of the century—the commercial illustrator who captured the moment's ideal of womanhood: great winsome eyes that always looked surprised, heavy, fringed nylon-and-natural glue-on eyelashes, silly sun hats, slim limbs, windblown hair, ready for fun. In *All About Girls*, a book he wrote in 1962, he describes his ideal:

> She may be allergic to yellow, mad for dill pickles, unafraid of mice, experienced at balloon ascensions, anesthetic to pepper, superstitious about the number seventeen, well-read on meristematic plant tissues, an authority on affine geometry or slightly deaf in the left ear. She may collect Strasbourg faience or dime store earrings. She may have fallen in love with her fiance, like one girl I know, "because the back of his neck was so adorable." She may get dizzy on second floor balconies and seasick on carousels. She may be unable to spell words with e,i, or i,e, in them. She may have a passion for parades, the Permian Period, Peridots, or the game of pelota.

Thirty years later, this seems like a description of a thoroughly annoying and neurotic woman by an equally annoying, compulsive man. But to the sixties, such a collection of zany traits—accompanied by the shimmer of long shiny hair, a skipping gait, and a carefree, come-what-may smile—added up to perky perfection.

She behaved as if she were on camera, always ready if, by chance, some handsome guy with a Nikon should catch her doing a spontaneous thing like jumping into the fountain in front of the Plaza Hotel, or taking a ring from a box of Cracker Jack into a fine jewelry store for engraving. She posed herself in special ways designed to make her look as if she were rushing frantically from one fun activity to another: mouth agape with an exultant *"Oh!"* and eyes wide with surprise; bent around at the waist as if caught dancing the twist with knees akimbo, or fingers snapping and heels kicked back like a "Hullabaloo" go-go girl; throwing her hat in the air; jumping straight up, all four limbs outstretched with glee.

Did anybody really live like this? Goldie Hawn did, in *Cactus Flower*. Jane Fonda did, in *Barefoot in the Park*. As for real women living real lives, they could only try. They could hope to exorcise glum thoughts and mundane situations from every moment of their lives by choosing upbeat cosmetics and the most ebullient apartment decor. Perky girlhood was less a real life style than it was an ideal, something to strive for. It was a public image, a way of presenting a happy face to the world. It was a façade of optimism possible only in an era that had yet to invent such concepts as finding oneself and self-realization. In the pre–Me Generation days, it was a worthy enough goal to simply radiate cheer with the constancy of the sun.

In fact, it was these irrepressible girls, working as shop girls in boutiques, who first began telling their customers—other young perky girls—to *have a nice day*.

And why shouldn't you have a nice day if you were young and wide-eyed in 1960? You didn't need a crystal ball to know that the next ten years were

*Twiggy and a plastic mannequin*

going to be *so much more fun* than the drab old girdle-pinched, station-wagon fifties.

Even cars were getting cute. Customers had tired of the finned and chrome-laden Bulgemobiles that lurched through the 1950s; they were beginning to buy a lovable little import called a Beetle. To counteract it in 1960, GM and Ford introduced small cars with swift names—the Corvair and the Falcon.

Social dancing was restyled, too, away from bulk towards briskness. To replace the elaborately choreographed lindy that had been the fast-dance standard through the fifties, the new decade hurtled onto the dance floor with an onslaught of kooky new steps such as the twist, the mashed potato, the watusi, the loco-motion, the swim, and the hully gully: pure fun! To dance these dances was to ride the wave of brash, anything-is-possible energy that launched the sixties and animated the perky girl.

Along with new dance steps came a revolution in underwear. Sheer stockings were antiquated; "lively legs" hose with patterns and textures was in. Garter belts and girdles made way for pettipants, then tights, and finally the grand climax of leg liberation, pantyhose, which let girls show their whole leg right up to the crotch. In pantyhose, you could do the monkey on the dance floor or twirl along a city street like a dervish (oh, how perky girls loved to skip and spin as they moved!), letting your skirt ride high. By 1967, the revolution had succeeded: "You need to know the new leg language," *Redbook* told its readers in an article called "Young, Wild, Wonderful" about "the wild new look in stockings—new lengths, textures, and designs and a rainbow of colors—glittering gold, silver, copper, and bronze."

So, too, the world was ready for a new ideal of womanhood—cuter, quicker, and more streamlined than the overupholstered model that had reigned through the fifties. Swollen cleavages, Shalimar-scented lingerie and lace, big cherry-red-lipsticked mouths, and baroque skyscraper-high heels with seamed stockings appeared as suffocating to the sixties' pared-down feminine aesthetic as Lolita's mother was to Humbert Humbert's fantasies.

Contrast Twiggy, supermodel of the sixties known for her adolescent body and first-day-of-creation eyes, with the fifties' premier model, Suzy Parker, whose serpentine hips and knowing smile epitomized what preperky women were supposed to be. Twiggy (née Lesley Hornby), a sixteen-year-old cockney high-school dropout with long legs and no bust, was the prime symbol of postvoluptuous femininity. "Completely disarming and charming," *Vogue*'s Diana Vreeland declared. "She is the mini girl in the mini camera." Along with the right looks, Twiggy manifested the proper silly attitude of a perky girl. Asked how much money she had made as the world's top cover girl, she bubbled, "A skillion dollars."

It was impossible to be too buoyant. Goldie Hawn parlayed an ability to giggle into pantheon perky status in her appearances as the Sock-It-to-Me Girl on television's "Laugh-In." With turquoise eyes wide open, mouth locked in a permanent squeal of delight, short yolk-colored hair ruffled happily, she was known for teeny bikinis that left plenty of skin visible and on which were painted icons of sixties cheer: hearts, daisies, peace symbols.

Perky girls were free and happy, but not quite yet liberated. Young, slim charmers with shiny, unfettered hair and tastefully worn miniskirts, they braved the world with their cute little chins thrust forward; but when the going got rough, they were kittens, and they collapsed adorably into the strong arms of daddy, hubby, or boyfriend.

As television's "That Girl" between 1966 and 1971, Marlo Thomas, playing bachelorette Ann Marie, was the penultimate example, topped only by Mary Tyler Moore. According to the show's theme song, her life is one of diamonds and daisies; the credits show her whirling along Fifth Avenue wearing a wide-brimmed bonnet, an A-line dress coat as short as a little girl's, and childish white tights. She spins and hugs herself with glee; she gambols around the Plaza fountain; she feeds the pigeons; she winks at a department-store mannequin dressed in a bridal gown (the mannequin is her exact double!); and she frolics on her merry way.

There is no doubt in Ann Marie's mind that she will be somebody's beautiful bride, but not quite yet.

*Goldie Hawn*

For now she is enjoying the heady fun of being young and single in a big city. Meanwhile, she has her doting daddy to bail her out of such madcap situations as when she gets her toe stuck in a bowling ball. And she has a handsome boyfriend to have semichaste fun with. In the evolution of the single woman on television, "That Girl" was the midpoint between the crackbrained lunacy of Margie Albright in "My Little Margie" and the attractive aptitude of Mary Richards in "The Mary Tyler Moore Show."

It was Mary Tyler Moore who set the gold standard for perky perfection. She began her career, fittingly enough, playing the Happy Hotpoint pixie on stove commercials during "The Adventures of Ozzie and Harriet" in the fifties. Mary wore a leotard and danced around Harriet's kitchen, calling out in a squeaky voice, "Hi, Harriet. Aren't you glad you bought a Hotpoint?" In 1959, her legs had a featured role in "Richard Diamond, Private Detective." Then, as Laura Petrie, Dick Van Dyke's wife on "The Dick Van Dyke Show" (1961–66), Mary hit her perky stride. She played a young housewife who favored Jackie Kennedy–style sheath dresses and was always getting herself into trouble (dying her hair platinum blond, setting up Rob's friends on blind dates, adopting a herd of revolting dogs) but who never lost her toothy grin or got a run in her pantyhose.

It was in "The Mary Tyler Moore Show," which made its debut in 1970, that perkiness found its fullest expression. Mary Richards is a single girl in hip-hugger slacks with her first job in the big city. She lives in a kooky studio and has friends as colorful as her toss pillows: Rhoda, the insecure Jewish girl

from upstairs; ditsy Phyllis, the landlady; Murray, the kindly schlep; and her bearish but adorable boss, Mr. Grant. As the sit-com characters evolved, and Mr. Grant was divorced, this momentous question arose but was never resolved: Would Mary sleep with Mr. Grant?

Did perky girls sleep with anyone? That was one of the sixties' great enigmas. Unlike their skinny, high-hemmed spiritual forebears, the flappers of the twenties, perky girls did not reek of "It." They were not hot youths. In fact, sex in all its sweaty, fleshy heat was antithetical to perky girls' squeaky-clean personalities.

And yet it was a confusing situation, because perky girls had something no other women in history

*Dick Van Dyke and Mary Tyler Moore,*
*"The Dick Van Dyke Show"*

had had: a convenient method of birth control. On May 9, 1960, the Federal Drug Administration declared Enovid—the first birth-control pill—safe for prescription sales. Within six years, one out of five women of child-bearing age had a prescription. Sixties people were infatuated with "the pill" (no need to say "birth-control pill"; in the sixties, there was only one pill that mattered). It was a prime symbol of modern life in general, and modern women in particular.

Thanks to the pill, carefree sex became yet another of the futuristic possibilities that the new decade offered. A girl on the pill could have sex any time she pleased; she was always ready; she could do it, if she wanted, just for fun! Later in the sixties, hippies would extol the pill as their permit to make free love. For the perky girl, it was not so simple. She didn't want to overthrow morality; she was not a slut. But neither did biology require her to be a prude anymore. The existence of the pill became an essential ingredient in the perky girl's coquettish personality. Clairol began to ask "Does she or doesn't she?" (about hair dye). You never quite knew for sure about a perky girl.

It is for this reason that Doris Day, a pioneer of sunshiny cuteness, lost her cachet in the age of perkiness. By the mid-sixties, Miss Day was broad in the beam, dressed in matronly bouclé suits and looking very middle-aged. But the real problem was her fabled virginity. It hung in the air like a stale cloud. Although never trampy, perky girls were much too modern to make such a fuss about their hymens.

Feminine idols of past generations had at least a few years to grow regal with age. But because her appeal was that she was garden fresh, the perky girl's moment of perfection was as short-lived as a cut flower's. At the first hint of a varicose vein showing through her fishnet stockings, or a tummy bulge in the poor boy, she was as useless as a worn-out paper dress.

Permanence, like seriousness, was regarded with contempt as being so old-fashioned and boring. Good things in the go-go world were designed to evaporate fast. Happenings were groovy because they self-destructed as they occurred, leaving no fusty old art to hang on a wall. Aluminum foil was more fun than sterling silver; and once word got out that Andy Warhol (master of impermanence) papered his studio walls with it, cheap silver paper became *the* material of choice—for walls, book and magazine covers, body paint, and bikinis. Outrageous costume jewelry was ever so much wiggier than diamonds; disposable dresses more of a kick than any Chanel original.

No commodity was more perishable than youth, and so perky girls were the most beloved objects of all. Everything about them suggested perishability; they strove to seem as evanescent as a soap bubble: weightless and so full of pep and dithery non sequiturs that if you gave them a helium balloon to hold, they might just float off into the ether.

In fact, the basic perky hairstyle was designed to make a perky girl's head resemble a balloon. It was called "the bubble." It was round, or slightly tapered with a nose-cone top, no bigger than a football helmet. The bubble

*Perky girls wore perky girdles.*

was teased, but only enough to give it body—never so much that it acquired the kind of weight flaunted by the sculpted 'dos of the vulgarians. A bubble had sides that swept down in front of the ears, forming cheek curls, known as "guiches"—sweet little wisps of hair stuck in place with hair spray or clear nail polish. As a single, out-of-balance accent, a klippie bow might be secured on one side over the temple.

The most popular variation of the bubble was the artichoke. The artichoke got its name because if you stood on a ladder looking straight down at a perky girl's head, you would see petallike symmetry that resembled the leaves of an artichoke all around the nape, towards which the entire unit tapered inward.

Close to the head, off the neck and forehead, the bubble circled and framed the face like the petals of a flower. It was girlish rather than womanly (so unwomanly in some versions, such as those worn by Judy Carne and Goldie Hawn, that you might even call it boyish). It seemed carefree; compared with the rigorous dips and contours of classic fifties hairstyles, or with the baroque extremes of the beehive, it was streamlined, with a distinct less-is-more modernity. It was nearly impervious to bad-weather fallout, allowing for uninhibited skipping and splashing through any kind of rain or humidity. On the other hand, the bubble was tidy and indisputably within all bounds of propriety. It was a perfect symbol for the morality that saturated so much of the early sixties: saucy and fun but in no way intemperate.

Long hair was old-fashioned and ladylike, wadded up in chignons and French twists—not appropriate for pixies. "Wear a 'little head' look," advised *The Hairdo Handbook* in 1964. "Remember that men most often like 'little women.'"

For achieving the cute-little-head look, the only choice other than the bubble was the flip.

The flip, also called the Dutch flip, was a style in which the hair was cut all one length and hovered somewhere above the collarbone, where the ends flipped up and out neatly and evenly all around the circumference. Consider the name: "flip." There you have its meaning: up, up, and away; on the move; flippant and flirty. The flip was freer than the bubble, but that is not to say it wasn't tame. A good flip, like the perky girl who wore it, could be happy and bouncy, but it was ultimately well behaved.

There is no better chronicle of the flip's evolution than Mary Tyler Moore's progress though the sixties. As Laura Petrie, Mary began in 1961 with a flip so modest and short you could mistake it for a bubble with a ragged edge around the bottom. Five years later, during the last season of "The Dick Van Dyke Show," Mary sports a full-bore flip, lush and extravagant down to mid-neck level. Its only flaw as a paradigm is that it appears heavily sprayed (homage to the early sixties' taste for stiff coiffures) rather than bouncy. By the mid-sixties, bounciness was a vital element of the true perky flip. For the debut of "The Mary Tyler Moore Show" in 1970, flipped curls hang in a luxuriant semicircle just above Mary's shoulders; her hair is free and swingy enough to bounce at every tilt, dip, spin, and twist of her peripatetic jaunt through life.

It hardly seems fair, but despite Mary Tyler Moore's role in hair history as a flip pioneer, the prize for the finest rendition of this archetypal hairdo must be given to Marlo Thomas. Playing Ann Marie in "That Girl," Marlo was outfitted with an exquisite flip. It was flawlessly symmetrical, shoulder length with brow-brushing bangs, crowned by a colorful headband, and as glossy as a wet otter. It didn't hurt that this amazing piece of hair artistry was complemented by the most significant set of eyelashes in the annals of perkiness. (Eyelashes were second only to hair in their importance as perky-girl signifiers.)

The flip presented major problems for the white perky girl with frizzy hair. She resorted to straightening cream, formerly the exclusive province of black people, who used such emollients to create "conk jobs" in pre-Afro days. If a chemical fix didn't work, she ironed it on a board: set the iron for "silk" (not too hot), rest your head on the ironing board, and press away, section by section. The other alternative was to wrap the hair tightly around the head immediately after shampooing and clamp it into place with a triangular hair net. After unwrapping, the former frizzhead would have hair that was temporarily silk smooth and suitable for merry flipping from side to side while gallivanting down the avenue.

By the late sixties, hair fashions were in turmoil; and although many a true-hearted perky girl remained

loyal to her bubble or flip, a new
perky hairdo took center stage: the
long, blunt straight cut, ironed flat.
Whereas a few years earlier, short
hair had been considered girlish
and long hair matronly, the tables
quickly turned in 1966 and '67.
Short hair seemed constrained.
Long hair was beginning to look
unfettered and fun.

By the time Pat, Tricia, and Julie
Nixon hit the White House in 1969,
tightly styled little coifs reeked of
hair repression. Many perky girls
had begun to grow long hair to signify a free spirit. Long hair also had
the distinct advantage over the pixie
bubble in that it could be gathered
into adorable pigtails and tied with
brightly colored bows and ribbons.
However, this shiny Alice-in-Won-
derland coiffure which became a
late-sixties perky-girl favorite must
not be confused with hippies' long,
natural hair. Nor does it have any-

*"That Girl": Marlo Thomas*

thing in common with sophisticated chignons and French twists of the late
fifties, or long hair pulled back into a tight, Bohemian bun.

A perky girl's long straight hair was cut just below the shoulders, always
freshly shampooed, the ends trimmed with military precision, every last bit of
spring and curl expunged, and brushed to a gleaming polish. It was a true
test of youthfulness, because no woman over thirty could wear it and not look
idiotic.

Perky girls applied makeup using the same principles that determined
hairstyle. The purpose was to create the appearance of lightness and fresh-
ness. Nature's idea of fresh, however, was not nearly good enough. So the
perky girl invested heavily in un-cosmetics: sheer lip gloss in "nude" shades
that masqueraded as the glow of moist young lips; transparent face powders
that added no extra color but just a shimmer of light. These subtle unguents
were applied to the blank canvas of a face rendered squeaky clean by a scrub
with Love's Fresh Lemon cleanser—which reminded the user that its key
ingredient, the lemon, "makes your hair squeak, martinis shriek, now makes
your face shiny."

Lemons were the love apples of the sixties. Their scent and image pervaded
the cosmetics counter. The citrus tang of Jean Naté cologne was ubiquitous.

High-rolling perky girls liked the lemon-scented essence so much that they bought it packaged in bottles a foot and a half tall.

The uncomplicated astringency of lemon was a perfect scent metaphor for perky girls. It was neither fragile and feminine, like gardenia, nor aggressively overripe, like rose. It had a sunny essence that was squeaky clean rather than sticky sweet. This is not to say that the lemon scents of the sixties were subtle. They were loud and bright; they were aromatic hullabaloos. Love's Lemon Cologne, for example, was not a traditional verbena with an elusive acidic top note; it was a strident lemon-oil elixir that could leave its enthusiastic user smelling like a room full of just-polished English furniture.

Once a perky girl's face was citrused clean of all impure oils, refreshed by Pink-A-Dolly-Pink Beauty Mask, blushed and powdered into a pale maidenly hue, it was time to focus attention on the eyes.

Everything else about the face was diminished in order to accent the eyes. Eyes were the key to the essential look of sexy innocence—big, soft eyes shadowed by makeup applied with the dramatic adumbration of a Dutch master. Eye makeup was the one area where the values of fresh and natural held no sway whatsoever. In the pursuit of the look of wide-eyed innocence, eyes were outlined, sockets shadowed and painted, brows plucked out and redrawn, undereyes inscribed with lashlike patterns, and—the ocular pièce de résistance—lids were hung with gigantic, flirty sets of false eyelashes. Perky girls loved the tickle of eyelashes on their cheeks, the swoopier the better.

Thick, heavy lashes that stayed put were, however, a beauty challenge. "The care and application of false eyelashes can be very baffling," advised Virginia Graham in her 1967 beauty guide, Don't Blame the Mirror. "Those two little hairy strips seem to lead a life of their own and leap about like mercury." The perky girl worked as skillfully as a surgeon, trimming and feathering the lashes, applying just the right amount of surgical adhesive with an orange stick from a manicure set, then blending the attached lash to the real one with a dry mascara brush. Teenage perky girls in Florida in 1963 gave themselves an extra challenge by starting a fad of making lashes out of their boyfriends' hair, woven with nylon thread, permanent-waved, then shaped and trimmed before the grueling application process even began. Was it worth it? Beauty tipster Ellen Peck, author of How to Get a Teenage Boy and What to Do with Him When You Get Him, thought so. She declared eyelashes "the number one weapon in the arsenal of female flirtation."

The best example of eyelashes in action were those worn by Marlo Thomas in "That Girl." Watch any episode and you will gasp in awe at the close-ups of her looking right, left, down, and up. She is like some grand Kabuki actor —batting and flipping and lowering and hoisting the lashes, rolling and crossing her eyes (signifying cute zaniness). That Girl's multitiered lashes and painted eyes were the mirrors of the ever-active perky girl's soul.

In the soul: that was where the perky flame had to twinkle. Hairstyles and

makeup were only its outward signs.
The key ingredient in persuasive
perkiness was a girl's character, and
this was something that could not
be learned or faked. Look at all the
celebrities who tried but failed to
make the grade. Being perky was a
vaunted ideal, but for every That
Girl and Mary Tyler Moore, there
were a dozen grumpy stars who
strived in vain to persuade the public they were as fresh and young as
springtime.

Nancy Sinatra wore vinyl boots,
had a long, sassy mane of blond
hair, and looked smashing in size-
four miniskirts. She even had hit
records with "These Boots Are
Made for Walkin' " and "Some-
thin' Stupid" (the latter a duet with
her father, Frank). All the elements
of perkiness were there . . . except
for a black hole at the heart of her

*Nancy Sinatra: too tough to be perky*

strangely dolorous personality. Instead of helium-filled balloons of pretty colors, hearing Nancy sing in her strange, flat voice brought to mind a long suck
on an ether mask. No matter how hard she frugged (with co-star Elvis Presley
in *Speedway*) or tapped the heels of those calf-hugging boots, she appeared
to be a grim individual whose shoe-inspired repertoire appealed more to
fetishists than to aficionados of girlish bounce.

Lucille Ball and her daughter, Lucie Arnaz, were also washouts as perky
girls. In the fifties, as Lucy Ricardo in "I Love Lucy," Miss Ball had created
a character far too willful, relentless, and ingenious to ever be reduced to
mere perkiness. But when she returned to the small screen for "The Lucy
Show" (in 1962) and "Here's Lucy" (in 1968), she adjusted her demeanor to
fit the times. Scheming wives were passé, so Lucy got cute—unmercifully
cute. All of the energy that had gone into making Lucy Ricardo so hilarious
was now applied to the Herculean task of playing perky as a middle-aged
widow in a polyester pantsuit with a cigarette-ravaged croak of a voice. Lucie
Arnaz played her short-skirted, high-booted daughter in "Here's Lucy," but
like her mom, Miss Arnaz had a sandpaper voice and a belligerent acting
style that gave her attempts at perkiness a disturbing bawdy-house quality.

Also unable to pull it off were girls who were simply too rich and famous
for the lightness of character being perky required. Princess Margaret, the
thick-waisted, jowly, Hermès-babushkaed younger sister of Queen Elizabeth,

tried valiantly to be footloose and carefree during the mod years of the sixties, zipping about London on motor scooters, hobnobbing with the Beatles, and boogying in nightclubs. The queen disapproved; and although there was something wiggy about a member of the royal family doing the watusi, it was also a bit embarrassing. Anyone who hauls the history of the British empire on her shoulders can never appear truly lithe and carefree. Perky royalty is an oxymoron, or maybe just moronic.

Lyndon Johnson's daughters, Luci Baines and Lynda Bird, had similar problems. The soigné Kennedys were an impossible act to follow when the LBJs entered the White House in 1963, so the gals from Texas aimed for perkiness. After a battery of makeovers, Luci glowed: "Suddenly it's teensville on Pennsylvania Avenue," *Life* announced as she enthusiastically demonstrated the finer points of the frug and the hully gully on the White House lawn. Meanwhile, older sister Lynda played Eliza Doolittle to George Hamilton's Henry Higgins. George swept her into a jet-set life ogled by movie fan magazines. The problem was that in every picture of the two of them, Lynda looked clumsy and uncomfortable; it was George who played it perky to the hilt.

It was not easy to achieve perkiness, but the good news was that any hopeful young girl who wanted to try had at her disposal one of the most rousing lifestyle guidebooks ever written: *Sex and the Single Girl* by Helen Gurley Brown. Published in 1962, it formally introduced the world to perky girls with these words: "Far from being a creature to be pitied and patronized, the single girl is emerging as the newest glamor girl of our times." By its title alone, the book was guaranteed to raise eyebrows. Linking "sex" and "single girls" was simply taboo. Before the sixties, any single girl who admitted a comfortable acquaintance with sex was regarded, to be blunt, as a whore.

*Sex and the Single Girl* was an international best-seller, published in twenty-three countries, translated into fifteen languages, and made into a movie starring Natalie Wood and Tony Curtis. It was the first sixties manifesto for women in general, perky girls in particular.

Published two years after the

*Lucie Arnaz and Lucille Ball: too corny to be perky*

birth-control pill became readily available, it posited that not only do single girls have sex; they sometimes have sex for reasons other than to find a husband. They might actually have sex because it is fun! The fun factor made it far more scandalous than the old-fashioned kiddie-producing sex that was within the reach of their married sisters.

"When a man thinks of a married woman, no matter how lovely she is, he must inevitably picture her . . . fixing little children's lunches, or scrubbing them down because they've fallen in a mudhole," Ms. Brown wrote. "When a man thinks of a single woman, he pictures her alone in her apartment, smooth legs sheathed in pink silk Capri pants, lying tantalizingly among dozens of satin cushions, trying to read but not very successfully, for HE is in the room—filling her thoughts, her dreams, her life."

This was a revolutionary idea: being single might, in some cases, at some times, and in some situations, be better and more fun than being married! Not that it was bad to get married. The understanding in *Sex and the Single Girl* is that, of course, every woman wants and needs a man. But until that happy day comes, single life can be a great adventure.

*Sex and the Single Girl* created a new feminine ideal: the young, freewheeling girl who mesmerized men with her uninhibited antics. She was so full of

tricks and surprises and charm, no guy would notice that she wasn't rich or pretty. "Ride a Vespa!" Helen Gurley Brown advised. "Have a memorable beach hat or two. Carry a controversial book at all times. Paint your car hot orange or shocking pink." *Sex and the Single Girl* contains no advice for knitting pipe-holders or cooking pot roast. This new way to a man's heart was not by using such traditional womanly skills. It was by being perky.

Helen Gurley Brown pinpointed the true nature of the sixties perky girl because she was one, proudly self-created. She describes herself as being born in poverty in Arkansas, "homely, plagued with acne, flat-chested, not brilliant, and at times mean and cranky." She redid herself by force of will and re-emerged as the hair-tossing coquette that women envy and men fall in love with. She became slim and sexy and positively oozed upbeat thoughts. She was the girl whose office desk blotter was sunny yellow instead of drab green, who could whip up a Caesar salad for a hungry man or make a conversation piece out of a funny hat.

She had used her own life as a drawing board; and having gotten the formula right, she was passing it along to her readers. Her tone was that of a friend taking you aside to whisper the secrets of the universe in your ear, then cheering you on as you lived by them.

The genius of *Sex and the Single Girl* was that it gave hope to throngs of "mouseburgers"—Ms. Brown's pet phrase for the saggy-stocking set, who, she promised, could have it all if they simply learned the revised rules of man hunting. The new secret was this: no matter how hard you must, in Ms. Brown's words, "work like a son of a bitch" attaining perkiness, the image you present to the world must be as carefree and lighthearted as a butterfly.

After the success of *Sex and the Single Girl*, Helen Gurley Brown assumed editorship of *Cosmopolitan*, formerly a staid magazine aimed at married-with-children readers who were concerned with family life. Under her direction, *Cosmo* became a showcase for the new perky sensibility, filled with breezy, sexy advice for single girls who wanted to have fun.

*Cosmopolitan* regularly featured writers such as Nora Ephron, Gael Greene, Jill Robinson, Jeannie Sakol, and W. H. Manville, all of whom went on to more elevated subjects than "Why I Wear My False Eyelashes to Bed" (by Laura Cunningham, 1965). But in the heady days of perky primacy, they, too, were busy helping to define the lively style. Typical of their efforts was an article written by Veronica Geng titled "Scorn Not the Street Compliment," in which Ms. Geng tells readers how to walk down the street in such a manner as to provoke catcalls like "Hey, mama, you lookin' fine!" Her tips include: "Look alive! The archetypal spontaneous compliment lure is Julie Christie in her sashay down the street in *Billy Liar*, hair bouncing, legs swinging . . . fresh, free, energetic, opened up to the world." And: "If you *must* go out while down in the love dumps, please try to put a pleasant face on your mood for the people you'll see."

Because the *Cosmo* girl was taught to have a life NOW rather than wait for marriage, the magazine was chocked with advice about how a perky girl ought to decorate her apartment. The design principle was to clearly set the occupant apart from her married friends and parents; to celebrate that merry moment in life between college-dorm sloppiness and settled-down nest building. A perky apartment was as harebrained and fun-loving as a girl's budget allowed. It was assumed that the reader was squeaking by on a tiny salary, so most suggestions emphasized cleverness over cost. Ferns hung from macramé holders knotted to look like big-eyed owls. Bathtubs and toilet-seat covers were festooned with Rickie Tickie Stickies—glue-backed daisies that made boring old bathroom fixtures come alive. Fun rugs, like white long-haired flokatis, helped cover over a sad linoleum floor, and a lemon-scented freshener gave the air a happy citrus tang.

The perky girl's palate for home decoration was shades of screaming citrus. The prime color was yellow, the brightest possible yellow of lemons and sunshine and Smiley the happy face. Wowtones such as tropical orange and stinging pink were feminine and helped give the perky girl's digs a jolt of eccentricity in contrast to contemporary split-level family homes that featured brown pine paneling and appliances in Harvest Gold. That was the essential rationale behind every home-decorating decision: to distance yourself from the stodgy and conservative, to serve warning that you were young and carefree.

Furniture was chosen with an eye towards establishing the status for which all perky girls strived: being fun and "different." The perky girl did not want a Chesterfield sofa or a Barca-Lounger. She chose vinyl chair-shaped bean bags as squishy as a down pillow or inflatable rubber couches that got blown up with a bicycle pump. Or just pillows . . . nothing but pilllows! "I like them in all sizes," wrote Leslie Uggams in her *Beauty Book* (1966). "To sit on, lie on, or lean on." Not only were they delightfully ding-a-ling, such furnishings demanded that anyone who tried to sit or relax in them literally roll and pitch and rock—i.e., *move*—rather than sit still. In the apartment of the perky girl, movement equaled a good time.

Wall decor was employed to suggest the limitlessness of the perky girl's far-flung world. Swirly bright Peter Max posters told you how out-of-the-ordinary she was. Blowups of

COSMOPOLITAN
December, 1968
50¢

WHAT THE PILL
IS DOING
TO HUSBANDS

SINGLE GIRL'S
CHRISTMAS

WHY I DATE
OLDER MEN

SAMANTHA
EGGAR
COMES ON
STRONG

LBJ AND
WOMEN

THE MAN-TRAP
APARTMENT

STUNNING NEW
MYSTERY BY
FRANCIS CLIFFORD

Marcel Marceau in whiteface evoked France, which, despite a bent towards ruinous intellectualization in the sixties, remained a romantic Mecca for perky girls. Any travel poster was good in this respect—a reminder that the girl who furnished the apartment was an adventuress, bags packed and ready for fun. Helen Gurley Brown admitted to "a TWA matador over my kitchen stove that's really goosebumpy."

The item of preeminent perkiness in any apartment was the avocado plant. *Don't Swallow the Avocado Pit—and What to Do with the Rest of It* not only offered directions for growing that nutty tree out of yesterday's lunch (what a conversation starter!) but suggestions for Avocado Eye Refresher ("place avocado crescents under each eye—goodbye puffiness"); how to use your avocado plant as a Christmas tree; and how to meet men at competitive avocado-plant shows. An avocado tree was living proof that its modern young owner saw beauty in what other people thought of as garbage (the pit).

The best way to make an apartment truly perky was to do it all yourself. Creativity was an esteemed quality in the sixties; it was evidence of a fresh eye and a love of novelty, both of which proved one was modern. Making something cute from nothing was one of the fundamental perky-girl talents. The queen of the genre was a kicky young thing from Chicago named Sari, host of her own TV show, "Sari the Junkshopper." Nobody had more fun ideas for turning garbage into interior decoration than she did. In her book *Junk Shopping with Sari*, she shares a moment of personal triumph with her readers: "I remember a mirage of Beautiful People . . . people in granny glasses and fur boas, minks and silk hostess pajamas. . . . I could have felt lost in this crowd, but I had risen to the occasion. Not with my gown, but with a special 'junk shopper' touch—beautiful four inch long crystal earrings made from an old chandelier!" *There* is perkiness in action!

There were other good reasons to go junk shopping. Rummaging through refuse offered yet another clever way to meet a man, almost as good as an afternoon at an avocado-plant contest. Sari suggests "rubbling" as a fun activity for young lovers. "Rubbling" was her name for wandering through deserted tenements in search of that special newel post or discarded shingle.

Farm-bound perky girls had Rubye Mae Griffith and her husband, Frank, authors of *How to Make Something from Nothing*, to suggest ways to make life in the middle of nowhere nearly as kooky as breakfast at Tiffany's. Perhaps their cleverest idea was the "Dancing Dolphin" fountain sculpture, which *only* a farm girl could make. "If you don't happen to live on a ranch where the carcass of a cow may turn up in your stream bed, you may not be able to adorn your garden pool with this frivolous 'Flipper' made from the jawbone of a cow," they cautioned readers. "Surrounded by polished rocks, this flippant little fellow becomes an interesting attention getter—guaranteed to astonish your friends!"

Perky girls did not have gourmet kitchens in their apartments; being so active, they lacked the attention span needed to follow the laborious cooking techniques of Julia Child. They entertained by serving fun things to eat: foods with a dash of exotic flavoring that required little culinary skill but were as amusing as driving an orange motor scooter to work. Pauper's pizzas, chablis cheese spread, guacamole, and wiki-wiki hamburgers are some of the fun dishes suggested in the 1965 cookbook *Saucepans and the Single Girl.*

Written by Jinx Kragen and Judy Perry, *Saucepans and the Single Girl* was (according to its dust jacket) "guaranteed to do more for a bachelor girl's social life than long lash mascara or a new discotheque dress," with "all the ingredients for that light-hearted leap from filing cabinet to flambé."

Oh, envy those junior executives who showed up at Jinx and Judy's door, chilled bottle of Mateus in hand! How could they ever know the strategy of girlish wiles that created the meal they were about to eat?

According to *Saucepans and the Single Girl,* if he "drives a small red sports car, sails, skis, sips Irish coffee, or peruses the centerfold of a man's magazine," then he must get the meal entitled "Food Fit for a Man in a Brooks Brothers Suit": Flawless Fondue, Spinach and Bacon Salad, and Strawberries with Kirsch.

What do Jinx and Judy have in store for the epicurean snob who sits at dinner discussing Sub Gum Yuk and Fromage Glacé? Dazzle him with a "Gallant Gourmet" meal of lobster thermidor made with frozen rock lobster tails underneath handfuls of grated cheddar cheese!

Here is a recipe from *Saucepans and the Single Girl,* designed to impress all bachelors—especially if it's served by a hostess clad in Pucci printed palazzo pajamas, preceded by a very dry martini, and accompanied by a stack of "cool jazz" records piled on the turntable.

CLAM   BLOBS
1 package (3 ounces) cream cheese
1 can (7 ounces) minced clams
Dash Worcestershire sauce
Dash curry powder
Onion salt to taste
Garlic powder to taste
Toast rounds

Mix everything together but the toast rounds. Pile mixture on toast rounds and stick under broiler for 3–5 minutes. Sprinkle with paprika and serve now. Better triple this recipe!

With all the effort they applied to being attractive, having a charming apartment, making decorative fountains out of cow carcasses, and cooking things that made men swoon, it was inevitable that perky girls, no matter how coy, would ultimately confront the question of sex. *Cosmopolitan* tackled it head-on, offering copious bedroom tips for nice girls. In the same smiley tone that only a few years earlier would have instructed single misses how to press a dress hem, the magazine offered bachelorettes "The Etiquette of the Orgasm," including suggestions of when it is appropriate to fake one: the first time you go to bed with him, on an anniversary, when he's depressed, when he tries spectacularly hard.

Even freaky sex was part of *Cosmo*'s brave new world. "Pow! Bam! Splat! —Girls Who Like to Get Punched" warned of romantic entanglements with sadists. And "Things to Do with Your Hands That Men Like" offered such suggestions as "Brush him lightly all over with your face-blusher brush," "Take his temperature," and the ever-popular "Make a sandwich out of him and two pillows."

When *Cosmo* got downright raunchy, its basically lighthearted sensibility made everything seem clean. After all, the young woman it advised to "frolic in a man's chest hairs" was not some old tart. She was a fresh-faced perky girl with shampooed hair and sheets that smelled of Jean Naté cologne. In the world described by Helen Gurley Brown, sex had gone from nasty to merely naughty, and was on the verge of being nice.

Helen Gurley Brown followed *Sex and the Single Girl* with *Sex and the Office* in 1964, which celebrated the fact that at least until they got married, perky girls worked at jobs. Fun jobs, preferably, like dog walker, or balloon peddler at the children's zoo; but even for a drab office, Ms. Brown suggested a hundred ways to brighten up the desk with such female accessories as "sharpened pencils in a blue delft jar, a Can-can dancer's bronze foot for a paperweight, a cigarette box that is glass and gilt, red lacquer trays on which you keep two pretty teacups and a pot."

Of course, there was no need for such effort if a girl was lucky enough to land the greatest and most glorious of all feminine jobs, the pinnacle of perkiness in the sixties: *stewardess*. Make no mistake, being a stewardess was hard work. The hours were irregular, and the pay was about three hundred dollars a month—small potatoes, even by 1960 standards. Nonetheless, being a stewardess at the dawn of the jet age had cachet only slightly less than that of the astronauts themselves; and as for femininity, the image of the stewardess was right up there with Playmate of the month as a paragon—modern womanhood at its most beguiling.

"Can an earthbound girl become a jet-setter?" asked *Flying High*, a book that promised to tell what it's really like to be a stewardess. "Can she fly to the Bahamas for a weekend, buy her shoes in Paris, arrange to work when she wants and play when she wants? Can she possibly find Prince Charming, adventure, and happiness gift-wrapped in a shiny steel bird?" The author, Elizabeth Rich, formerly of Maine but now of New York, London, and Paris, says YES! Flying around the world was kicky enough; flying on a planeload of interesting people—eighty percent of them men—made being a stewardess the optimum way to partake of all the benefits of jet-age modernity (and get a man while you were at it). "DANGER! Keep away from airlines," warned *Teen* magazine, "under penalty of finding a zingy, zwingy perfect job!"

*Lighthearted stewardesses show off their new uniforms, 1969.*

You might think that because stewardesses lasted an average of two-and-one-third years before resigning (in 1965, eighty-five percent of all resignations were for marriage), there would be plenty of openings. Wrong. Out of every one hundred girls who applied, only four made the grade.

The job requirements as specified by American Airlines required that an applicant be a "wholesome all-American girl type, between ages 20 and 26, 5 feet 2 inches to 5 feet 8 inches in height, with proportionate weight not to exceed 130 pounds. She must be single, in excellent health, attractive, and possess considerable personal charm as well as a high degree of intelligence and enthusiasm." American also required that girls have "long arms to reach overhead racks." Pan Am demanded its girls be able to swim. Western Airlines required "poise, speed, stamina, and smilability."

Delta insisted upon grace under stress and a clear complexion. Slenderness was of utmost importance—especially in the hips, which spent so much time at passenger eye level. With the exception of the long-arm proviso and the ability to swim, these requirements pretty much define perkiness.

Girls accepted into stewardess college joined what American called "the high flying beauty set." Their first assignment: a personal-appearance analysis, including a list of things they needed to accomplish, grooming-wise. They learned to purge themselves of such unperky mannerisms as "aimless gazing and staring, repetitive stroking of chin, clearing throat, and chewing gum in public." They were taught how to tuck in their derrières and how to pluck out their eyebrows. Experts determined their most flattering hairdos and makeup.

If they graduated, the job was sheer perky heaven. When twenty-two-year-old Jo Keeling, "a pretty, perky, blue-eyed blonde from apple country," describes her life as a stewardess to Sheila Barron for a *Teen* article called "Hostess with the Mostess," she "bubbles over . . . her eyes light up and she seems to glow." At home in New York, Jo dabbles with fresh flower arrangements, dances the minute the music starts, bakes lasagne, plays guitar, window-shops, reads a book a week, plans her wardrobe, and grooms herself.

("Grooming is not a sometimes thing with a hostess," she notes. "It's a day in and day out, night in and night out necessity.") On the job, Jo is even busier: "There might be a lunch date in one city and a swinging party in another—all in the same day! Zowie! What a life!" Jo says she wouldn't give it up for anything . . . "except 'hanging out diapers.' "

Being a stewardess afforded perky girls a glamorous existence that presixties women hardly could have imagined. Sandee Boots described her life as a stewardess for *Teen*: "I live on Sunset Strip. My roommate and I date some movie people; we go to premieres, races, and occasionally ride in Rolls-Royces. We regularly migrate to Acapulco in the winter. We spent this spring in the South Pacific and most of the summer in Europe." Who but a wealthy jet setter or a stewardess would have access to an outfit such as that designed by couturier Emilio Pucci (for Braniff) consisting of bright-raspberry A-line dress and stretch culottes, Pucci printed head scarf, and helmet-shaped bubble hat with built-in wraparound sunglasses!

The question that drove men wild in these days before the sexual revolution made such thoughts truly dopey was "Are stews nice girls or swingers?" Helen Gurley Brown wrote, "There is something sexy about being sequestered 20,000 feet above the earth almost as close to a strange man as a banana to its skin, motors humming (yours and the plane's) and nothing to do but get to know each other." Books, movies, and cartoons in *Playboy* magazine were absolutely obsessed by these high-flying perky girls who, unlike the dour flight attendants of today, were perceived as the epitome of the sexy single girl. The question was "Do they or don't they?" To be a stewardess was to be the perpetual subject of this question: exactly the situation in which perky girls thrived.

*Coffee, Tea or Me*, written in 1967 by Trudy Baker and Rachel Jones, was billed as "the uninhibited memoirs of two airlines stewardesses" and purported to give the real scoop on the private lives of stews. It sold over a million copies; but true to perky-girl morality, it was mischievous rather than downright sexy. Trudy and Rachel are cheerful sorority sisters who take us on a nonstop tour of a GP-rated "mad, mod world" with just a "pippy poo" (to use Helen Gurley Brown's favorite phrase) of naughtiness. They always manage to stay one step ahead of horny captains, randy salesmen, girl-chasing soldiers, and all the other "stew-bums" who took Helen Gurley Brown's banana-and-skin metaphor a little too literally.

An earlier (1960) book called *Girl on a Wing* by Bernard Glemser (subsequently republished as *The Fly Girls* to cash in on the success of *Coffee, Tea or Me*) was advertised as "the no-holds-barred novel of the stewardesses who swing in the sky—and on the ground!" The book is prefaced by a warning from the publisher: "Some may be shocked. Others will believe this is a wildly imaginative novel. But, mothers, whatever you think, hold on to your long-haired, wide-eyed daughters until you've read this book. Mr. Glemser has obviously known a 'stew' or two and—shocking, kooky, wild or wicked—he tells it exactly like it is!"

Despite the dire admonition, "the fly girls" are the most innocent of swingers, their antics no more risqué than a pillow fight at the dorm. Oh, yes—there is one stewardess who has sex. She's the Italian one. The voluptuous one with big breasts and swelling hips. The one who won't cut her hair to regulation length, and who wears her stewardess cap at an angle that is sexy rather than perky. She is drummed out of the corps and subsequently dies in an accident. You know she'll come to no good as soon as she is described in her black silk nightgown, "smelling to high heaven of perfume." In the high-flying world that put perkiness on a pedestal, such a woman was doomed. Perky girls could flirt, tease, and cavort; they might even, under the right circumstances, have sex. But to be sensual—to ooze lust instead of cuteness—was a cardinal sin against the commands of perkiness.

There was one calling that presented even greater possibilities for perkiness than stewardess. That was being a nun. There was already a venerable tradition of mining cuteness out of convents and monasteries, in movies such as *Come to the Stable* and *The Bells of St. Mary's* and in Bill O'Malley's merry cartoons about Sisters Maureen and Colleen, who appeared in newspapers as "O'Malley's Nuns." But suddenly in the sixties, nuns were the most adorable crackpots since Auntie Mame. Phalanxes of rollicking postulants invaded popular culture—singing, flying, riding motorcycles, and strumming the guitar. Even perky princess Mary Tyler Moore got into a habit for her role as a plainclothes nun in the Elvis movie *Change of Habit*.

Here comes the wiggiest pop star of 1963, Sister Luc-Gabrielle of Belgium, a.k.a. Soeur Sourire, known worldwide as the Singing Nun, riding her turquoise-blue Vespa motor scooter! She travels with trusty "Sister Adele" (her guitar) slung over her shoulder, gunnysack style. The wind whips her vestments and sends a string of rosary beads rattling out behind as she whizzes along a country road, scattering geese, cattle, and automobiles.

*Sister Luc-Gabrielle, the Singing Nun, reads about herself.*

Unlike grumpy old-style nuns who saw kids as targets for beatings with a ruler, Sister Luc-Gabrielle was a true sixties perky girl. As portrayed by Debbie Reynolds in *The Singing Nun* (for which her name was simplified to Sister Ann), she is eager, impulsive, happy-go-lucky, and she loves to play games with the boys and girls in the playground—rough-and-tumble games full of pep, like the Kennedy family plays when it gets together for a happy afternoon of touch football. It is in the playground that she meets a lonely waif named Dom and composes a lilting song to cheer him up. (He needs cheering because his father is a drunk, his mother a whore.) The song, "Dominique," becomes a monster number-one worldwide hit! (It happened in December 1963.) *Mon Dieu!* It is a miracle! Like Elvis and the Beatles, the Singing Nun performs her hit song on "The Ed Sullivan Show." No wordly perky girl ever had such a breathlessly successful career. (After the success of "Dominique," Sister Luc-Gabrielle quit the convent and tried in vain to launch a lay singing career with an ode to birth control called "Glory Be to God for the Golden Pill.")

Nuns were so popular after Sister Luc-Gabrielle's real-life triumph on "Ed Sullivan" that record racks in stores overflowed with other singing nuns eager for a piece of the action.

The Singing Nuns of Jesus and Mary from Hyattsville, Maryland, unable to go on tour because convent rules forbade travel, released an album featuring their own version of "Dominique" as well as "The Happy Wanderer." A song stylist called Sister Adele (yes, the same name as Sister Luc-Gabrielle's guitar) released an album titled *Dominique.* Sister Adele's songs, like Sister Luc-Gabrielle's, were cheerful, childish, and rustic in that special French- (or Belgian-) nunnish way that the record-buying public so adored: "It's Raining, Little Shepherd Girl," "Shepherd Maiden," "Where Are You Going, Little Shepherd?"

The Medical Mission Sisters of Philadelphia came out with an album called *I Know the Secret,* on which the liner notes describe lead singer Sister Miriam Therese Winter as "vibrant and sure in flowing blue, a silver cross suspended from her neck. She snaps her fingers to and fro, her heel tapping as the guitar and marachas [sic] take up the beat." Although introduced as a "pert, young troubador," Sister Miriam's description in the liner roles stretches the limits of perkiness, portraying her more like Mick Jagger in a habit: The "lithe elfin woman with frisky brown eyes . . . starts snapping out a rhythm, her head tilted, swaying slightly, the long blue veil flowing down her back. 'I love the guitar,' " she says. " 'It's really real.' "

The last word in perky nuns, and arguably the perkiest girl of the sixties, was Sister Bertrille of the convent of San Tanco in San Juan. Sister Bertrille was a fictional character created in 1965 in a book by Tere Rios, who introduced her this way:

> Of all the nuns in the world, Sister Bertrille was probably the smallest. She had dark eyes, brows like gull wings, a small nose with one freckle; and she hurried all the time—partly to keep up with all the big people surrounding her, and partly because she was just a natural-born hurrier. . . . There was clearly an invisible sparkle and twinkle in the air about her that was pure American. This comes, some theorists say, from vitamins, ice skating, braces on the teeth, dancing lessons, and liberal doses of free air.

Did perkiness ever have a more exquisite avatar?

Sister Bertrille arrives in Puerto Rico, waving gaily from the ship's rail at Sister Placido, the stern mother superior, who never waves at anybody. She tells Sister Placido how much fun she had on her voyage, singing with the sailors and playing cards. Sister Placido does not sing or play cards. As they walk to the convent along a narrow, cobbled street, men call out—not lewdly, but to remark on how pretty Sister Bertrille is, how tiny, and how cutely she walks. Men do not call out to Sister Placido.

As they near the convent, atop the highest hill in San Juan, a gust of wind begins to rattle the nuns' stiff-starched white bonnets.

> Sister Bertrille's wide white cornette, folded like a paper airplane with the point at the front, was a perfect airfoil; she was running to keep up, which gave her thrust; her tiny body was very little load, and practically no drag. So when she skipped up over the highest hill in San Juan and turned the corner and lifted her head and ran a bit to catch up, that gust lifted her right into the air. She was airborne; and THE FLYING NUN was born!

Sally Field, the original TV Gidget, traded her bikini for a habit and starred in eighty-two TV sitcom episodes of "The Flying Nun." At five foot two, ninety-seven pounds, she was perfect for the role. Indeed, Sally was one of the decade's beacons of perkiness. It was not possible to write about her without using three or more of the following adjectives: pert, perky, cute, nutty, snub-nosed, giggly, freckle-faced, sprightly, lively, chipper. Ironically, the star of "Gidget" was distraught at being so cute. At the same time Screen Gems (where she would be known as "Sister Terrific") was pursuing her to play Sister Bertrille, Sally was testing for the Katherine Ross role in Mike Nichols's *The Graduate*. When she didn't get the important movie role, she reluctantly signed on for the frivolous TV show (after upping Screen Gems's offer from $1,500 to $4,000 a week); but she regretted it. As squeaky-clean Sister Bertrille, Sally was ostracized from the hip Hollywood of 1967. "Everybody was into dope and granola," she sighed, "and saw me as part of what they were fighting against." Nevertheless, inspired by the Singing Nun's success with "Dominique," Sally Field cut an album of her own, titled *The Flying Nun Sings*. It featured the theme song from the show, "Who Needs Wings to Fly?"

The popularity of zany nuns was the most conspicuous expression of a larger trend in perky-girl heroines, which was a perverse fascination with abnormality. As the sixties got freakier and extravagant behavior became more common (among hippies, for instance), ordinary perky girls were ever more limited in their ability to turn heads. To use a favorite term of the time, their kookiness was getting coopted.

Perky nuns were one good solution to that problem, because it was inevitably amusing to see a woman

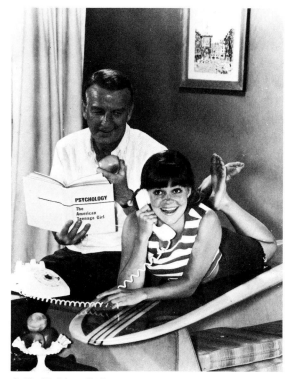

*Sally Field as Gidget*

in a habit break the customary rules of nun behavior. It was even more fun if she transcended the laws of physics and flew. Nuns in general and the Flying Nun in particular revived perkiness by restoring its essential element, *idiosyncrasy*.

In order to maintain the WOW! factor in perkiness, it became necessary by the mid-sixties to create perky girls who could, like the Flying Nun, go beyond the bounds of ordinary human behavior. So it happened that "Bewitched" became one of the most popular television shows in history. "Bewitched" mined eight seasons of amusement from the basic situation of an ordinary suburban junior executive married to a witch. Although she is married and in fact desperately wants to be normal, Samantha (Elizabeth Montgomery) is driven by her witchy nature (or sometimes by her meddling mother) to create new, supernatural levels of perkiness. For instance, Samantha puts a hex on husband, Darren, so that every time he tells a lie (even a little one), his ears grow longer; she brings Napoleon back from nineteenth-century France as a house guest, then cannot get rid of him; she attends a dinner party with her husband's boss while under a spell that makes her speak only in rhymes.

The success of "Bewitched" begot "I Dream of Jeannie" the next season, about a beautiful genie who is the mischief-making servant of an astronaut (Larry Hagman). Barbara Eden, who played genie Jeannie, was described by Tim Brooks in his *Complete Directory of Prime Time TV Stars* as "pert, shapely, and with a sexy twinkle in her eye." Also in 1965, Bob Cummings of "Love That Bob" fame starred with Julie Newmar in "My Living Doll." This one was about a psychiatrist with a live-in patient who happened to be a wide-eyed, leggy robot. As late as 1973, the formula was recast for "The Girl with Something Extra," about a husband (John Davidson) who learns to live with a wife (Sally Field, again!) who has ESP. By 1973, however, the number-one show on television was "All in the Family." The magic charms of perkiness were long out of date, and far too fragile to survive in the vulgar, insult-riddled early-seventies world of Archie Bunker. "The Girl with Something Extra" barely lasted until the end of the season.

Even more than Marlo Thomas and Mary Tyler Moore in their perky heydays, more than Sally Field as Gidget, more than any stewardess or nun, there was one girl who was perkier than all the others. You would say she was perky to the bone if she had bones. Like the others, she has since moved on to more serious endeavors; but in the sixties, nobody embodied the spirit of perkiness better than Barbie.

Barbie always had fun. She was always dressed in a cute outfit. As a "teenage-fashion model" (first molded in 1959), her profession was as perky as could be. Her flexible little body was put together so that she could assume a multitude of pert poses; she was always ready to kick a leg out gleefully or flip her hair in a way that was sure to turn Ken's plastic head. (Ken, by the way, was introduced in 1961, when Mattel, Barbie's maker, realized that there was little use in being perky without a guy around to react properly.)

No matter what Barbie did, she did it with flair, always heeding the cardinal rule of perkiness—which was to put yourself in a cute setting. The "Barbie Goes to College" ensemble featured a cardboard backdrop of a malt-shop soda fountain. The July-August 1962 *Barbie* magazine invited readers to "Join Barbie and Ken at a Twist Party." In 1965, she appeared in a "Disc Date" outfit, complete with miniature record and record player. The same year, she was ready for a "Hootenanny." Even Barbie's British perky pals, Stacey and Casey, came ready for action in their own elaborate paper "Fashion Boutique."

Although plastic, Barbie had all the fashion smarts of her flesh-and-blood sisters. In 1961, she abandoned her trademarked swirl ponytail and adopted a bubble hairdo; and in 1964, "Barbie's Wig Wardrobe" went on sale, including three shades (blond, brunet, and titian) available in the bubble-on-bubble and side-part flip styles. Soon, like every other perky girl in town, Barbie was wearing her hair in a long flip, called "The American Girl."

In 1966, Barbie faced a great crisis. Like real girls with too many curves for skimpy sixties fashions, she suddenly began to look outdated. Her status as queen of all fashion-model dolls was threatened by, of all people, her own cousin, Mattel's Francie. Francie was diminutive, with a smaller bust, and looked younger than Barbie. Her hair was longer and swingier. According to *Barbie* magazine, she used Beatle slang like "fabby" and "gear"; she wore crazy-patterned stockings, and she loved pigging out on fudge sundaes (which didn't show a bit on her girlish figure).

While tradition-bound Barbie wore a pink "Fashion Luncheon" suit that looked like something from Jackie Kennedy's closet, Francie capered about in a micro-miniskirt and thigh-high red boots, or her stylish "Go Granny Go" ankle-length granny gown, or "Swingin' Separates" such as "Fur Out" (1966), "Pazam!" (1968), and "Culotte-Wot?" (1968).

*Barbie and Ken in their salad days*

The awful truth was undeniable. Barbie, the original perky girl, had peaked and grown stale. She valiantly struggled to stay cute. Her "Slumber Party Set" included a book for her to read, *How to Lose Weight.* She had a makeover in 1967—wider eyes, super-long lashes, ironed-flat hair, and a waist that twisted so she could dance the San Francisco free style. Despite all this, there was no denying the march of time. She faced yet another even perkier competitor in 1967: Mattel's Twiggy. Twiggy was an effigy of the popular English fashion model whose 31–23–33 figure was sending young women across America and England into anorexic fashion shock. (In fact, Twiggy was actually a surplus Francie with the head of another Mattel doll, Casey.) Twiggy made her debut with close-cropped blond hair and painted-on mod eyelashes, wearing a blue, yellow, and green minidress with bright yellow boots.

The final blow to Barbie's reign as perky queen came in 1967, when Ken disappeared! He was gone, left no forwarding address, out of stock, no longer in production. (Barbie biographer Billieboy suspects Ken was lured away by Barbie's younger and perkier sister, Midge, who also went out of production in 1967.)

There is a happy ending to the story. Ken returned two years later with an expanded consciousness. The new Ken doll was hip, and decked out in a "Guruvy Formal"—a bright red Nehru jacket over shiny white pants. Barbie was up to Ken's fashion challenge, coming out in 1970 in her own "Maxi 'N Mini" ensemble—a Lurex-striped miniskirt, maxicoat, and high-heel Mylar boots. The perky days were over. High fashion was back in style.

# PLAYBOYS

WHILE MANY sixties people were learning to hang loose or to fight a good fight, a tireless legion of men squeezed themselves into knife-crease, no-cuff, no-belt, no-pleat, low-rise, pipe-leg, bolero-pocket perma-press Life O' Ease trousers with Securoslax Recoil Stretch Fortrel waistband, slapped their cheeks with palmfuls of Hai Karate Oriental Lime cologne, and strode into the world searching for sophistication. The prosperous new decade offered up abundant regalia of the Good Life: stereophonic FM tuners and flaming Kahlúa Crepes Bresilienne, jet package tours of Morocco, and erotic movies imported from Europe. A guide to all this sophistication was within reach of any man with fifty cents for a copy of *Playboy*.

First published in December 1953, *Playboy* magazine had hit a million in circulation by 1962, when publisher Hugh Hefner commenced the Herculean task of delineating "The Playboy Philosophy" by reminding readers, "The magazine was never intended for the general public—it is edited for a select audience of young, literate, urban men, who share with us a particular point of view on life."

*Playboy* was not by any means the only arena where this point of view was particularized. But it was so ardent in its efforts that it became the supreme sourcebook for a decisive image of masculine modernity. The image was built upon a belief that moral taboos and social barriers at long last could be abolished. The libertine life once available only to pashas, European Casanovas, and movie casting directors was there to be grasped by any guy who followed *Playboy*'s advice to wear a satin smoking jacket, listen to winners of its annual jazz poll on large speakers, have an open mind abounding with literate, cultured, liberal thoughts, and smell of lime or leather-scented cologne. "Our philosophy is that you should work hard and play hard, and strive to get into the sophisticated upper crust," Hef announced.

Maybe it was the right magazine in the right market niche at the right time, or maybe it ought to get credit for establishing a lifestyle that might not otherwise have come along: whichever is the case, Hugh Hefner's *Playboy* was the most potent cry of yearning in popular culture since rock and roll proclaimed the secession of teens from adult society. *Playboy* was not about being fresh and rebellious, however. It was the voice of the upwardly mobile adult male with acute hungers to be modern and to see nude women.

Condemned by enemies as a girlie magazine with a crass materialistic undertow, *Playboy* defended its cheesecake and its materialism with religious zeal. (Clergymen got a seventy-five percent reduction in their subscription rate if they ordered *Playboy* on church letterhead.) By the end of the decade, *TV Guide* was the only magazine that topped its circulation of over six million.

The jet-age playboy (we'll use a lower-case *p* to talk about him outside the pages of the magazine) wanted to be new and improved. He ached to liberate himself from anything that was square. He surveyed the coming decade and inhaled a deep, tantalizing whiff of all the freedoms that stretched before him. He was free to look at bare bosoms and bottoms in Swedish films; he was free to read *Lady Chatterley's Lover;* he might even find free-of-any-obligation sex thanks to the pill. He could travel around the globe in a jet plane; and thanks to miracle fibers, he never had to worry about wrinkling his suit.

The playboy strove to be well traveled, well dressed, and well groomed. He might be frisky, but he was never unruly. He never, under any circumstances whatsoever, lost composure. If a little old lady in a hunkering Nash Rambler gouged a dent in his Jaguar XKE *gran tourismo* coupe, or if he dribbled hot fondue on his silk ascot in the presence of his fair companion, he knew how to keep his cool. Being a sophisticate meant being as slick as an ice cube in a pitcher of dry martinis.

Playboys dug jazz at midnight; they savored the image of Sinatra with his bow tie loosened, shirt open, jacket slung over his shoulder, singing "Come Fly with Me" in a smoky lounge. They wanted to hear Lionel Hampton play vibes on their favorite late-night jazz broadcast while they dined *à deux* on flambéed duck with sauce à l'orange in their penthouse apartment high above the city's lights.

In the comfort of their pad, they lounged in turtlenecks instead of ties, Jiffie Squire leisure slippers (whose advertisements promised they were "like walking on marshmallows") instead of lace-up

brogues; they preferred lordly Peach Brandy pipe tobacco or cigarillos to plain, quarter-a-pack cigarettes. The serious playboy slept in a bed with light dimmers and motorized drape controls recessed into the headboard. And of course, he aimed to share that bed with a date who had enormous breasts.

Rather than worrying that such fantasies were symptoms of arrested adolescence, playboys savored the idea that they were doing no less than defining the ultimate Good Life for all contemporary, up-to-date, fully equipped, broad-minded, sexually adventurous adults. They were the quintessence of modern malehood, so they postulated; and their particular brand of off-the-rack sophistication, combined with righteous self-indulgence and a ceaseless effort at self-improvement, has flourished in upscale "men's magazines" ever since.

The most onerous thing in the world to playboys was repression—anything puritanical that inhibited modern life. They swore by the power of intellectual, spiritual, oenophilic, sartorial, culinary, and sexual enlightenment. They loved to stand foursquare against such evils as *conformity*, *sacred cows*, and *stultifying traditions*. They were against censorship. They were against prudery. They were for the free exchange of ideas; and they were for sex as a pastime whose time, at last, had arrived after centuries of grim and joyless procreation.

Like so many iconoclastic sixties people, the playboy regarded himself as a lifestyle pioneer at the vanguard of a revolution. In his case it was the sexual revolution, and he was fighting for the right to enjoy himself. But he didn't like to think of his quest for pleasure as ignoble hedonism. "The Playboy Forum," which printed letters from readers, was loaded with praise from ministers, professors, psychologists, and other high-status arbiters of taste who applauded *Playboy* for its liberating message. "As long as ignorant people are in a position to impose their views on others, our task will be incomplete," wrote Walter D. Himmelein (of the University of Pennsylvania) to the "Forum" of May 1966. Mr. Himmelein included a check for the Playboy Foundation, whose goal was "social and legal reforms" in the fight for free expression.

"*What is a Playboy?*" a subscription card to the magazine asked in 1956:

Is he simply a wastrel, a ne'er-do-well, a fashionable bum? Far from it: He can be a sharp-minded young business executive, a worker in the arts, a university professor, an architect or engineer. He can be many things, providing he possesses a certain *point of view*. He must see life not as a vale of tears, but as a happy time; he must take joy in his work, without regarding it as the be-all and end-all of living; he must be an alert man, an aware man, a man of taste, a man sensitive to pleasure, a man who—without acquiring the stigma of the voluptuary or dilettante —can live life to the hilt.

So, let the sixties begin! Down with grandfatherly Eisenhower and gray-faced Nixon and moralistic country-club Republicanism! Hurrah for Jack Kennedy, who is so young and worldly and good looking and eats French food and reads Ian Fleming novels and even pals around with Sinatra and the Rat Pack and has a young wife with Continental breeding and managed (so the rumors say) to get a piece of Marilyn and Jayne and Angie, too! Hurrah for living life to the hilt!

With their fanatical devotion to strict detail, attitude, and appearance (note all the "musts" in the *"What is a Playboy?"* credo), playboys were hopelessly incompatible with the *la dolce vita* jet set. Nonetheless the jet set, with their ability to flout humdrum life and their glamorous ingestion of pleasures all around the world, from sunning in Saint-Tropez to skiing in Gstaad, became the playboy's most exalted role models.

Even if he might only take a jet from Chicago to Pittsburgh on business or to Miami Beach to visit his mom, or even if he only got around the neighborhood in his spirited little Corvair Monza Spyder and never ever took a plane, the playboy counted jet travel among modern life's great rewards.

Remember how glamorous flying was in 1960? Jets made it eminently contemporary, and virtually anything contemporary was an essential element of the playboy's sustaining fantasies. The aspiring playboy could easily see himself "in shirtsleeves, smoking a pipe, lounging comfortably or even taking a stroll down the long, plush-carpeted cabin, enjoying the soothing strains of a Strauss waltz drifting muted and pleasant from hidden speakers." That's the way Martin Caidin described a typical man on a typical jet flight in his nearly evangelical observance of the dawn of the passenger jet age, *Boeing 707*, published in 1959.

"Is it truly any less than a miracle?" Caidin asked. In 1959, it seemed miraculous; but within only a few years, the high-flying freedom that was once the prerogative of the idle rich could be had by nearly any working stiff with a two-week vacation and a few dollars to shell out for proliferating cut-rate fares. Imagine: ordinary guys could now hobnob with the sexiest women on earth—stewardesses!

The playboy's adventuring fantasies were only a discount fare away. For one hundred nine dollars in 1966, he could spend a frolicsome week on Corfu or Tahiti, at Club Méditerranée—where business quadrupled between 1960 and 1970. As early as 1961, a book called *Views to Dine By* offered culinary instruction.

> . . . for the seasoned traveler who has, at last, graduated from the prerequisite omnibus guide book—who now has time to linger, and enjoy the beauty of the land. No longer does he have a quota of birthplaces, fountains, monuments, churches and museums he *must* see.
> . . . He may sit back and "make like a native" and share with the great the views which have given them respite and moral fortification.

Published by Alitalia Airlines, *Views to Dine By* has but one standard upon which it judges restaurants for inclusion: do they have a view? It is impossible to overstate the importance of *the view* to the playboy's sense of self. The view was everything, and there was only one place to get it: way up high. Let life's drones travel in subway tubes and live in basement flats and scurry along the sidewalks. The playboy wanted to live above the mundane: zooming through the clouds in a 707 to some swinging pleasure capital, seducing a voluptuous woman in his penthouse above the city, and, most deliciously, indulging in fine cuisine and oenophilic pleasures somewhere on top of the world. Dining-with-a-view, while certainly not invented in the sixties, reached its apotheosis as an expression of the playboy's ceaseless quest for altitude and the mastery it implied.

The final entry in *Views to Dine By* is a restaurant not yet built, but destined to open in 1962. The restaurant was a rendering of the playboy lifestyle in culinary terms, and symbolizes the whole gastronomic revolution that ran a parallel course with playboyism in the sixties. It had a view that one promotional brochure described as "unequalled in American dining"—550 feet above the earth, through outward-sloping windows, of the Olympic and Cascade mountains, Mount Rainier, Mount Saint Helens, Puget Sound, and the whole city of Seattle. *It was a 360-degree view!* This was the Eye of the Needle revolving restaurant atop the Space Needle at the Seattle Century 21 Exposition world's fair of 1962.

The revolving restaurant was an idea proposed by Eddie Carlson, head of Western International Hotels and world's fair chairman, after he made an inspiring visit to the 445-foot-tall (nonrevolving) restaurant in Stuttgart, West Germany. "How painlessly went the coins for the elevator ride, how delightfully gay was the dinner hour high above the outward-stretching lights of the city," Carlson recalled in *Space Needle, USA*, the souvenir booklet about the fair's main attraction, which authors Harold Mansfield and George Gulacsik offer as a symbol of man's "wanting to rise high above his surroundings."

The awe-inspiring thing about the Space Needle was the way its central supporting tower was invisible from the panoramic windows. Dining there was even better than a penthouse; it was like dining on a cloud, or in outer space! Hostesses wore stewardesslike blue uniforms, supplemented with capes in a color they described to guests as "Re-entry Red."

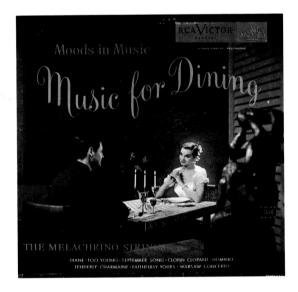

The most futuristic aspect of the restaurant itself, and the one most pertinent to an understanding of the high-gear lifestyle sought by the gourmet playboy, was its menu. Here, too, was a reflection of the fair's efforts to show the world of 2000. One brochure described future foods as "frozen exotic fruits, meats and herbs flown from all corners of the world to be combined in gourmet dinners." You could order exactly that at the Eye of the Needle: frozen beefsteak served with "delicate sweet onions grown on the Hawaiian Island of Maui, brought across the Pacific"; frozen breast of chicken Taj Mahal; frozen strawberries Almavivia, soaked in kirsch.

In the jet age, gourmet food was foreign food. Knowing how to say "coq au vin" or "moussaka" was evidence that you were cosmopolitan, you had tasted the world's riches, you weren't a bumpkin. Knowing how to cook them put you in the uppermost echelon of pleasure seekers. This was the beginning of the modern food revolution in America, and a return of the kind of ostentatious cookery that had been in eclipse since before Prohibition. Being fancy was fashionable again.

In the fifties, the common image of a gourmet had been someone with an abnormal fascination for food that ordinary folks considered repulsive or inedible: chocolate-covered ants and grasshoppers, candied flower petals, snails, sheep's eyes, goose-liver pâté, and the like. Even such fifties-vintage continental favorites as boeuf bourguignon and French onion soup were mostly the province of lace-hankie types like Vincent Price and Adolphe Menjou.

By the early sixties, a taste for gourmet food was becoming a symbol of the kind of manly, globe-trotting derring-do that playboys wanted to exude. Knowing your way around a continental menu and a wine list revealed that you were a discerning connoisseur who circled the earth to find its choicest prizes. Ten years earlier, such finicky behavior might have been considered effeminate by most meat-eating American men; but in the soaring sixties, when the world was the playboy's oyster, the fussier a guy was about his fancy food and elaborately formulated cocktails, the more masculine he seemed.

The unenlightened masses ate food and drank drinks. Playboys didn't *eat*, they *indulged their palate*, and not with food and drink, but with viands, victuals, potables, and libations. The gourmet tides that flooded into the sixties with the publication of *Mastering the Art of French Cooking* in 1961 (and Julia Child's appearance as "The French Chef" on television in 1962), then Time-Life's twenty-six-volume Foods of the World series, made continental cuisine accessible to anyone with the will to rise above the dull routine of meat and potatoes. Playboys found prodigious opportunities to realize their goals of living life to the hilt (or at least fantasize about it) at New York City's palaces of conspicuous epicureanism, the Four Seasons (opened in 1959), and the Forum of the Twelve Caesars (1958), the latter described by the 1960 gourmet guidebook *Great Restaurants of America* as "a Neronian weekend orgy where flames leap from great platters on every side of the room."

For those who lacked the resources to enjoy a night on the town, RCA offered a record album called *Music for Dining:* a soup-to-nuts program of mood music designed to match your gourmet meal. The album's liner notes promise "a dozen musical courses to accompany your delectation. . . . Pâté de foie gras is offered (with truffles, of course), to be nibbled at while the orchestra presents a lush treatment of 'Too Young.' For the somewhat more autumnal touch of Kurt Weill's 'September Song,' a chilled dish would be most fitting. Perhaps a lobster mayonnaise." Onward goes the fabulous repast, through duckling à l'orange accompanied by "Clopin Clopant" and a pastry tray announced by the *Warsaw Concerto.* Finally, the gourmet evening concludes with "murmured whispers over candlelight and the romantic melodies of 'Faithfully Yours.' "

Short-lived *Gusto International* ("A Magazine for the Modern Epicure") featured advertisements telling readers "the secret of the best chefs in town" (they serve frozen South African rock lobster tails) and "how to enjoy a taste of Mexico even if you didn't make Acapulco this winter" (serve Mariachi tequila). One *Gusto* article explains that the American picnic is really just a secondhand version of the ever-so-more-soigné French *pique-nique,* the Italian *pic-nic,* and the German *Picknick;* other stories describe the cuisine of London, the martini mystique, and the joy of eating out of jars and cans: "By simply opening a jar of brandied cherries, we can remove ourselves from the hum drum and savor a fine Italian dessert. Canned kumquats can take us to Cathay. Pâté de foie gras to Paris and sausage sticks to Copenhagen."

Exoticism reigned. And what could possibly be more exotic than flambéed food? "To cook without blazing spirits would be like cooking without butter or cream or stock," Thomas Mario, *Playboy*'s resident gourmet, announced in the December 1962 issue, which featured a meal in which *every dish* was ignited: Onion soup flambé, lobster Provençale in a pool of blazing cognac, mushrooms and peas with burning rum, and an omelette soufflé set ablaze with Grand Marnier. (After dinner, to continue the pyromaniacal theme of the evening, *Playboy* suggests basking in the "ruby ember of your postprandial panatella and the euphoric crackling of a roaring hearth.")

Sixties cookery was defined by its opportunities to be different. "Mainland Americans are thoroughly familiar with European hors d'oeuvre," sighed Anita Prichard in *Fondue Magic.* "But now, blowing in from the West on easterly winds from the Islands, comes a new term for appetizer, fresh as to taste and visual appeal: the elegant and often elaborate pupu tray." Ms. Prichard notes that the great thing about the pupu tray, which is customarily accompanied by heavy rum potations and served with skewers so everyone can cauterize his or her own morsels of food in the fire, is that it is an "eat/drink/be merry simultaneously phenomenon." That was what made fondue so popular in the sixties. "Guests gather round the fondue pot, searing and dunking flavorful chunks of bread, beef, cake or fruit—that's the fun of it! And those bewitching dips conjured up from all over the world—that's the saucery."

The problem a playboy might have with fondue cookery was that it was for four or more people, not for a cozy twosome. Fondues were more a perky girl's kind of thing, anyway, with their dainty forks and little nibbles of food. For guys, especially single guys on a swinging date, the great gourmet cooking discovery of the sixties was the hibachi grill.

Hibachi cooking was especially favored in the playboy's pad because it was so *intime*. Unlike the jumbo backyard barbecue grill with its suburban patio-wife-and-two-point-seven-kids connotation, the hibachi was at its best cooking for two in a smart apartment, indoors (put it in the fireplace) or out (on the balcony). It was better than the fondue pot, too, because it was suited for large, masculine pieces of food, such as a steak or rock lobster tails. Best of all, it demanded the time-honored and most manly of all cooking rituals: the igniting of a charcoal fire. "A hibachi is perfect for the man who likes to play with fire," suggested Thomas Mario in a *Playboy* article about "The Indoor Picnic." *Honorable Hibachi*, a cookbook by Kathryn Popper published in 1965, suggests that the hibachi is especially wonderful because it is quick, maneuverable, and fun—just like a foreign sports car as opposed to a bloated American sedan (or outside barbecue grill).

Gourmet playboys had a how-to guide for their culinary sex fantasies in *The Seducer's Cookbook*, published in 1962, which promised "recipes with which to bait the trap . . . advice about decorating the apartment appropriately, decorating yourself, avoiding detection if there is an unsuspecting hus-

*What woman could resist a playboy's well-appointed pad?*

band or wife involved." Author Mimi Sheraton, who later became the restaurant critic for *The New York Times*, described her reasons for writing *The Seducer's Cookbook:* "1) To enable men to get the answer they want—Yes. 2) To give women a better reason for saying it. 3) To keep America from becoming, sexually, a have-not nation." Ms. Sheraton even managed to borrow *Playboy*'s alliterative prose style when she worried that sophisticated seduction was becoming a lost art in this sexually liberated era of people "pushing, pulling, pleading, and promising" in order to get a bedmate.

In addition to sexy recipes (including such unlikely aphrodisiacs as hamburger Provençale, English muffin pizza, and fried liver with bacon), *The Seducer's Cookbook* warns against menu faux pas: sardines, tripe, or beer. The author recommends good places to pick somebody up if you have no one special to seduce: museums, the library, department stores, stockholders' meetings, and foreign trade fairs ("staffed by native beauties"). She suggests keeping terrycloth robes in the bedroom, so that after the first round of sex, when you want more food, you and your date don't have to cook and eat in the nude.

All this fuss over getting someone into bed was rendered as jolly good fun in *The Seducer's Cookbook*. In *Playboy*, it was the pinnacle of suavity. Whatever its tone, the process of seduction always began with cocktails. Few subjects were doted over so fastidiously by would-be playboys.

Observe, for example, playboy role model James Bond and his elaborate martini. He was peremptorily obsessive about it: "Three measures of Gordon's, one of vodka, half a measure of Kina Lillet. Shake it very well until it's ice-cold, then add a large thin slice of lemon peel." So he commanded in the book *Casino Royale*, further requiring that the drink be served in a deep champagne goblet, then suggesting that the bartender might do even better if he used vodka made with grain instead of potatoes.

Whatever happened to guys who drank whiskey straight—maybe poured into a glass, maybe not? There was no mixological mumbo jumbo about the way Humphrey Bogart or John Wayne took his liquor. But by the sixties, John Wayne was old and Bogie was a campy cult hero. Martinis, which had evolved from the intoxicant of the twenties' Lost Generation to the drink of underweight Ivy League pansies and desk-bound executives, were reborn in the sixties as the most macho cocktail of all. As sophistication became an ever-more attractive attribute of manliness, the flawless martini became the preeminent symbol of the savvy drinking man. Whiskey, straight, began to look like an oaf's drink. An oaf was exactly the kind of man the playboy wanted to prove he was not.

Naturally, because drinking to excess, being able to hold your liquor, and getting a girl drunk are all time-honored symbols of masculinity, *Playboy* was filled with liquor advertising. A large proportion of the ads were for gin, many touting gin's dryness, coolness, keenness, and civility—exactly the qualities that the playboy himself sought to emanate. The martini was his liquid metaphor, and lore about attaining ultimate dryness (hence, extreme potency) permeated playboy culture. (At the Dearborn Inn in Michigan, where big auto-company executives gathered, vermouth was added with a single spray from a perfume atomizer; joke methods for attaining the utmost dryness abounded, such as chilling the gin in the shadow of a bottle of vermouth.) In 1965, Johnny Carson summed up the role of the martini in the life of modern man in *Happiness Is a Dry Martini*, a little gift book with urbane Whitney Darrow, Jr. illustrations. It was nothing but jokes about getting drunk (e.g., "Happiness is . . . finding two olives in your martini when you're hungry").

Drinking well was an essential quality of all playboy role models: not just James Bond but Sinatra and the lounge-lizard Rat Pack (especially Dino), who were always sloshing about with highballs in their hands but always cool, and Jacqueline Susann's jut-jawed Robin Stone in *Once Is Not Enough*, the high-powered executive who exists on a diet of nothing but blood-rare steaks, dry martinis, fast sex, and success.

The conspicuous exception to this rule was Hugh Hefner himself—the one and only, the ultimate, the authentic and original playboy, who drank little other than a dozen Pepsi-Colas every day.

Hef was one of the decade's great eccentrics, who managed to turn his own nearly agoraphobic craving to control the environment into an enviable symbol of supreme coolness. He didn't leave his house for weeks on end; sometimes he didn't even leave his bed. But, you see, he didn't need to! He bought the world's goodies and brought them all home. By almost anybody's standards in the leisure-worshiping early sixties, Hef had it made in the shade: "I don't have to arrange my life by other people's *hours*. I don't always have to be in some boring conference. I don't have to go through business lunches and a lot of formalities. I don't even shave if I don't feel like it. I don't have to get dressed. I don't have to put on a shirt and tie and suit every day. I just put on a *bathrobe!*" That's what he told Tom Wolfe, who described Hef's reclusive life at the Playboy Mansion in Chicago as "just paradise; a bed, a fortress of smooth wood, windowless walls, and dials."

All dedicated readers of *Playboy* knew the details of Hef's paradise because the mansion—with its tropical indoor pool (including a secluded Woo Grotto), its round-the-clock room service, its population of Bunnies and Playmates and jazz musicians and witty party guests, its eight-and-a-half-foot vibrating, rotating circular bed in the master bedroom, its twenty-four ceiling-mounted spherical stereo speakers, its live-in Ampex engineer for Hef's (then futuristic) bedroom videotape outfit—was a regular attraction in *Playboy*'s pictorial stories about swinging parties and nude girls. Hef lived The Life! TO THE HILT! You could see him doing it nearly every month in the magazine. *Playboy* press agents insisted that he never be photographed in public without a Bunny on each arm.

He puffed serenely on his pipe, he wore slippers all the time, he stayed up all night and slept all day, he was surrounded by beautiful girls currying his favor, he thought erudite thoughts for "The Playboy Philosophy," and he had every electronic toy and modern convenience known to man.

The dream life wasn't there merely to supply readers with vicarious thrills. *Playboy* sought to play a real part in helping shape men's behavior. Like *The New Yorker*, which had introduced itself to the stylish twenties as "not for the old lady in Dubuque," *Playboy* wanted to be the essential magazine for modern sophisticates, who as a matter of principle rejected little-old-lady mentality. Rather than simply offer urbane entertainment as *The New Yorker* had done, *Playboy* also provided philosophical vindication of its new style of urbanity, plus methodical instructions. It was aimed at all the *boys* in Dubuque who wanted to know how to be civilized. It was their monthly lesson in living life to the hilt.

A first easy step was buying *Playboy* products. As of 1967, there were at least ninety, including a tie, a tie tack, a tie bar, a card case, cuff links, an ID bracelet, a money clip, a key chain, a billfold, blazer buttons, a Bunny hand puppet, an "Order of the Playmate" garter for milady, a liquor caddy, a giant-size "Executive" cigarette lighter, a cocktails-for-two set, personalized Bunny matches, a party pack (swizzle sticks, picks, napkins), Bunny decals for boat prow or car window, a steel-shafted putter with a Playboy Rabbit on the bronze head, a Playboy sweater with matching turtleneck bib, a Playboy Bunny-tail wall plaque (it says "Caught Live at the Playboy Club"), a Leroy Neiman art portfolio (six dramatic prints in full color), and an ascot ("for that more than casual occasion") in olive, gray, wine, or navy.

Writing in the *Journal of Popular Culture* in 1967, sociology professors Walter M. Gerson and Sander H. Lund observed that *Playboy* supplied its readers "a goal to achieve, a model of behavior to emulate, and an identity to assume." The identity was that of the "sophisticated, cosmopolitan, urbane, diverse, affluent, intellectual, promiscuous (if that is the word), mature bachelor." The professors noted that a vast majority of *Playboy*'s articles were instructive: "what to wear and how to wear it, what cars to drive, what food and drink to consume, how to throw parties, and where to travel." Even *Playboy*'s remarkably high-tone fiction (Kerouac, James Baldwin, Nabokov, Graham Greene, etc.) served a purpose: "The Playboy becomes multidimensional. He can quote Ibsen, Sartre, and Mailer. He is at home at formal dinner parties and hippie beer bashes, and as a consequence he seduces with equal facility sophisticated debutantes and female bohemians."

A dramatic example of the educational function of the magazine happened on "Playboy's Penthouse" and "Playboy After Dark," the two syndicated television shows Hef hosted (the first in 1959, the second in 1969). They allowed viewers to *actually attend a party at Hef's mansion!* They were no routine television variety shows with that hoary old stage-and-performer format left over from vaudeville days. They were extraordinary, and to this day unique, applications of television intimacy.

The camera is first person. The camera is I. It arrives in a limo at night, it

*Party at Hef's. Shel Silverstein plays guitar.*

whisks in the door. Here's Hef! He welcomes me. He's just like I've seen him in the magazine—pipe, smoking jacket, slippers. He looks me right in the lens like we're old friends and tells me about some of the other guests who have already arrived: Elke and Miles and Federico and Shel are here, so let's go on in. We track into the festivities and guests peek at us to see who's arrived. Some wave. Hef waves back for us.

Here's the pool table, and here's Sammy Davis, Jr., shooting a game. Hef walks me right up to the table. "Hi, Sammy!" Hef says. And Sammy looks up, says hi to Hef, then winks at me. Think Sammy'll ask me to join him for a game of snooker? No time for that, because now Hef's taking me over to the piano, and now he's coaxing Mel Tormé into singing for all of us good friends at this swinging soirée. There are Bunnies everywhere in fishnet stockings and powder-puff tails. Wall-to-wall celebrities. Jazz musicians. Famous writers. Beautiful people. (I'm so glad I know Hef!) There is dancing, too (during which the camera I hangs out in the middle of the dance floor without a partner). There are toasts. A crackling fire. Brandy. Cigars. A view of the city. The party goes on for ninety minutes (including commercials).

This was an experience beyond voyeurism and titillation. It was an explicit lesson in how to behave at an elegant party. It was all so personal, it could seem painfully embarrassing if you were not able to fully suspend your disbelief. Consider: the shows were usually broadcast on Saturday night, late. What if you were home alone without a date, wearing a smelly T-shirt, eating bologna, and drinking beer from a can? Did you rush to your closet and grab your silk jacket and ascot? Did you defrost a Stouffer's Lobster Newburg dinner to go along with Hef's caviar and toast points? Did you pour a snifter of brandy and click it against Pete Fountain's glass, which was close to the TV screen during the merry midnight toast? Did you answer out loud when Hef asked you how you liked the party?

Who knows how viewers reacted? Hef's television parties, which went so far beyond the boundary of ordinary video aesthetics, lasted only one season in each incarnation.

But the very same principle of bringing the outsider smack into the Good Life made the magazine flourish. The Playmates, for example, were never aloof, sexy, hard-to-get girls. They were friendly. They always posed looking right into the camera with inviting eyes.

Janet Pilgrim (Charlaine Karalus), "Playboy's Office Playmate" of July 1955, was the first to step out of the anonymity in which earlier Playmates had been shrouded. She was described with these tantalizing words: "We suppose it's natural to think of the pulchritudinous Playmates as existing in a world apart. Actually, potential Playmates are all around you: the new secretary at your office, the doe-eyed beauty who sat opposite you at lunch yesterday, the girl who sells you shirts and ties at your favorite store. We found Miss July in our own circulation department."

From the time of Janet Pilgrim, one regular aspect of the Playmate profiles was their description of the kind of man the Playmates liked. Their requirements never included wealth, power, status, or fame. Miss December 1966 prefers dates "who take her to her favorite beaches and cozy restaurants rather than gaudier showbiz scenes." Miss July 1965 likes "a guy who doesn't try to make an impression." Miss November 1965 is a homebody looking for a "sincere guy." Nor did they demand someone who was handsome. Miss May 1964 wants someone "tall, dark, and assertively masculine." Miss November seeks a man who is "tall, fair, and smart." Miss February 1965 likes "tall, dark, and sincere." Miss October prefers "tall, blond, ambitious, and dominant." Obviously, only short men had anything to worry about.

*Playboy* wanted to make readers comfortable about the racy lifestyle it advocated. "We try to edit *Playboy* with the adult directness of a good foreign film," Hugh Hefner said. In other words, there were bosoms and bawdiness, but all in good taste; no drooling sleaze allowed. From the beginning, Hefner rejected all the pitiful kinds of advertising that had been customary in earlier men's magazines: acne cures, elevator shoes, trusses, earn twenty-five dollars a week in your spare time, miracle hair restorer. "It seems to me," he said, "that when a guy goes out and plunks down seventy-five cents for a magazine [the newsstand price by the mid-sixties], he doesn't like to be told he is fat, poverty-stricken, uneducated and a generally unpleasant fellow by all kinds of ads telling him how to improve himself."

In fact, the ads in *Playboy* did little else *but* tell men how to improve themselves; but they did it with utmost discernment; they used flattery rather than intimidation. In most ads, the audience is addressed as an in crowd privy to the special knowledge that only playboys have . . . more important, that all playboys *need* to have. The advertising composed a meticulous course in the lifestyle—month after month of two- and three-hundred-page, ad-packed issues filled with details about how to live like the "select, young, urban" man.

## *How to Smoke*

Cigarettes are déclassé. Perfumed pipe tobacco is the connoisseur's choice.

"'Masterpiece Pipe Tobacco is so man-of-the-world,' says Eva Gabor. 'And so masculine!'"

"Klompen Kloggen's natural tobacco bouquet works on a woman the way the subtle essence of a fine perfume works on a man." A beautiful blonde looks into the camera and asks, "Please, may I sniff your Klompen Kloggen?"

## *How to Dress*

The playboy's cardinal rule is: NO WRINKLES! James Bond never showed a crease or pucker in his custom-tailored suits because he was so cool. Ordinary guys who try to live the unrumpled life achieve what they hope is the 007 look by encasing themselves in wash-and-wear, wrinkle-proof, strain-resistant, airtight miracle fibers such as Arnel triacetate, Daroglo (Dacron and mohair), Darolite (Dacron polyester), Daro-Poplon (Dacron worsted poplin), Zantrel Polynosic High-Modulus Rayon, Lustrana ("a silky-to-the-touch fabric of Dacron polyester and cotton poplin treated with Zepel to scoff at stains"), or Bancora ("Go ahead, throw it in the machine!").

The goal is to look not only wrinkle-free but long and lean, with a low-low rise between belt line and inseam. In the early sixties, this was a problem, as only blue jeans of-

fered the low-rise look; and jeans, being a teen favorite, were definitely not approved playboy garb. Many slacks designers had not yet caught up with the new continental low-rise preference; they were still producing pants with a vast frontal area left over from the pleated-pants epoch. The result, without the pleats, was trousers with gigantic, smooth crotch regions, a full twelve inches between inseam and waist.

That changed in the mid-sixties with the advent of bolero pockets. The low-rise look became firmly entrenched; the playboy fashion in pants was lank and ultrasmooth, with only enough room in the crotch region for a tastefully distended basket. "Total neatness" was the Dacron promise and the playboy's clothing credo.

"Whatever his intentions, no man in a baggy suit should rescue fair maid," instructs PBM, makers of "the suits with the built-in paisley handkerchief."

Although long-crotched by today's standards, Sansabelt trousers were a sixties playboy ideal, described in ads as "the most talked about idea in men's slacks in years. The result of Sansabelt's ability to fit you so easily, so comfortably, so well, is a 'look.' Sansabelters naturally call it the Sansabelt Look. It has become the most talked about look in men's slacks in a quarter century."

"Looking for that l-o-o-o-n-g lean look?" asks Higgins, the makers of Hilton Club Luxury Trousers and Permanently Pressed Sebring Slacks. "It's the look that pares you down for action! That's Higgins styling!! Young, active, vigorous. There's nothing more 'fitting' than a pair of Higgins slacks."

"Forward-thinking get-out-of-townsmen plan for a quick weekend take-off by smartly dressing for business in threads that easily convert to country club casual wear," observes a caption for Bill Blass Double-Duty Garb. Picture number one shows an "executive decision maker" in his office, dressed in blazer with extension waistband slacks, cotton shirt, silk tie, and Italian silk pocket square; in the second shot (later that day at the golf course), he has taken off his tie and turned the pocket square into an ascot!

## How to Smell

Playboys want to smell like leather, lime, teak wood, or bay rum. Their scents are packaged as cologne, after-shave, after-bath, skin bracer, refreshant, friction lotion, powder-keg talc, instant lather, all-purpose lotion, soap-on-a-rope, and shaving balm. To distinguish them from feminine perfume, the bottles come wrapped in burlap, tied with rawhide, or, in the case of Jaguar, packaged in a bamboo cage with a

for men...
exhilarating elegance ..

JADE EAST
COLOGNE AND AFTER SHAVE

padlock and key. Because—let's face it—there is something rather sissy-boy about a man overly concerned with his perfume, scent advertising is the most aggressively masculine of all:

- "It takes more than martinis to build an image, mister." (Sir)
- "A dashing dry-martini of a fragrance" (Lyme By George!)
- "Extra dry with a twist of lemon" (That Man)
- "It's frosted with a twist of lime!" (Old Spice Lime)
- "So make her cry a little." (Studd)
- "Shiver her timbers." (Seven Seas)
- "If you have any doubts about yourself, try something else." (Brut)
- "Liquid virility" (Dunhill)
- "A hauntingly virile cologne for the man on the prowl" (White Hunter)
- "What Scandinavian men have" (Teak)

The most powerful weapon of seduction is the playboy's pad, to which *Playboy* devoted a series of breathtaking photo essays throughout the sixties. Each article profiles an enviable lair and is replete with suggestions for ordinary readers who, while perhaps unable to afford such pricey real estate, might at least borrow a few interior-design hints.

In August 1965, we were taken "high amid the towering spires of New York, where free-lance photographer Pete Turner combines an office and a home into a top-floor bachelor pad apartment ideally suited to his jet-propelled life as one of the busiest camera artists on the international scene." The globe-trotting lensman is a hi-fi buff with speakers in every room—including the bathroom!—and two tape recorders, on which he listens to bossa nova sounds he recorded on a trip to Rio. The lighting is all recessed and operates on rheostats, which lets him establish whatever mood he wants. His "master's bedroom" has a control panel on the headboard of his king-size bed to regulate not only the lighting but also the speaker system, the house intercom, and the drapes. Next to Mr. Turner's bed is a handy reservoir just big enough for two glasses and a champagne bucket.

Not all the dream pads were city penthouses. In October 1966, Jim Tittle shows off his "single man's deluxe retreat," which happens to be a wooden shack in an oil-company storage yard in Abilene, Texas. Does the less-than-soigné location stop Mr. Tittle from living life to the hilt? No way! Inside, "atmospheric underwaterlike light" is created by a stained-glass window. Teak chairs and white shag rugs surround a central fireplace with a great copper chimney. All the light is indirect; all the walls are covered with burlap.

The greatest of all playboy pads (other than Hef's own mansion) is a fantasy home described in an elaborate set of architectural renderings titled "The Playboy Town House—Posh Plans for Exciting Urban Living," created when the magazine assigned architect-designer R. Donald Jaye the task of conceiving the ideal urban living space. The goal was "expansive, nonconfining elbowroom, legroom, and luxurious living room,'' plus a two-car garage, a full-size indoor swimming pool with adjacent recreation area, integrated dining room-kitchen-bar, plenty of fireplaces, "all appurtenances automatically controlled," a roof sun deck "for summer simmering," and, of course, a generously proportioned master bedroom with oversize bath, dressing room, and rotating bed.

There it is, drawn with the utmost architectural sleekness, haloed by city lights: fieldstone and teak, fountains and fireplaces, Willem de Kooning's *Duck Pond* on the wall, unbelievable stereo gear: why, it's just like Hef's! . . . only smaller.

The most engaging thing about the "Town House" article is the text, which is written in the form of a date scenario. What a fantasy! "Guiding our guest to the right rear of the carport, we unlock the Rabbit-escutcheoned teak door and lead the way down a richly grained teak-walled passageway." Later, "we pause at the bar for a sampling of the preprandial potables and some quiet conversation, and then continue on with lightened gait." Across thick wall-to-wall Afghan carpeting, beneath a skylight that shows the setting sun, into the master bedroom, we guide our *"vis-à-vis"* finally to the marvel-of-mechanical-ingenuity bed, its headboard "fully outfitted to fill any needs of its bedded owner: reading, late hour supping or sipping , listening or viewing, at one's fingertips."

Amazingly, the tour barely pauses at the bed. We and our guest then go·on to admire the compartmentalized teak clothing closets, a bathroom of Olympian proportions, a chess table (teak, natch), a twenty-one-inch color television, and a bubble lamp next to a sofa. We wind up in the living room in front of the fire. "In showing our companion about, we've reaffirmed our belief that the Town House represents the best of all possible worlds for the unattached, affluent young man . . . with an urbane outlook, a mind of his own, and a tasteful appreciation of the life of elegant ease."

*Playboy* did it best, but did not completely corner the market on creating the image of the sixties bon vivant. As titillating as Hef's life was, James Bond enjoyed certain privileges that even the supreme pasha of playboyism didn't have. Agent 007 of Her Majesty's Secret Service knew his way around a gal, a gun, and a fast car; plus he had a license to kill any bad guy he didn't like. Here was a man who truly lived life to the hilt!

In some ways, you couldn't find two men more different than the real Hugh Hefner and the fictional James Bond. Hef stayed in Chicago. He was thin, cerebral, and assiduous. He was waited on by hordes of staff, sycophants, Bunnies, and freeloaders. James Bond traveled the globe to its most glamorous locations. He was strong, aggressive, and (in the movies, especially) self-mocking. He had no staff, not even a partner.

In spite of their differences, Hef and 007 shared that *particular point of view* described in the first "Playboy Philosophy." They were modern men using the world for their pleasure: *men,* not Beach Boys or Beatles or any of that contemporary kid stuff. The playboy—through such heros as Hef, 007, and Sinatra with his ring-a-ding-ding drinking-smoking-womanizing Rat Pack—saw himself as a grown-up. This became an ever more prominent feature of his self-image as the decade's immaturities accelerated and youth became an issue as provocative as Vietnam. The playboy aspired to manhood. He worshiped sophistication, not youth.

Bond is sophistication personified. He is English, which by the mid-sixties, when London is the planet's prime source of savoir faire, is the innest nationality by far. He is a gourmet who drives a Bentley and an Aston-Martin; he wears Savile Row single-breasted dark-blue suits and shirts of sea-island cotton; he tells time by a Rolex; he carries a stealthy Beretta and has a license to kill anyone, anytime, anywhere. In the movies, which eliminate the suffering and self-doubt Bond endures in the books, he is a superhero of truly mythological proportions. His life is simply ideal. Like Hef's.

Women throw themselves at him, but they aren't run-of-the-mill gorgeous women; they are athletic, mysterious, and they like sex every bit as much as he. Bond doesn't merely travel the world for idle pleasure; he goes to all the most exotic places and stays in the best hotels and eats the most sumptuous foreign food (just as the playboy craves to do)—all the while conducting business, which in his case is *saving the world* from destruction. For anyone with a job that sometimes seems humdrum, and anyone annoyed by life's petty frustrations, James Bond is a vision of liberation.

By 1964 and the release of the third James Bond film, *Goldfinger*, the sixties were immersed in secret-agent mania. In May, *Newsweek* reported a multimillion-dollar rush on 007 attaché cases, trench coats, and cuff links in France. "In Australia, an athletic Bond buff can now thrash around the barrier reef with an 007 snorkel, later change to a Bond evening suit, stuff a Bond handkerchief in his breast pocket, give his date a box of Bond choco-

*James Bond's passion for martinis helped vodka sales soar during the sixties.*

lates—or even undies—and finally soften her up with Bond cordials." The Licensing Corporation of America approved the Bond imprimatur on a board game, shaving cream, men's and women's shoes, handcuffs, and bubble gum. A 007 brassiere was rejected as not in keeping with the sophisticated image. Advertisements for 007 After Shave assured purchasers that the scent gave "any man the license to kill women."

If playboys fantasized about living the high life à la James Bond or Hugh Hefner, they were in reality

*See-through fashions were a playboy's dream-come-true.*

satisfied just to see some bare tit. Ogling breasts was one of the Good Life's sweetest fruits. The *Playboy* reader was a breast gourmet: big zaftig ones in particular, with pink nipples or sultry beige areolas. Connoisseurship of such breasts made the playboy feel part of a great brotherhood of swinging guys who knew the score.

Content for so long to stare down cleavages in hopes of getting a peek at the promised land of the nipple, playboys suddenly found the millennium at hand in 1964. That was when Rudi Gernreich introduced the topless swimsuit.

Gernreich, a Vienna-born Californian, had been known as a bathing-suit mischief maker since the early fifties, when he exhibited a flimsy leotard suit at a time when most beach wear was armored Lastex with modesty panels and nose-cone bust supports.

His topless suit—knitted trunks held up by a couple of slight straps, fully exposing the breasts—was never meant as a serious fashion statement, Gernreich later contended. It was merely a whimsical prediction of the future . . . and also a challenge to the fashion press: print a picture of it if you dare!

The week Gernreich showed it, *Women's Wear Daily* published a very small picture of a model wearing it. *Life* ran a picture, but with model Peggy Moffitt's arms crossed strategically. *The New York Times* did not run a picture but called it "the most radical development in swimsuit design since the bikini."

Gernreich had intended to make only a few dozen copies, but store buyers ordered it by the hundred! (Eventually, three thousand were sold.) By July, women in Los Angeles and Chicago were arrested on the beaches for wearing it. WE PROTEST TOPLESS SUITS IN THE NAME OF CHRIST, said picket signs outside a Dallas department store. Even the mayor of Saint-Tropez, an uninhibited resort town where casual bikini-top shedding had allegedly inspired Gernreich's creation, threatened to patrol the beach with helicopters in order to spot exposed breasts and arrest offenders. "I never dreamed it would go beyond the fashion business into sociology," Gernreich marveled.

*Izvestia* declared the bathing suit a sign that "the decay of the moneybag society continues." France's minister of the interior called it a "public outrage." The Pope condemned it as a "desperate and senseless adventure of impudent shamelessness." Toplessness became a major news story of the summer of 1964.

Carnegie Models, Ltd., a British dress manufacturer, enlarged upon the concept with a topless cocktail gown; but a week after it was in the stores, a spokesman for the company rued the idea: "A joke's a joke. But this is promiscuous." In July, Rae Southern, an exotic dancer, wore a bare-bosom evening dress and fur stole to a fashionable restaurant, accompanied by an escort, a reporter, and a photographer from *The Sunday Mirror*. Mary Quant announced autumn plans for two topless dresses.

In the wake of his notorious bathing suit, Gernreich devised the no-bra bra, a filmy set of nylon cups without a single support bone or strip of elastic. (It was followed by the no-front bra, the no-side bra, and the no-back bra.) At the same time, Warner's lingerie company formulated the body stocking—skin-tight, flesh-colored nylon that eliminated any need for undergarments, thus opening up a world of see-through possibilities. "This is the year when women will have to re-evaluate their beliefs about underwear," *The New York Times* announced in the summer of '64. Fashion authorities suggested Band-Aids as modest camouflage for pointy nipples.

For playboys, these bosomy developments were Jubilation Day. "When the first topless bathing suits hit the beaches last year," *Playboy* wrote gleefully in April 1965, "we joined the rest of mankind in hailing the advent of an age of limitless revelation. . . . Today's woman, to the delight of males who suffered through the *femme*-concealing fashions of the Fifties, has rediscovered that sex and style can be synonymous." *Playboy*'s analysis of the nude look lauded the peekaboo effect, the fishnet top, metallic mesh lounging pajamas, the monokini, and the topless evening gown.

Could it honestly be true, as Gernreich declared, that "clothes are disappearing"? So it seemed! The micro-miniskirt, cut to just below the crotch, was replacing the mid-thigh mini. Italian designers were showing harem pants slit clear up to the waist. Bosoms, including nipples ("this year's most important fashion accessory," Gernreich proclaimed), were everywhere! "For men," *Time* stewed, "the big question is where to look, and how?"

The week Gernreich's topless bathing suit hit the news, Dave Rosenberg, a public-relations man for the Condor Club of North Beach in San Francisco, saw a cute human-interest picture in the *Chronicle:* a four-year-old girl had lost the top of her swimsuit at the beach. The tot's dilemma inspired Mr. Rosenberg to have a brilliant idea. He went to Pete Mattioli, one of the Condor's bosses, who had been having problems drawing customers with local rock-and-roll bands. "Want to pack the club?" Rosenberg asked. He suggested that the Condor's most ravishing cocktail waitress, a short, well-proportioned teenage blonde named Carol Doda, perform in one of Gernreich's topless suits.

On June 16, 1964, two weeks after the debut of the topless bathing suit, Ms. Doda began dancing topless at the Condor Club. Motivated by her stylish new costume and the instant notoriety it provided, she spent three thousand dollars for what was then a novel operation—silicone injections. "I got one shot a week in each breast for twenty weeks," she recalled. "It was sort of like going to a gas station and saying 'Fill 'er up, Mack.'" Her bust size grew from 36 to 44 double-D. Doda's expanded chest became what Tom Wolfe called the biggest "convention and tourist attraction in America, with the possible exception of Manhattan."

Her act was short and simple, choreographed to display the famous breasts. The lights dim, and "floating down from the heavens on a three-thousand-dollar grand piano" (the announcer's words), Carol Doda appears. First you see only her legs, atop the piano, ponying and mashed-potatoing and watusiing as the band plays a high-flying Chuck Berry song. When the piano settles on the stage, the music stops. "Now, ladies and gentlemen," the announcer announces, "Miss Carol Doda will perform the swim." The strobe light starts flashing, and she starts swimming. Noth-

*Silicone breast pioneer Carol Doda at the Condor Club in San Francisco*

ing shows off big breasts better than the swim, with its flailing arm movements and rhythmic chest thrusts. She bounces ten minutes; then the piano
ascends, carrying Carol Doda and her silicone breasts back into the heavens.
The show is over. The club is cleared, and the next audience is ushered in.
Doda did this show six times a day, seven days a week. It was a gigantic
success.

North Beach sprouted fifteen swim clubs, with topless attractions ranging
from Tosha the Glo Girl at Big Al's to Mommy Spiegelman (TOPLESS MOTHER
OF EIGHT! the marquee boasted) at El Cid.

In April 1965, the California Department of Alcoholic Beverage Control
issued regulations prohibiting bare breasts at nightclubs. Twenty-three dancers were arrested on April 22 for indecent exposure. The crackdown was by
no means the end of toplessness, but by the summer of '65, bare breasts were
old news.

As the sexual revolution that *Playboy* forecast and promoted gathered momentum, a sad thing happened. Playboys, with all their seductive rigmarole
—their knife-crease slacks and shaken-not-stirred martinis and revolving
beds and flaming gourmet cherries jubilee—were left behind. They got
stranded in the early sixties! By the end of the decade, they weren't the cool-
cat cosmopolites anymore; they were horny guys in creepy lounging jackets
and three-year-old pairs of Sansabelts, proffering syrupy Drambuie cocktails,
smelling of English Leather and honeyed pipe tobacco and listening to some
once-hip jazz recording on a clunky old reel-to-reel tape deck, while everybody cool was wearing jeans or wide-whales and grooving on eight-track acid
rock and teenyboppers with Twiggy-size bee-bite tits.

Whereas in 1964, a mere peek at bouncing boobs made topless clubs the
hottest entertainment in the West, now there were topless *and* bottomless
clubs, there were Broadway plays where you could see completely naked
bodies, there were hippies not only parading around in the raw but offering
all the free love you wanted! And there was *Penthouse* magazine, which
showed not just breasts but pubic hair and labia, too. *Playboy*'s role as standard bearer for the daring, but always polite, new age of libertinism was
dramatically superseded by radical lifestyles that made Hef's erudite "Philosophy" look positively prudish. The moral revolution of the late sixties called
*Playboy*'s bluff.

It was a dilemma for playboys, and for *Playboy* magazine. For a few
blithe years, the magazine thrived on the decade's conspicuous titillations
such as the spicy singles scene (swingers' apartment complexes, computer
dating), hippies (because of their sexual openness), psychedelic drugs (because of their alleged aphrodisiac powers), and radical politics (down with
censorship!). A few end-of-the-sixties Playmates even declared some
vague affiliation with the counterculture: Miss May 1970 said, "I can't do
the nine-to-five bit. . . . I want to feel free." Miss December 1969 "decided
that the nine-to-five work routine was a down trip." Miss August 1967 even

worried about the war in Vietnam: "I just hope that it really *is* worth it."

The playboy had far too much invested in his car, his pad, his wardrobe, and, most important, his civilized self-image, to join the new anarchistic multitudes of sloppy, licentious hippies and rebels and freaks . . . even if they did get a lot of sex.

But don't you see, there's the confirmation of what Hef had been saying all along: the playboy lifestyle wasn't fundamentally *only* about big boobs and sex. It was more about being cultured and suave and polished (and also about big boobs and sex). "If girls were the only motivation for buying our magazines," Hef said in 1961, "they wouldn't sell. People would buy sheer smut. We, on the other hand, are Taste City." Hippie types, however ribald they might be, did not belong in Taste City. They were slobs with wrinkled clothes and uncombed hair, smelling of b.o. instead of Brut. They knew nothing of life's sophisticated pleasures; they tried to act childlike, not mature.

That is why, despite getting superannuated by the sexual revolution, playboys continued to live life to the hilt *their way.* Their nemesis was no longer little old ladies; it was vulgar youth.

Even as *Playboy* magazine left its sixties attitudes behind, the smoking-jacket-and-cool-jazz way of life many readers discovered in the glory days of James Bond and Hef's first twenty-five "Philosophies" remained a vivid ideal. Heck, it *still* is an ideal, blissfully oblivious to twenty years of social dislocation. If you don't believe us, look at who's driving the next Porsche you see.

# YOUNG VULGARIANS

YOUNG VULGARIANS were street-smart teenagers from hardscrabble neighborhoods such as South Philadelphia and the Bronx. In the early sixties they created a spectacular style.

Unburdened by middle-class rules of good taste, young vulgarians positively dripped with splendiferous cheapness. If you want a quick mental picture of what they looked like, think of Priscilla Presley in 1963, when Elvis acted as her personal cosmetology consultant; or remember the sassy kids in John Waters's movie *Hairspray;* or flash back to continental doo-woppers such as Dion and the Belmonts. Young vulgarians flaunted huge bouffants, heavy eyeliner, pounds of Vitalis, and black leather coats over sharkskin trousers.

The look was hoodlum baroque, combining a city-tough attitude with formal hairdos as ornate as the chandeliers at the local catering hall. This was a look that was bigger than fashion. It expressed a turgid universe of teenage passion and despair.

Any teenager could tune into the universe of young vulgarians simply by watching "American Bandstand" every afternoon on television, to see which "regulars" were dancing the slow dances together and what they were wearing. You could get into the young-vulgarian world by listening to radio stations such as New York's WINS and WMCA, where disc jockeys Murray the K and Cousin Brucie spoke the true language of teens . . . and made everyone else on the air sound like Arthur Godfrey.

Girl groups like the Shirelles and Shangri-Las were mentors. Far from being perky, young-vulgarian girls approached romance with the same delicacy they used applying makeup. They knew that love was not as light and carefree as a soap bubble; and with each ID bracelet they flung back at a two-timing boy, they proudly sacrificed their Cleopatra eyeliner to cry at the lyrics of songs such as "Chains" and "I Wanna Love Him So Bad."

Young vulgarians were important not only for their breathtaking style but because they were the swan song of teenagers. They reigned from 1960 to 1964, before the Beatles made everyone want to be young again.

Before the Beatles, the world of teenagers was a small-time affair. Major merchandisers had not yet learned to aim their wiles at teens. And so teens were pretty much left alone to wallow in teen fads and fancies, to which the adult world was oblivious.

Out of this privacy was built a true subculture, a world apart from the prying eyes of grown-ups, who wouldn't think of watching "Bandstand" or buying the tawdry gimcracks sold to teens: dollar charm bracelets from the back of *Love Confessions* magazine, or pink fur dice to hang from the jalopy's rearview mirror. Teens were the ones who cared about Clearasil, Maybelline eye pencil, fuzzy mohair sweaters, and leopard-skin sneakers. Young vulgarians put together the best of the worst of it, and made it fashion.

Like most subcultures, young vulgarians lived by a strict code. Being a young vulgarian meant being cool at all costs. For boys, coolness was exemplified on a junior level by singers Frankie Avalon, Dion DiMucci, Fabian, and Bobby Rydell—good neighborhood boys from South Philly who had massive doses of white soul and major-league pompadours. The senior level was headed by Frank Sinatra—Mr. Las Vegas—whose silky singing was less important to male young vulgarians than the fantasy of his life: white Lincoln Continentals, smoky nightclub lounges, and fabled connections to Mafia royalty. Second only to the Chairman of the Board was Bobby Darin, never photographed without a cigarette held street-style, and a wicked look in his eyes that spelled as much trouble as his song "Mack the Knife."

Looking *continental* was the goal. It defined a kind of suavity adapted from the world of adults who wore big cuff links and brocade tuxedos. It combined an attitude of utter unflappability, the vague dark threat of a junior mafioso, and the smarmy ease of a headwaiter. A guy who was continental cool talked as little as possible and never smiled. He danced the dirty bop with fast, tight moves, keeping his eyes focused on some distant point in space—anywhere but on his equally sullen girlfriend. Eye contact would have looked far too warm and vulnerable.

To aid in the elimination of eye contact, wraparound sunglasses were a vital part of the ensemble. Shades made a guy look not only cool but dangerous. Standing on the street corner, eating a soft pretzel from a vendor, a teen in wraparound glasses and a tight sharkskin suit or a three-quarter-length leather raincoat looked like a real tough guy rather than a high-school student. He wanted you to see him as one of the kind of big-time hoods that police refer to as gentlemen.

Because life for young vulgarians was a continuous adolescent soap opera of love, revenge, and redemption, looking or acting happy was a signal that you were really out of it. Teen life was serious business. Perkiness was anathema. A young-vulgarian girl approached her role in life with the gravity of a diva digging into *Medea.* She strove to look emblematic of all the passions of the brink of womanhood. Facial animation was taboo; too much goofy smiling was unsexy and looked childish—and anyway, it disturbed one's makeup.

Boys, too, had much to learn. For example, they had to be accomplished make-out artists. That meant being able to leave any girl with a personalized monogram: a huge hickey on her neck. Walking around with a purple neck bruise was a perfectly acceptable fashion for teenage girls who did not strive to affect kitten-soft femininity.

For girls, the single most important signifier of vulgarianism was the hairdo. In some cases, the face appeared to exist for little reason other than to provide an anchor for it. The best of them were as ceremonious as Marie Antoinette's—lacking only miniature sailing ships stuck up among the combed, back-combed, sprayed, ratted, and teased work of art.

Nineteen sixty-three was the climactic year for the beehive, the crowning hairdo of the young-vulgarian era. (Some grown-ups wore their hair in this style, too, but only on teenagers did it tend to grow beyond the one-foot mark.) The beehive was a soaring cylindrical bouffant that resembled a beer keg, a tornado, or eponymously, a beehive. Although it was sprayed so stiff it looked like ironwork that could withstand a hard blow from a wrecking ball, its looks were deceiving: this confectionary coif was a fragile monument to the art of hair ecclesiology; it took hours to erect, and once raised, it was extremely volatile. Whenever the hairdo and its owner returned home, the gossamer mountain was cautiously wrapped with yards of toilet paper to preserve its shape.

Being a young-vulgarian girl was not easy. It meant exacting hours of hair-do maintenance on a daily schedule. To have some appreciation of the industry and elbow grease that went into the making of a really superb beehive, we have assembled these basic procedures from hair-styling books of the time:

When construction begins, the first task is overcoming the hair's cleanliness. Just-washed hair is limp, and so it must be slathered immediately with setting gel to give it body and texture. While damp and still tacky from the gel, the hair is rolled onto big plastic rollers (preferably pink) and covered with a triangular hair net.

Now the hairdo is dried. While its owner reads a fan magazine in a chair, the curled and wrapped coiffure on her head is snugged into a giant metal-domed hair dryer and baked with currents of hot air for about as long as it takes to cook a chicken. When thoroughly dry, it is ready to be combed out.

Shaping begins. Section by section, using a rat-tail comb, the hair is cordoned off and back-combed mercilessly, tuft by tuft, until it becomes a dozen or more weedy clumps standing out from the head. Each matted clump is saturated with a heavy-duty spray such as Aqua Net until it is as malleable as a bundle of solder wires. As the clumps dry, more back-combing further fluffs out any hair that might have wilted under the salvos of spray.

Now a hairbrush is used to gingerly create the familiar beehive or keg shape, then even more carefully arrange the uppermost layers of the matted tangle into a halo as delicate as spun sugar. The spire is then sprayed once more to make certain it keeps its place.

No one knew more about the aesthetics of beehive hair than Ingerid of Boston, author of styling classics *How to Comb Five Different Tops from Only Two Rows of Curls; The French Twist, Asymmetric, the Chignon, Extra Hair Pieces, Pony Tail Variations, and Braids;* and the seminal treatise on teasing, *Ingerid's Combing Techniques.* Ingerid invented the "Cleopatra Backcomb" —a surefire method of sliding-and-stretching-and-teasing with a comb that created an enormous hairdo guaranteed to stay put. (With each stroke of the comb, say to yourself, "One—two—three, comb smooth. One—two—three, comb smooth.")

She was not only a hairdresser but something of a cosmetological philosopher as well. Under the headline THESE ARE MY THOUGHTS ON BACK-COMBING, Ingerid comes out foursquare against "vicious" back-combing, or back-combing with gestures and facial features that give "the impression of a sadist at work with fiendish delight." Ingerid says she is not at all impressed when a customer comes into her salon with a huge ratted hairdo and boasts that "she hasn't combed her hair in three weeks." Back-combing is an art, Ingerid says; and when done right, it "looks like French pastry."

Maintaining a majestic hairdo was an exercise in self-sacrifice, and a classic example of the adage that beauty knows no pain. In 1963, when Elvis Presley wanted a picture of his girlfriend, Priscilla, in the compact car he gave her, she posed sitting in the driver's seat, but had to lean awkwardly out the door because there simply was no room inside the car for her hair. There was no way anyone could sleep on a ratted beehive and expect it to survive; and so serious wearers of the hairdo spent the night propped upright on pillows in semi-repose. With luck, the beehive that greeted its owner in the morning would need only a bit of coaxing with the sharp end of a rat-tail comb to lift the pouf where it sagged, plus a few coats of hair spray to keep it in place for the day.

Because every young vulgarian knew well the demands of achieving such a hairdo, it was proper etiquette to display a work in progress. Girls unblushingly went about town with their hair rolled in massive curlers with a chiffon scarf tied under the chin, babushka style. Indeed, some girls wore their curlers so long and so well that that became a style unto itself. They would shampoo and roll up their hair, then leave it that way until the next shampoo. When, if ever, the hairdo was unfurled from the rollers, it was inevitably a letdown from the perfection of its promise.

The beauty of properly rolled hair on display was that it did two things well. If you used jumbo rollers and then added a big scarf, your hair was already a good six inches up in the air without a single bit of back-combing. Secondly, if you used a hair net instead of a scarf, you could display another bit of artistry from the beauty-class curriculum: a virtuoso display of perfectly rolled and clipped hair, end papers neatly placed, and pin curls symmetrically secured in front of the ears.

Because girls with big hair avoided body-depleting shampoos until absolutely necessary, teen culture was rampant with beehive apocrypha. It was common knowledge that out of unwashed beehives crawled all the worst types of cooties: roaches the size of lemons, beetles the size of oranges, and spiders the size of grapefruits. Even more awful than the poor, trapped insects who yearned for a glimpse of daylight were the legions of mutant rodents who fed on the chemically rich hair spray and grew large and crazy, tunneling deep into the hairdo wearer's ear canals. No one who went to high school in the early sixties was spared the cautionary tale of the girl with the unwashed beehive who mysteriously collapsed and died at her desk. When the school nurse parted the girls unyielding high rise, she found a nest of rats busy munching their way into the girl's skull.

In a more realistic vein, young-vulgarian girls were famed for their ability to carry contraband in the manner of native women who tote baskets on their heads. Beehive hairdos provided useful cubbyholes for switchblade knives, zip guns, stilettos, blackjacks, brass knuckles, and small flasks. It was the one place the principal always forgot to look . . . or was he afraid of looking?

Young-vulgarian boys had their own hair goals, every bit as difficult to achieve as the towering ratted beehive. Their hair was worn long—so long, in fact, that without pomade it would have flopped over their ears, Beatles style. But it never did. It was secured with enormous amounts of unguent such as Brylcreem, Dixie Peach, Pomatex, or, in an emergency, Crisco straight from the can. The critical quality of any hair grease was extremely low viscosity. It had to be thick enough to show comb tracks in perfect, parallel relief. Ideally, each cord of hair, composed of a hundred or more cilia, appeared to be a single black rope, like a dripping-wet licorice whip.

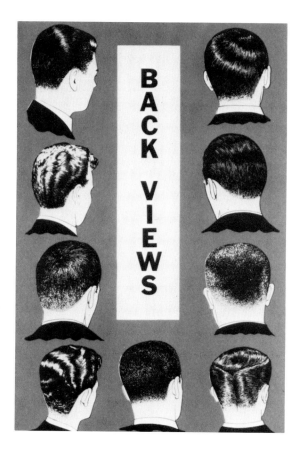

*A manly hairdo was built upon a foundation of grease. For rock-and-roller Wayne Cochrane (opposite page), a little dab was hardly enough.*

The most devilishly hard part of a boy's hairdo was getting the back of the head right. Stylish teens turned up their noses at anything as passé as a fifties ducktail, preferring an elaborate arrangement that crisscrossed the hair across the back of the skull in an overlapping pattern from nape to top of head. Perfectly done, it resembled hundreds of fingers intertwined in prayer.

The front and sides presented problems of their own. The best hairdos featured a forelock forward and then *whoosh*, flipped back so that it lay on top of itself, forming a lordly prow that jutted out, hovering half a hand's length in front of the face. Another popular style looked like a sideways S: the forelock rose, dipped dramatically at the brow, then rose up again. Another option resembled the vortex inside a wave: a giant curling tube of greasy hair was pulled forward between the eyes—simple yet inelegant.

How to make the front fit with the top was the most important issue faced by the young vulgarian with a comb. In some cases, they were fashioned as a single unit, like Edd "Kookie" Byrnes's hair on "77 Sunset Strip." He whipped the wave around, then used the flat of his palm to press it out and forward, at the same time blending the wave with the top. That was easy: a unitary look. But the more popular style was to fashion the wave as a distinct entity at the very front, curling over—exactly like a breaking ocean wave—and jutting as far out as possible. It was high enough so you could not see the brink where the base of the wave met the top of the head; but if you did manage to get an aerial view, you would see that it resembled a movie-set façade, with nothing behind it but enough hair piled up as needed for support. In this case, the hair on top of the head had to be glass smooth, without even the tine marks of a comb to disturb its sleekness.

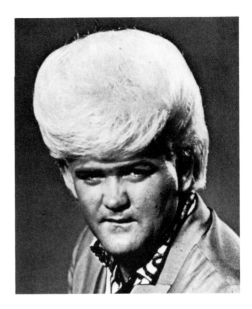

Similar problems were faced when dealing with the sides. Old-fashioned fenders, combed as a separate entity, above the sideburns and below the sculpted top, were no longer a valid fashion statement. Sides had to be integrated into the whole coiffure, including sideburns, which young-vulgarian boys wore no longer than mid-ear level.

Boys, like girls, hated to wash their hair; after all, they had a fortune in grease invested in it. So minor unpleasantness such as dandruff simply had to be accepted. Flecks of white stuck into the grease all along the waves and furrows of an elaborate hairdo added a festive touch, similar to a souvenir glass ball filled with snow.

None of these boys had a beard or mustache. Shaving was a big deal, since it was only on a clean canvas that hickeys could be adequately displayed. As for skin, there was no great pride in having a blemish-free complexion. A few zits on a guy were the mark of heavy hormones. You didn't want a big rash of gooey pimples, but a few tasteful dots here and there were fine. Globs of Clearasil with its distinctive sepia coloring added a bit of variety to the otherwise pasty pigmentation.

The girls had pimples or they didn't, but no one ever knew. All flaws were hidden beneath a washcloth-thick veil of pancake makeup. The goal was colorless, opaque skin, achieved with Max Factor Pancake Number Two or pan stick. Girls applied it with a sponge, layer after layer, building up the surface like an artist with a can of gesso. The correct amount was achieved when the entire surface was reduced to a smooth, beige blanket. It was especially essential that lips were negated. Lips in their natural state were repugnantly healthy, wet, and pink. The only feature approved of by real teenage girls were eyes, so lips were sponged away or, even better, blotted out by a heavy coat of Erace—a lipstick-shaped blemish concealer. Over the Erace went dead-white lipstick, rendering the wearer's lips as bloodless as a corpse's.

It is hard to explain to those who missed the sixties, or perhaps lived through them on a farm in Iowa, just how shocking this beloved hard-core vulgarian look was. It was like a negative of a living person. Eye sockets were coal black and hollow, and dead-white lips made even the healthiest teeth look yellow; combined with dyed black hair and blanched skin, the effect was as ghastly as a fiendish host of a TV spook show. In 1962, *Seventeen* magazine tried to steer readers away from white lipstick by recommending instead a subtle wash of Max Factor's Essence of Pearl in combination with another pastel shade, suggesting that it was better to look "subtle, not scary." To the teenager working to create an awe-inspiring cheap face, subtlety equaled failure.

Once her natural color and features were all blotted out, the good parts were redrawn. Eyes first, matched to the lips with chalk-white eye shadow. Black liquid eyeliner was applied at the lash line in a thick ribbon that started at the inside corner and grew in width to the outside corner, where it extended a half-inch beyond the eye, ending with a sharp, upturned doe-eye effect. Finally, the inside bottom rim of the eye was penciled with a black eyebrow pencil, finalizing the creation of a hard, black little orb that looked dangerous and sexy.

Before applying eye makeup, it was important to remove the eyebrows. Shaving off the brows was essential because nature never provided a pair of them sufficiently arched and black. Using a Woolworth's five-and-dime eyebrow pencil, sharpened with a safety-razor blade, girls drew their brows a good inch above the path of the old ones, heading on a forty-five-degree angle upwards to the outer corners.

After completion of the toilette, it was time to get dressed for school. A pointy padded bra was hooked on, a few extra Kleenexes stuffed into the cups if they sagged. The most daring young-vulgarian girls saved their allowances and sent away from the Frederick's of Hollywood catalog for the "On-the-Shelf" brassiere, which "pushes up and

*Shaved eyebrows and teased hair: an example of young vulgarian beauty*

pushes in" and promised to "lift your entire bosom . . . put it on the shelf . . . utilize all possible cleavage!" Over the bra went a white nylon "pussycat" blouse. The front of the blouse had a double row of ruffles, like the tuxedo shirts worn by musicians who play at bar mitzvahs. Because the blouse's white fabric was on the sheer side (sexy!), it was a nice touch to wear a black bra underneath, a constant reminder to all lookers of the wearer's femininity. The bra glowed seductively through the fabric, as did the wearer's small gold crucifix.

Young-vulgarian girls loved jewelry almost as much as makeup; all good jewelry had symbolic resonance. Lockets containing pictures of dreamy singers such as Dion or Cliff Richard intertwined around the neck with favorite religious icons. On her wrist, the well-accessoried teen sported her boyfriend's oversized ID bracelet, made of thick, coarse silver links with the boy's first name engraved on the flat metal surface in front. Ankle bracelets, worn under the nylons, were ubiquitous; also popular were a boyfriend's class ring, dog tags (with his name), and a pink or blue beaded bracelet that replicated the ID bracelets worn by newborn babies in hospitals. Dime-store bangle bracelets clattered merrily against it, and a costume jewelry birthstone ring was worn on the middle finger of a hand whose bitten fingernails were painted with pearlescent white polish.

The pussycat blouse was tucked into a short, tight black skirt, cinched at the waist by an elastic black belt with a gold buckle. On her legs, the high-school fashion plate wore sheer black nylons, even more trampy when they had a run in them. Black stockings were worn with black shoes with pointy toes and curvy Cuban heels an inch high. Made of low-grade Leatherette, they fell apart after the first rainstorm or an afternoon of doing the pony.

An acceptable alternative to slutty shoes and runned nylons were sneakers and "poodle socks." Not—ugh—athletic sneakers as worn by the pink-cheeked cheerleaders in phys-ed class; the proper sneakers were pointy-toed and came in purple, leopard skin, tiger stripes, or black. If white sneakers were worn, they had to be covered with the names of cute boys or teen singers scribbled on with a blue ballpoint pen. Under the sneakers were poodle socks, made of heavy white spandex Vyrene as thick and lumpy as a chenille bedspread. The texture of the cuffs was like hobnail glass, all nubbly white bumps.

Over the whole ensemble went a huge cable-stitched mohair cardigan in pinky peach or turquoise blue, or a high-school jacket with white Leatherette sleeves and the name of the school spelled out in felt letters on the back: SCRANTON VOCATIONAL TECH. On the breast pocket, in loopy white letters, was embroidered the owner's name or, better, nickname: BOOTSIE, LUCKY, or TWINKIE. Under that might be another row of script announcing to the world her chosen major: NAIL CARE, COSMETOLOGY, or HAIR REMOVAL.

Before a real teenage girl left the house, she slung a big handbag over her shoulder. The best bags were black Leatherette. They were copious because

*Television's "American Bandstand," starring Dick Clark (above), made real Philadelphia teenagers into celebrities. On opposite page, regulars Kenny and Arlene do the stroll.*

teens had a lot of equipment to tote around. First came a big nylon hairbrush and a rat-tail comb, then a can of hair spray. A makeup kit held pancake makeup, a sponge, extra Erace, eyeliner, and duplicates of everything used for the morning toilette. The purse was also the receptacle for issues of the latest teen mags, such as *16*, *Dig*, or *Tiger Beat*—plus a few 45 records to trade with friends, candy bars, a dozen pieces of Bazooka bubble gum, a tube of Clearasil, lucky rabbit's feet, a bus pass, and, finally, a bloated wallet.

The young-vulgarian girl had remarkably high wallet consciousness. The wallet itself was nothing special—you could get one for $1.95 at the corner store. But the plastic picture folder contained the depth and breadth of her social life. The thicker the wallet was with pictures, the more popular a girl was. Snap open that compartment and there you saw the population of her world—picture after picture of other teens posed in front of the romantic pastel studio clouds that were the mark of the yearbook photographer. Each was autographed, some with the favorite inscription, "Love ya!" Girls' *i*'s were topped with round, hollow dots; handwriting tended towards the fat and bulbous style that foreshadowed the penmanship of today's urban graffiti artists. Boys' messages—often in the form of innuendo about hickeys and make-out parties—were generously sprinkled with the interjection "ha!" to signify the writer's contempt for warm, fuzzy sentiment.

The world at large might never have known about young vulgarians if it hadn't been for Dick Clark's television show, "American Bandstand." Its cast of pale, zitty South Philadelphia kids, with their lopsided bouffants and black eyeliner and continental fashions, riveted a nation of young viewers.

The show was called "Bandstand" when it began in 1952 on WFIL-TV in Philadelphia. It was hosted by Bob Horn on a set designed to look like a record shop, and featured thirty minutes of local kids dancing to popular records. In 1956, Dick Clark, a radio disc jockey, became the host of the show; and a year later it had become a national hit, carried by sixty-seven ABC affiliates. "Bandstand" soon became the premier showcase for every aspiring rock-and-roll act. Its ability to make hits was legendary.

It was a simple show. There were bleachers for kids to sit on when they weren't dancing, an autograph table for guest stars, Dick Clark's podium,

and a board that listed the top ten songs of the week. Its resounding success was due neither to the stars it attracted nor to the charisma of Dick Clark. "Bandstand" resonated in the hearts of loyal legions of teenage viewers because of the unvarnished reality of its ensemble of dancers. They were kids just like those on any city street corner, except for the fact that their daily doings were beamed each afternoon into your living room.

This was not a case of art imitating life: this was real life as art. No wily theatrical producer could have cast such perfect specimens of urban teenhood as Frani Giordano, Carole Scaldeferri, or Denny Dziena. These were the genuine article, teenagers just like you or the kids next door, dressed as if they had just come from school (they had), wearing their favorite shaggy mohair sweaters and tight pants, looking goofy-eyed at each other in the throes of adolescent passion.

Five days a week, viewers tuned in (many to stations that carried the full ninety minutes of the show) and saw a real-life soap opera and street-fashion show. Each day brought new intrigue: Would Bob and Justine break up? Would Carmen Jimenez's mom allow her to keep that spectacular white skunk streak in her jet-black hair? Would Frankie get over his wild crush on Angel Kelly and find happiness with Frani G.?

By today's elevated standards of teen beauty, the "Bandstand" kids looked positively rodentlike: small, pinched faces with too much makeup and too big hair. They were snaggle-toothed and their clothes were cheap and their nylons sagged at the ankles. When they posed for pictures in *Teen* or *Dig*, it was always on the front stoop of their parents' brick row house in front of an aluminum-screened front door. All those things that now seem tacky were what made them great. "Bandstand" kids were nothing less than young vulgarian royalty. At four o'clock each weekday, they took center stage and did the greatest after-school job any kid could imagine. They twisted and slow-danced and drank Pepsi and played rate-a-record: "I give it an eighty-nine—it's got a good beat and you can dance to it." "Bandstand" kids had it made. They were professional teenagers.

Like every high school, Dick Clark's little world had its standard cast of characters: the beauties, the brains, the playboys, the heartbreakers. "Bandstand" was a microcosm in which all that mattered were teen things. Although the roster of kids changed constantly, there were regulars who left indelible impressions. Carole Scaldeferri, a Connie Francis look-alike, was known as the cover girl of "Bandstand" because of her aspirations to be a model. She was famous for precision dancing and a meticulous wardrobe. She was so fastidious that sometimes she would sit out important dance numbers rather than go on camera with a wrinkle in her skirt.

Jimmy Peatross was the fastest dancer on the show. As slim and light-footed as an inner-city Fred Astaire, Jimmy went through partners like popcorn, exhausting all the girls with his lightning-fast jitterbug. He became a favorite when he overcame the trauma of his first Spotlight Dance. Moving to his favorite song—"Tall Cool One"—he accidentally punched his partner in the ribs with his elbow.

The first regular to get star treatment was Arlene DiPietro, the daughter of a sheet-metal mechanic and a bank employee, whom Dick Clark fancied because she constantly flashed a big toothy smile at the camera. Arlene's claim to fame was that she had poise, even when the "Bandstand" cameras filmed her hasty retreat to the sidelines to let the house physician, kindly Dr. Dick, remove an eyelash from her eye.

Less beloved by Dick Clark, but an audience favorite, was Carmen Jimenez. Carmen did not look like a model, nor was she as poised as Arlene. She had "street kid" written all over her. She was small, compact, and tough looking. She liked tight black skirts and black shoes with straps and buttons. She and her sister Yvette had matching skunk streaks—big, thick white

stripes running down the middle of their jet-black hair. After her success on "Bandstand," Carmen settled down to a career as a clerk in a Philadelphia dime store.

The heartbeat of "Bandstand" came from its couples, and the happiest among them were Frani Giordano and Frankie Levins. Frani was a high-energy girl with a big, womanly body, buck teeth, a mound of teased blond hair, and a splashy wardrobe of dresses, all of which appeared to be covered with huge black and white dots. Frani won the pony contest after weeks of grueling competition. Dimpled Frankie, also a blond, was her main squeeze and the target of many home viewers' crushes. Ultimately, Frankie proved to be not man enough to hold on to the tempestuous Frani, who dumped him after she got mad when he asked her to carry the birthday cake Dick Clark had presented to him on the air.

Without a doubt, the most famous of all couples were Bob and Justine. Justine Carrelli started dancing on "Bandstand" back in 1956, when it was a decidedly local program with no eyes on the big time. Bob (Robert Harry Clayton) was a viewer who fell in love with the beautiful blonde on the show and commuted from his home in Wilmington, Delaware to Forty-sixth and Market Street in Philadelphia (the "Bandstand" studio) to dance on the show.

Because he was a good dancer, and cute, he made it on the air ... but Justine wanted nothing to do with him. She was going steady with handsome Tex Conners. Bob was nothing if not persistent, and in time he wooed her to be his dance partner and date. Viewers swooned as Bob's passion for Justine grew stronger and slowly, week by week, dance by dance, she fell for him. Soon they were inseparable, looking moonily into each other's eyes, pressed tightly together at each slow dance. Like the bride and groom atop a wedding cake, they looked perfect together. Justine was only five foot two, with light blond hair. Bob towered over her at five foot seven. He was blond, too, but according to "Bandstand" regular Pat Mollitieri, "His hair seems darker because of his hair lotion."

Finally, to the horror of the viewers, after two years of public going steady and after more dreamy looks and sweaty dances than anyone could remember, Bob and Justine split up. There was not even a birthday cake to blame it on. They just went their separate ways, and everyone watched in sorrow as they danced side by side with new partners. By 1963, both Bob and Justine had left the show, Justine to try her luck as a singer with a band in Las Vegas, and Bob to settle down as a "retail trainee" back in Wilmington.

Unlike other teen celebrities, who parlayed their early time in the spotlight into a career, most "Bandstand" kids left the show and returned into the ether of anonymity from which they had come. In 1963, *Teen* magazine scouted out what had become of the golden boys and girls of the dance floor only a few years after their heyday. Carole Scaldeferri was working as a receptionist in a modeling agency; Myrna Horowitz (who had conquered polio to dance on "Bandstand") was an office worker for the city of Philadelphia; Billy Young was working in a supermarket; Bob Durkin, who worked in a pizza parlor when he wasn't dancing on the show, was now a full-time pizza baker. Carole Crossin was a beautician and Joe Fusco a hairdresser. The biggest success story *Teen* found belonged to Kenny Rossi, one half of one of the all-time-great couples, Arlene and Kenny. Kenny had cut a record, which was reported to be "getting heavy play in Georgia."

In a world that had little prepackaged teen culture, no brat-pack movies, no MTV or *Sassy* magazine, "American Bandstand" was one important teen touchstone. AM radio was the other. Radio was the way teens knew what was going on. They communicated with each other by calling in record dedications, and listened closely for the deejay to say, "This is going out to Bobby from Vonetta, who wants her lover boy to know . . . 'There's a Moon Out Tonight.' " They squealed at the mention of their school's name, and scribbled down any information about rock-and-roll concerts about to come to town.

None of this would likely have happened if it weren't for transistor radios, the first of which was a bone-white Sony not much larger than a cigarette pack with a gold circular speaker disc in front. "Look . . . No Cords!" the Sears catalog enthused in 1960, raving about the colorful, unbreakable Dur-Pac Mighty Midgets that go anywhere and pull in stations miles away. Listening to the radio was no longer a family affair. Teens could tune in while in their rooms supposedly doing homework, or in the corridors of school. They no longer had to endure corny shows their parents liked, such as "The Breakfast Club." Any teen able to scrape together $16.50 for the cheapest two-by-four-inch Silvertone had the power to secede from the adult world at any time.

Disc jockeys became a new kind of celebrity. These were not the silky-voiced platter spinners of old; they were jivey cats who played songs like Ernie K-Doe's "Mother-in-Law" and followed up each hit with a barrage of crazed patter all their own. The number-one kingpin of them all was a middle-aged Jewish bopper named Murray Kaufman, who went by the name of Murray the K. As host of the "Swingin' Soiree" on New York City's WINS, Murray helped spread haute-vulgarian culture throughout the east.

Murray the K knew that kids wanted to be different than grown-ups, so he invented a secret language to share with his listeners. An old record was a "golden gasser." Finding a secluded place to neck on a date was "submarine race watching." He called the language "Meusarray"—a gibberish translation of his own first name.

Meusarray was in fact a variation of old-fashioned carnival slang. In his book *Murray the K Tells It Like It Is, Baby,* he offers this example of Meusarray morphology: "Heusave Feusun weusith theuse leusnageusage eusand meusake seusure yeusou leusisten teuse WEUSINS. Eusi weusill seusee yeuso seusoon!" ("Have fun with this language and make sure you listen to WINS. I will see you soon.") Teens who became fluent in this crazy tongue had a powerful secret. They could gab frantically on the phone, telling all kinds of secrets in front of befuddled parents.

> Mur-ray, Mur-ray the K-ay
> He's the Hul-ly Gul-ly man.
> Tune in the Swingin' Soir-ee
> And Mur-ray, Mur-ray the K-ay. . . .

So began each night's program, as Murray the K introduced himself with a strong bleat of "Harrumm Bay," an African-style chant that had the rousing effect of a football cheer at halftime. Sounding as breathless as if he had just chased the Supremes around the block, Murray shouted out, "This is Murray the K telling it like it is, baby; and you're what's happenin', baby. . . ."

Murray came face to face with fans twice a year during his holiday shows at the Fox Theater in Brooklyn, known casually as the Brooklyn Fox. At Easter and Christmas, he put together knockout concerts that had kids ricocheting off the walls at the baroque old movie palace. These were among the last great neighborhood rock-and-roll shows—before the quantum escalation in scope that happened when the Beatles played to sixty thousand fans at Shea Stadium in 1965. Grand as it was with its vintage velvet seats and crystal chandeliers, the Fox was simply a movie theater with a stage in front of the screen. Teenagers could sit in the fifth row and bounce up and down in their seats and scream as Wilson Pickett sang "In the Midnight Hour" or Lesley Gore moaned, "You Don't Own Me." It was safe and familiar; and even if an occasional scuffle broke out and pocketbooks got trampled and hairdos mussed, it was a gas.

The playbills for these concerts provide a vivid picture of New York City teen life in the early sixties. Scattered among the studio photos of singers such as the Del Satins and Cannibal and the Headhunters are pictures of platters of cold cuts—ads from Regina Caterers of 6401 11th Avenue, Brooklyn; ads for clothing that "guarantees pants that hug you tight" and stores that promise "Man—the selection is hepzee . . . with the most boss lookin' duds you ever saw." Thom McAn offers shoes in a style called the Voodoo ($4.95), which boasts a "tiny stacked heel that sends out signals."

The shows began with Murray the K walking onstage to signs of MURRAY WE LOVE YOU, MURRAY FOR GOVERNOR, and LUV MURRAY FOREVER. When he paced back and forth, trails of flying love missives followed him—Jujubes, jelly beans, gum balls, change purses, compacts, and combs. He launched into a string of hyperboles to tease his audience about the show they were about to be bombarded with; then, to the delight of all young vulgarians, he trotted out the Murray the K Dancers, led by his wife, Jackie the K.

Jackie's bouffant hairdo soared toward the proscenium arch, scarcely jiggling as she frugged her way across the boards. Jackie the K wore some of the heaviest eye makeup in history—jet black to match her hair. She was an utter fox —a pale-lipped minx all dolled up in bell-bottoms and Cuban-heeled boots.

Here was a role model for all young-vulgarian girls! She was exactly what they wanted to be. No one in today's world even ap-

*Jackie the K*

proaches it, except perhaps Elvira, the sexy host of TV horror movies. Jackie the K did not even have to frug to elicit oohs and ahs. Simply standing center stage was enough: the spotlight outlining her immense hair, whitening her pale face, glinting off her long nails, and shimmering against her skin-tight sequined clothes.

Jackie was beloved because her hair and makeup exuded vulgarianism. There were other inspirations, such as Liz Taylor in *Cleopatra*, whose eye makeup was magnificent; but Liz's haughty Hollywood aura prevented her from becoming a true vulgarian queen. The stars who got closest to young vulgarians' hearts were the girl groups who really seemed to live the vulgarian life and sang about it in Homeric dirges about unrequited desire and eternal tragedy. Their oratoriae were declaimed so persuasively that today their names alone evoke the world of teen extremism: Shirelles, Crystals, Angels, Chiffons, Ronettes, Jaynetts, and Shangri-Las.

They were groups of brutally real teenagers, rough around the edges, with street smarts and a hungry attitude. Under the tutelage of record producer Phil Spector, that edge was kept intact and even sharpened (as opposed to Motown's policy of sending girl groups, such as the Supremes, to charm school in order to remove any taint of ghetto funk).

The girl groups' biggest hits were melodramas set in a volatile world of rebellious boyfriends, conniving rivals, and repressive parents. They were sung with the kind of urgency young vulgarians loved to use to define the traumas of their lives. And as much as the lyrics to songs such as "Leader of the Pack" and "Not Too Young to Get Married" conveyed the high drama of teen life, the *look* of the girl groups said it all. They summarized the fashion of young-vulgarian feminity.

The Ronettes, for instance: the combined height of their three matching bouffants was at least four-and-a-half feet tall. Their eye makeup was a study in black-and-white impasto. They wore high, tight, side-slit skirts and stiletto heels. Mainly, they perfected the attitude that every hard-core teenage girl slaved to achieve: nasty, uncouth sensuality.

The Ronettes were the best-known girl group. (The Supremes, although more famous, were *women*.) They began as go-go dancers at the Peppermint Lounge, served as dancing girls for Murray the K's shows at the Brooklyn Fox, then met Phil Spector in 1963. Spector fell in love with their looks (and later married lead singer Veronica Bennett). (Of course he liked the way they looked: Phil was himself a definitive vulgarian—short, rodentlike, known for pegged pants, Cuban-heel shoes, and round-the-clock sunglasses.)

The greatest asset the Ronettes had, other than their devastatingly slutty appearance, was Veronica's (Ronnie's) majestic voice. It was lush, burly, and resonant, yet painfully plaintive: made to sing tales of teenage woe and passion. When you listen to the Ronettes sing, you hear three girls with big hairdos pleading with a mohair-sweatered greaser boyfriend to "Be My Baby" or telling him "Baby, I Love You." They are not hit paraders or studio-

*Girl groups Reparata and the Delrons (upper left), the Shangri-Las (upper right) and the Ronettes (above) sang songs full of teenage melodrama and established new heights in hairdos.*

perfect vocalists. They're girls on a street corner singing about the things that matter to them.

The Shangri-Las were even more convincing: not just real but *real bad.* Marge and Mary Anne Ganser and Mary and Betty Weiss were authentic street kids from Queens who possessed what Aida Pavletich, author of *Rock-a-Bye Baby,* calls the "Nyaaah street sound." They didn't merely sing their songs. They testified them; they shouted; they cried; they acted out hysterical playlets (complete with studio sound effects such as screeching seagulls, squealing tires, and—the best effect of all—a shouted "MMMWAAA!" to simulate the action in a song called "Give Him a Great Big Kiss").

The raw intensity of the Shangri-Las was the zenith of girl-group music and a definitive statement of the young-vulgarian sound on record.

The reign of the girl groups was short; their flame-out was engineered in some degree by the producer who launched them. Phil Spector's "wall of sound" made hits like "Da Doo Ron Ron" and "Then He Kissed Me" high-water marks of musical extravagance: long, blurred chords sustained by horns, vamping pianos, violin glissandi, throbbing maracas and castanets, boinging glockenspiels, fuzz boxes, echo chambers, and half-a-dozen guitars all strumming in unison. It was delirious and exhilarating: Spector's motto on record labels promised "Tomorrow's Sound Today"; he was taking rock-and-roll music where it had never been before.

How far could he go? The sound got bigger and more bombastic as Spector grew more confident of his genius. Even the preposterously big emotions of the lyrics were overwhelmed. Ellie Greenwich, who with Jeff Barry coauthored many of Spector's greatest hits, described the fatalistic penchant: "Everything got bigger, bigger, and bigger until there was no more record. He wanted to go further, get bigger and bigger, *but there was no bigger.*"

The same eulogy applies to the beehive hairdo—and to the lifestyle of the devout young vulgarian who lived in its shadow. Once the ultimate is reached, there is nowhere left to go.

# SURFERS, TWISTERS, AND PARTY ANIMALS

LIKE MANY OTHER inhabitants of their decade, surfers, twisters, and party animals yearned to escape the status quo. But they had a quicker and cleaner way to reach bliss than either psychedelic drugs (too confusing) or political struggle (too hard).

The most efficient method was to chug a keg of brew, blast "Louie Louie" on the stereo, lie out in the sun until your hair turned blond and your skin turned brown, or simply dance until your backbone cried for mercy.

When people look back wistfully on how much fun the early sixties were, most likely it is the world of these pioneering party reptiles they are remembering. The movie *Animal House*, made in 1978 but set in 1962, is a good portrait of a time that was a golden age of devilish hijinx and kamikaze-style fun.

Social dancing was a necessary skill for anyone under wheelchair age; chiropractors bought Cadillacs with the profits that rolled in from swarms of dancers who slipped discs while twisting. The beaches of Florida and California were besieged by college students on spring break, dangling from motel balconies and barfing beer on each other.

The sixties had an obsession with escaping from the humdrum world of the Organization Man. Routine was bad; adventurers were idolized. Being free was everybody's goal.

Riding waves equaled freedom. "Surfing is a release from exploding tensions of twentieth-century living," wrote Frederick Wardy in *Surfer* magazine. "[It is an] escape from the hustling, bustling city world of steel and concrete, a return to nature's reality." The Beach Boys sang it more simply: "Catch a wave and you're sittin' on top of the world."

The surfing craze that blossomed between 1961 and 1965 distilled California beach life to a sunshiny essence. It wasn't only about the sport of wave riding; it was a whole carefree cosmology of twanging guitars, hot-rod cars, the smells of suntan lotion and sizzling cheeseburgers at an oceanside drive-in, and girls in bikinis and guys in tight white Levi's dancing the twist and the surfer stomp on Muscle Beach. The image of surfing swelled into a way of life, a point of view, a pose. The surfer transformed from a vaguely irresponsible beachcomber into a lifestyle pioneer who had discovered the holy grail of the decade: a fountain of eternal youth, represented by the ocean's waves and a sun that always shone.

The surfer who captured the imagination of the world in the early sixties was a physical ideal: lanky; sun-bleached and/or peroxided blond hair; skin that was tan but basically so Caucasian it never looked ethnically dark; pale, dreamy eyes with sun-bleached brows; a nose covered with zinc oxide; and an *attitude*. He was cool and he knew it. You could see it in the way he sauntered—didn't walk—real unbuttoned and easy in his baggies (outsized shorts) and wide-striped Pendleton shirt and tennies (sneakers). He was psyched; he had the kind of hang-loose savoir faire that you could get only by facing down an eighteen-footer in stormy surf. This boy *knew* nature.

Surfers were vitality personified, with their young muscles glistening in the salty spray and their round-the-clock search for pleasure. They were mostly

white and middle-class, and they had plenty of time and enough money to buy paraffin to wax their boards and suntan lotion for their bodies. They lived in a different universe than that of the brooding folkniks with their furrow-browed worries about the bomb and civil rights. They lived to party. In fact, Tom Wolfe told of a bunch of L.A. surfers who attended the Watts riots just for fun and spent the night drinking beer until they were kicked out by blacks for being just too damned rowdy.

Before anyone had heard of Vietnam or LSD or Lee Harvey Oswald, at a moment when anything seemed possible and leisure time was ever more abundant, when a few dollars bought enough gas (at twenty-five

*The Astronauts captured the surfing sound in their hit song, "Baja," in 1963.*

cents per gallon) to take you from Malibu to Corona del Mar, the surfers' dream of life as an endless summer really did appear to be a possibility. For a few years on the cusp of the age of Aquarius, it was a seductive ideal.

Music is what sold it. The world discovered surfers because of surf music, which accomplished the remarkable feat of defining an entire way of life. "Currently, the United States, as well as a number of foreign countries, has erupted with a wild and most refreshing fad, SURFING," advise the liner notes on an album called *The Surfaris Play.* "It's a sport that has given birth to its own music, its own dance steps, and its own language."

Songs with surfer lyrics became so popular that millions of landlocked young people who would never get a chance to see Malibu or Waikiki knew such surfer terms as "cowabunga!" (the wavecracker's rebel yell) and "wipe out" (getting thrown off the board by a big wave). Kids in Peoria drove woodies (wood-paneled vintage station wagons, the fashionable means of transportation for surfboards). Working-class English teens, not yet bitten by the Beatles bug, danced to the Shadows' proto-surfer instrumentals, "Kon Tiki" and "Apache."

Surf music evolved out of the late-fifties/early-sixties twangy instrumentals of Duane Eddy ("Rebel-'Rouser"), Link Wray ("Rumble"), and the Ventures ("Walk—Don't Run"). Some of the best examples of this sound, such as Sandy Nelson's "Teen Beat" and "Let There Be Drums," actually seemed to capture the *feel* of the waves in danceable form. That is what many Southern California surfers believed as they stomped their way to ecstasy at beach-side dances and high-school sock hops in Orange County along the Pacific Coast in 1959–61. Foremost among the local instrumental bands was Dick Dale and the Del-Tones, described by *Life* as "chief purveyor of an ear-splitting noise called 'surfing music.' "

With Dick Dale and his reverb-equipped Stratocaster guitar setting the frantic pace, a surfing sound began to formulate in suburban garages up and down the Southern California coast. Mostly instrumentals at first, this music was frantic, devil-may-care, and totally danceable.

Unlike most rock and roll, which owed so much to rhythm and blues, the surfing sound was white. It was upbeat, charged with a spirit of freedom and aggressive optimism. Listen to Dick Dale's "Let's Go Trippin'," its pulsating guitar chords and raspy horns punctuated by the hollers and shrieks and "hey, yeah!"'s of surfers riding waves.

Dale played surf music for surfers. It was the Beach Boys who, by adding lyrics to the sound, brought surfing to the whole world. They didn't necessarily aim to capture the feel of the *sport* in their music. (In fact, Beach Boy songwriter Brian Wilson was scared of the water.) They set out to celebrate all the fun and glory and good times of the surfers' life.

They began as a high-school quintet, performing Everly Brothers and Four Freshmen numbers at sock hops and lip-synching top-of-the-chart hits they couldn't quite master. Only one of them, Dennis Wilson, was a surfer; and like most surfers in the L.A. area, he listened every day to KFWB radio, "the surfer's choice," which not only played surfer instrumentals by the Rublers, the Pyramids, the Challengers, and Dick Dale but also broadcast the surf conditions each morning. One day Dennis, Mike Love, and Dennis's brother Brian wrote down a bunch of the surfing terms they heard on KFWB, and out of them created a song called "Surfin'." Brian handed in the tune to his high-school music composition teacher, who had given the class an assignment to write a sonata. Brian flunked.

Undaunted by the bad grade, the fivesome named themselves the Pendle-tones in hopes that the Pendleton shirt company would give them free shirts (the surfers' favorite brand), and they cut a record of "Surfin'," backed by a teen party song called "Luau" on the flip side ("You don't have to go to the islands to have a lot of fun / Just pretend your patio's an island in the sun"). "Surfin' " established the vocal pattern that made the Beach Boys unique. They sang with an adolescent timbre that was the unmistakable sound of real kids, not song stylists trying to cash in on a sound. It was formulated in a dazzling package of complex harmonies and a Phil Spector–inspired orchestral wall of sound.

By the time "Surfin' " was released on the "X" label on December 8, 1961, the Pendletones had been renamed the Beach Boys so that everyone, not only surfers, would understand the happy life they were singing about. "Surfin' " hit number one locally and seventy-five in the national Hot 100. When Beach Boy Carl Wilson first heard the song on the radio, he celebrated by drinking milk shakes until he threw up. Brian bleached his hair blond.

In April 1963, the Beach Boys struck gold with "Surfin' U.S.A." Borrowing

*The Beach Boys first called themselves the Pendletones. By the time they posed for the cover of their first album,* Surfin' Safari, *they had changed their name but were still wearing Pendleton shirts, the surfers' favorite.*

a rollicking Chuck Berry tune called "Sweet Little Sixteen," they began with the wishful phrase, "If everybody had an ocean," then carried the fantasy to jubilant extremes, singing, "Everybody's going surfing, all across the U.S.A." They named every place along the California coast where the surfing craze had struck, implying in some raving, fantastical way that the same thing could happen anywhere. It was a dizzy notion that Danny and the Juniors had pioneered in "Twistin' U.S.A.," and that Martha and the Vandellas would soon use in "Dancing in the Street": taking the listener on a breathless trip through a nation enraptured by an ideal—in this case, surfing.

By mid-1963, the passion for surfing had gone far beyond athletic beach people who had mastered riding surfboards. Merely hanging out at the beach, enjoying the preciousness of summer, cruising the strip and dancing the latest dance: the whole scene was coming together in surfing music's delirious odes to the cloudless joy of being young and suntanned. Generated by the sinewy echo of the Stratocaster guitar and the Beach Boys' silken four-part harmonies, the image of the surfer and the life he led beguiled vast numbers of sixties people who were hungry for fun.

One thing that made the demanding sport of surfing so popular was how

*Fun on the beach: above, singer Bobby Freeman dances the swim; opposite page, Annette Funicello and Frankie Avalon in* Muscle Beach Party

easy it was to buy into the lifestyle without actually having to ride a wave. It was enough to hang around the beach. There, you could show off what the 1965 Montgomery Ward mail-order catalog advertised as "bold surfer styling," in the form of two-ply nylon surfer trunks ("the latest look in beach wear") for men; and the Yé-Yé Antron bikini with peek-a-boo pants from the California "Surf Beauties" collection for women.

Even if you had no plans to go to the beach, the sunny carelessness of the surfing life was yours if you wanted it. Just learn the lingo by listening to the Beach Boys and Jan and Dean, then send away for one of Ed "Big Daddy" Roth's Weirdo T-Shirts (BORN TO LOSE, CATCH A WAVE) that identifies you as a member of the beach/car culture. Wear chinos (without a belt) and a Pendleton shirt like the surfers, or boxer-style swim trunks and a horizontal-striped nylon windbreaker. Clomp around in flip-flops or huaraches (Mexican sandals) made out of rubber tires. Apply a Band-Aid to your lip, indicating terminal sunburn. Put a set of slicks (wide, smooth-treaded tires, for drag racing) on your car. Bleach your hair towhead blond and rub your skin with Man Tan for the instant sun-bronzed look. Most important, act carefree; be young; have fun!

At the same time the Beach Boys were defining the joys of being an all-American, clean-cut, teenage sun-seeker, the beach was becoming a major movie star. The first big beach movie had been *Gidget* in 1959, from a novel by Frederick Kohner, whose daughter Kathy had been hanging out at Malibu with a gang of surfers named Tubesteak, Moondoggie, and Pink. Because Kathy was only five feet tall, Tubesteak named her "Gidget," a contraction of "girl midget." Kohner's account of Kathy's beach-side adventures became a popular movie that inspired two sequels and a television series spin-off. ABC's "Hawaiian Eye" (1959–63) and "Surfside 6" (1960–62) featured detectives whose beat was the beach. *Where the Boys Are* extolled Florida beaches in 1960. The following year, Elvis co-starred with Hawaiian surf in *Blue Hawaii*, from a script originally titled "Beach Boy." It was his biggest movie hit.

The very idea of *the beach* had become so attractive that in 1963, the Viking Press published *The Beach Book* by Gloria Steinem—a massive ode to (in the words of the dust jacket) "making a kite, a sandcastle, a bikini . . . reading palms, rubbing backs, burying friends." Chapter 1 is eighty-four pages devoted entirely to "The Suntan," including notes on how to peel fashionably; and the inside of the dust jacket is reflective silver, for face tanning. Ms. Steinem's book also includes stimulating beach fantasies to have while lying around (" 'Yes, I'd *love* to swim in the nude,' says Sophia Loren") and exercises to help develop a beautiful bustline.

The year *The Beach Book* was published, American-International Pictures released *Beach Party* with Frankie Avalon and Annette Funicello, and songs by Dick Dale and the Del-Tones. It was the beginning of a cycle of movies that featured sand and surf, nonstop dancing, and some terrific music (*Muscle Beach Party* introduced "Little Stevie Wonder"; *Beach Ball* featured the Supremes, the Four Seasons, the Righteous Brothers, the Hondells, and the Walker Brothers). The plots were outrageously goofy: about the strife between surfers and bullying greasers, real-estate developers, or (in the case of *Pajama Party*) a handsome teenage Martian.

No one seemed to mind the bizarre antitype casting of Frankie and Annette, with their pasty South Philadelphia complexions and jet-black hair, as beach people; perhaps if real California surfers had been cast in the leads, the movies might have seemed like foreign films to beach-starved inland teens. Nor were audiences bothered by Annette's massively modest body-concealing swimsuits (Walt Disney, who still had her under contract

from "Mickey Mouse Club" days, had pleaded with her not to show her navel). In the wake of *Beach Party*, AIP released *Bikini Beach, How to Stuff a Wild Bikini, Beach Blanket Bingo*, and *The Ghost in The Invisible Bikini*, among others; and lesser studios put out dozens more, including TCF's *Horror of Party Beach, Surf Party*, and *Wild on the Beach*; fly-by-night exploitation filmmakers joined the fun with *Monster from the Surf, One Way Wahine*, and *It's a Bikini World*. None of these pictures lost money.

*New York Times* critics inveighed against beach movies' "idiocy" and "moronic intellectual levels"; they have since become a symbol of utter mindlessness. Of course, that was their purpose: to portray a life stripped of care and worry, focused only on pleasure. There are no parents in these movies, and few adults. In sequel after sequel, nobody gets any older; nothing changes. Here was a joyful image of what the sun-worshiping early sixties sought: an endless summer.

Characters dance, shimmy, splash, surf, run, roast weenies, and party all night long. "They're surf ridin' . . . skin divin' . . . sky jumpin' . . . drag racin' . . . beach bashin' boys and their bikini beauties," is how posters for *Beach Ball* (1965) described the subjects of the film. The best-known of all the characters was one named Miss Perpetual Motion, played by Candy Johnson, who made a career out of shaking the fringe on her scanty swimsuits.

While Hollywood movies helped create the popular image of the juvenile, hedonistic beach life, surfing hit its poetical climax in *The Endless Summer*, a low-budget movie by Bruce Brown first screened in 1964, released internationally two years later. Brown was a real surfer who began his motion-picture career as a teen in the late fifties by making short, plotless films starring terrific waves, which he showed to surfer audiences in the garage of his parents' home. By 1962, he had produced *Slippery When Wet, Surf Crazy, Barefoot Adventure*, and *Water Logged*—all feature-length pictures with plenty of wave-riding action but minimal story lines. In 1963, he conceived his grandest project, *The Endless Summer*, with a real plot: two surfers, Robert August and Mike Hynson, travel the globe in search of the perfect wave. His cinematography (in 16mm) was reminiscent of Robert Flaherty's awesome *Man of Aran*; film critics called Brown "the Bergman of the boards." His respect for the ocean's beauty reflected the sixties' yearning to find meaningfulness by going back to nature. His heroes' innocent global adventures are a consummate expression of pre-1968 confidence.

With the popularity of *The Endless Summer* (it earned a whopping 8 million dollars on an original investment of fifty thousand), surfing crested as a fashion. It was admired now not only by teenage record buyers and drive-in-movie make-out artists but by the art-cinema crowd as well. The surfer had become a genuine culture hero.

Like so many sixties fads, the widespread infatuation for surfing evaporated as fast as it appeared. Surfing's best propaganda, the music, was confronted in 1964 by Beatlemania and the British music invasion. The Southern

California sound's glorification of cars and beach-going was replaced on millions of record players by Merseybeat ditties such as Gerry and the Pacemakers' "How Do You Do It?," the Dave Clark Five's "Glad All Over," and the Beatles' yeah-yeah-yeah rockers. When the Beach Boys' "I Get Around" hit number one on the *Billboard* chart on July 4, 1964, it was the first single by an American male group to reach the top in eight months.

An ignominious symbolic end of the Beach Boys' reign as culture heroes came at the Monterey International Pop Festival in June 1967. The festival was conceived as a celebration of the "new sensibility" that was sweeping the country. The Beach Boys were invited to headline and accepted the invitation . . . but got so scared they backed out. "All those people from England who play acid rock," Brian Wilson worried. "If the audience is coming to the concert to see them, they're going to hate us." Otis Redding took their place. The music at Monterey defined the new sound of the sixties: Ravi Shankar, the Who, the Byrds; blues, folk rock, hard rock, and the "California sound" of the Mamas and the Papas, but a conspicuous dearth of surfer songs. During his hot-lick set on Sunday night, Jimi Hendrix paused while playing "Third from the Sun" on his fuzz-tone twelve-string Rickenbacker (a dramatic change from the surf sound's reverberating Stratocaster) and sneered to the audience, "You heard the last of surfing music!"

Changing musical taste was only a small part of the surfer's demise as a cool sixties person. The big story was the appearance of hippies. In some ways, hippies were natural heirs of a life surfers had pioneered. They, too, were drawn to California, and they, too, were white and middle-class and built a life around dropping out to be happy in the sun. The hippies' search for a greater reality via LSD trips expressed a mind-set not unlike surfers' questing for nature's truth atop a rolling wave. But while surfers were hunting up the perfect wave and the endless summer, winds of change swept across the land, and suddenly the surfer's idyllic existence was the worst of all possible things a person could be in the late sixties—*irrelevant.* Furthermore, surfers were clean-cut, which had become the epitome of square.

The last surfer hit song was "Wipe Out," which reached number sixteen in the *Billboard* Hot 100 in August 1966. This was its second appearance on the charts, three years after its first success. The second time, the maniac cry of "WIPE OUT!" and the Surfaris' frantic drum solo seemed to have an altogether different meaning. It hardly sounded like a surfing song anymore. The throbbing beat and cackling vocal war cry now seemed light-years away from the healthy surfer life. Instead, "Wipe Out" was more like an instrumental incantation of threat, rebellion, and suicidal danger. It was the same song, but the radical shift in meaning is easy to figure out: the surfer's yearning to escape had been co-opted by the drug scene.

## *Dance Mania*

Of all the hyperkinetic crazes of the early sixties, none was more frantic than dance mania. Surfing's halcyon years, between 1960 and 1964, exactly correspond to the great postlindy age of demented dance steps. Some dance fads actually came straight out of the surfer world: the surfer stomp, which replicated the movements of balancing a surfboard; the swim, which combined the twist with the arm movements of the Australian crawl; and the watusi, in which knee spring and hip sway created the impression of riding over a heaving surf. "Ocean waves seldom break in a straight line parallel to the shore," suggested John Youmans in his illuminating book *Social Dance.* "They usually break at an angle diagonal to the shoreline. This surfing phenomenon is represented by half-arc motions of the hip. A watusi dancer uses his hands and arms to pantomime various actions or objects that are usually associated with surfing or the sea."

The critical similarity between surf culture and dance mania, however, is not choreography. It is the passion for finding joy by shimmying and shaking and riding a surging rhythm—whether the ocean's or Chubby Checker's. Surfers did it on a board by day; twisters and hully gulliers got in tune with the swelling vibrations of the early sixties on the dance floor at night.

It all started with "The Twist," first recorded by Hank Ballard in 1959 as the B side of "Teardrops on Your Letter." The song (for which Ballard got the idea by watching some teens in Tampa, Florida, do a new dance) didn't even make the top ten, but Dick Clark liked it enough to convince Cameo-Parkway Records of Philadelphia (Fabian's label) to have local boy Ernest Evans record a cover version in 1960. Because Dick's wife thought Ernest looked like Fats Domino, he was rechristened Chubby Checker. His version of "The Twist," given plenty of national exposure on "American Bandstand," shot up to number one in September 1960 and became such a phenomenon that it was hailed as the most important music innovation since "Rock Around the Clock."

Anyone could do it. That was the significant thing about the twist as a dance step. It was easy! There was no restrictive Arthur Murray choreography to learn. You didn't have to coordinate steps with a partner. You were on your own. Twisting was the perfect dance for a time in history when people were hungry to break free of rules. It was a way to be literally footloose and proclaim independence on the dance floor.

These are Chubby Checker's instructions from his *Chubby Checker Twistin' Round the World* album:

S T A N C E :  Prizefighter position, one leg extended forward and arms extended forward from the elbow.

M O V E M E N T :  Hips swivel from side to side as if rubbing oneself with a towel. Knees are bent slightly. As hips move left, arms move to the right, and vice versa.

F O O T  M O V E M E N T :  Twist feet as if putting out a cigarette. Entire body moves forward and back and from side to side.

A D  L I B  V A R I A T I O N S :

- Bend knees as far as possible, then rise. Repeat.
- Extend one arm over the head, and twirl as if throwing a lasso.
- While twisting, lift one foot off the ground and return to place. Repeat.

Helen Wicks Reid of *Ballroom Dance Magazine* suggested that the best way to practice the twist is with a bath towel, held behind.

With both arms out and forward, feet about fifteen inches apart and knees bent, pull the towel with first one hand then the other as you pretend to dry yourself. Keep your shoulders steady as you move your hips from side to side. When you have "the feel," relinquish the towel so your arms will be free to move with your body—in as conservative or abandoned a manner as you may choose at any given time. Express yourself! Twist as enthusiastically as you wish. (Note: If you wish to work in harmony with your partner, the lady uses the right foot when the gentleman uses his left, etc.)

The twist itself was not such a big deal; musically, it wasn't significantly different from any of the fast rock and roll that preceded it. What made it a landmark in pop-music history was its emphasis on *the beat* and on fast, fast dancing and, most of all, the way it spread—according to the liner notes of an album called *All the World Is Twistin'*—"like some wild prairie fire out of control." Bobby Lewis followed Chubby Checker's record with an even harder-driving twister, "Tossin' and Turnin' "; then Gary U.S. Bonds added to the revelry with "Quarter to Three," "Twist, Twist Señora," and "Dear Lady Twist."

The twist went international when the American cast from the Paris production of *West Side Story* went to Chez Régine in Paris in 1960 with an armload of Chubby Checker records from America. Mme Régine had the Americans teach her how to twist, and she in turn taught the twist to her fashionable disco clientele.

The twist climbed up the ladder of social respectability in America at a most improbable place: a New York nightclub called the Peppermint Lounge. The Lounge was a shabby bar on West Forty-fifth Street frequented by leather-boy bikers, hookers, and street hustlers—"a flesh spa for the midtown beatnik crowd," according to *Time*. The house band was Joey Dee and the Starlighters, who played a lot of twist music, to which Peppermint Lounge waitresses rotated and gyrated between serving drinks.

To understand how it became the hottest nightclub on the planet in 1961, let us first introduce you to a tiny bunch of sixties people known as the jet set. More a figment of gossip columnists' need for copy than a momentous segment of society, the jet set (a.k.a. the Beautiful People) was an essentially irrelevant coterie of jaded American money, shiftless titled Europeans, and show-business notoriety, including hairdressers to the rich and famous, aging debutantes, fashion models, and assorted social climbers. "Everybody has a nickname," Arthur Herzog wrote in *The New York Times Magazine*. "Meet Kiki, Gigi, Ollie, Foozie, Flukie, Sukie, Squeekie, Shugsie, and Soupy."

The jet set had been identified in 1960 by *New York Journal-American* society editor Cholly Knickerbocker (Igor Cassini). Cassini had coined the term because

> *cafe society* is outmoded. You can't say any longer that well-known so-
> ciety people go regularly to night clubs because the usual night clubs
> are too dull for them. Jet setters are people who fly away for weekends.
> They are the avant-garde, the pace-setters. The jet set is people who
> live fast, move fast, know the latest thing and do the unusual and the
> unorthodox. The jet set has no fixed rules and standards.

In the spring of 1961, Cholly Knickerbocker's column mentioned that the Peppermint Lounge had been chosen as a favorite place for late-night gaiety by the jet set, lead by slumming socialites Countess Christina Paolozzi and Susan Stein (the former subsequently famous for being expunged from the Social Register when she posed topless in *Harper's Bazaar*; the latter subsequently famous as the force behind the nude-look fashions worn by patrons of the 1966 New York Shakespeare Festival). The Beautiful People arrived at the Peppermint Lounge in their limousines, drank cheap booze, listened to Joey Dee; and most important of all, they did the twist.

Once the word was out that it was *the* place to be, the Peppermint Lounge became one of the early sixties' biggest instant fads. So many aspiring jet setters crowded into the shabby lounge that there was no room left for the regular clientele, who were kept out by a newly hired squad of bouncers.

The twist was suddenly the epitome of chic. The press slavered over the nightly scene at the Peppermint Lounge: here come the Duke and Duchess of Bedford, Countess Bernadotte, Oleg Cassini, and Norman Mailer ("neither naked nor dead, but soaked in perspiration," according to *Time*). Even Greta

*Chubby Checker's recording of "The Twist" started the biggest dance craze in history in 1960. The twist was easy to do on the sand, as demonstrated by beach-party movie regular Candy Johnson.*

Garbo "hauled herself out of her myth-lined cocoon and appeared, lank-haired and bone pale, to snap her fingers and smile."

Killer Joe Piro (who had earned his moniker in the forties by jitterbugging partners to death) became New York City's most famous resident twist-meister. He gave twisting lessons to celebrities, organized twist contests, and became what *Life* called "the dance master of the discotheque." Killer Joe was a folk hero, glorified by a group called the Rocky Fellers in a song called "Killer Joe" and pictured in national magazines holding court at Shepheard's club in New York, where he twisted all night long. It was his moment of glory as a dancer, but Joe wasn't entirely happy. "Although the fox trot is our national dance," he lamented, "nobody knows how to do it anymore."

The twist established a course of cultural miscegenation that characterized the whole decade: the breeding of teen fads into mainstream fashion. NEW TWIST IN CAFE SOCIETY, *Variety* headlined. ADULTS NOW DIG JUVES' NEW BEAT. Suddenly dance crazes, which had been strictly kids' stuff until 1961, had escaped the world of youth and were embraced by adults striving to be modern and thereby prove they were not fuddy-duddies. (The same would soon happen with clothes, hairdos, even drugs and sex habits.) Ahmet Ertegun, president of Atlantic Records, explained the pattern to *The New York Times*:

> New dances originate in the American South, either with Negro enter-tainers or among their Negro audiences. A record is made, and white adolescents learn it. From here the dance (usually named for a song) goes to Europe where it is considered chic because it is foreign. The globe-trotting jet set picks up the dance abroad and brings it home for the rest of us to see.

From the jet set, the twist's popularity instantly trickled down the socioeconomic ladder. "A middle-aged man cannot hula-hoop," says a dancer in the quickie exploitation movie *Hey, Let's Twist*. "But he can twist. He can stand still, wriggle his shoulder to port and starboard, snap his fingers, and feel like a real go-to-heller."

In the sixties, being modern was the greatest thing anyone could be, even greater than being young. The twist, with its frantic, heedless choreography and its endorsement by the Beautiful People, *was* modernity—so much so that on December 31, 1961, Guy Lombardo's immemorial New Year's Eve broadcast was beaten in the New York City TV ratings by Joey Dee's New Year's party, featuring a midnight rendition of "Auld Lang Syne" with a twisting beat!

Joey Dee recorded "Peppermint Twist—Part 1" at the end of 1961. Chubby Checker followed an appearance on "The Ed Sullivan Show" that October by releasing his original 45 *again*. Astonishingly, *both* twist records hit number one on the *Billboard* chart in January 1962—Chubby's the week of January 13, Joey's the week of January 27. This time, it wasn't just teens aboard the twisting bandwagon.

They were twisting at the Locarno Ballroom in London, at Régine's New Jimmy's in Paris, at the Whiskey A Go Go on Sunset Strip, at the Anchor Bar in Saint-Tropez, and at New York's new hot spot, Le Club. To signify the twist's adoption by the jet set, Chubby Checker recorded twelve different international twist songs, each in a different country's idiom, including "Twist Mit Mir (Mus I Denn)," "The O Sole Mio Twist," "Alouette All You Twisters," and the "Hava Nagela Twist."

Cashing in on the phenomenal triumph of the twist came a deluge of kooky dance records: "Bristol Stomp" by the Dovells, "Mashed Potato Time" by Dee Dee Sharp, "The Monkey Time" by Major Lance, "The Wah-Watusi" by the Orlons, and "The Mouse" by Soupy Sales. Some of the dances that came and went were the pony, the frog, the frug, the hitchhike, the woodpecker (a favorite among London's "lively young aristocrats," according to *Life*), the jerk, the twine, the slauson, the shaggy dog, the skate, the limbo twist, and the calypso twist. In September 1963, *Newsweek* reported that the latest craze among London's "Modernists" (they meant "mods," but the term was not yet known in the U.S.A.) was the Philip, named because its deadpan expression, hands-clasped-behind-the-head posture, and twitching movements reminded young Brits of Prince Philip. A Buckingham Palace spokesman commented, "The Prince is not unfamiliar with the twist. But I don't think he'll be bothering with this thing."

Here are some of the choreographic notes from the back of record albums hoping to ignite new dance crazes:

- THE HUMP: "The Hump, close cousin to the Frug, is done with the hands behind the head and gyrations in the opposite direction." *(The Invictas A Go-Go)*
- THE WATUSI: "First, you must conquer your normal, erect posture to assume the basic Watusi Crouch. Good Watusi-ers start in a sitting position with their knees bent, their hips back, their arms extended to the front. As if that were not enough, you must keep the beat of the music not with your feet, but with your hips. To time with the music, vibrate your hips from side to side. That's the real trick: vibrating well." (*The Watusi* by Bobby Jay and the Hawks)
- THE SWIM: "Do the Twist with your hips and legs and do all sorts of swimming or diving motions with your hands." *(Swim with the Go-Gos)*
- THE FRUG: "The Frug is full of rhythmic, St. Vitus Dance styled seizures." (*The Frug* by the Nightcaps)
- THE HULLY GULLY: "Although it started as a square dance, there's nothing square about the Hully Gully. The foot movements are shuffle and kick steps with the arms jerking back towards the chest, much like pulling up on the reins of a horse. Now comes the real fun.

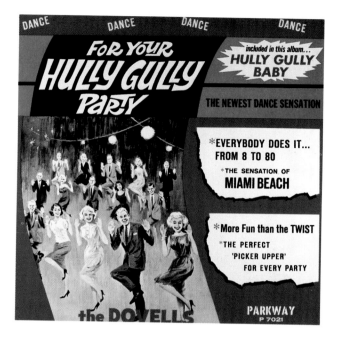

The Hully Gully is like a dancing charade. A take-charge person shouts out well-known names of people, places or things. The group reacts accordingly and mimics the subject called. The ideas are endless, but here are a few to start you off: *Frankenstein*—arms extended, stiffen up body; *Sonny Liston*—give 'em the old one-two; *Winston Churchill*—hold up your hand and make the famous V sign." (*For Your Hully Gully Party* by the Dovells)

Dance mania came to a fast end about the same time surfers were eclipsed by hippies. In 1965 and '66, such lighthearted steps as the watusi and the monkey (in which dancers pretended to climb palm trees, peel bananas, and drink milk from coconuts) gave way to the jerk. The jerk was less fun than it was *wild*. To do it, a dancer moved forward and back with clenched fists alternately pushing up and pulling down, the diaphragm expanding and contracting as the arms flailed. There was no happy-go-lucky pantomime to the jerk; it was simply a matter of feeling the music and moving to the beat. *Social Dance* called this "a radical departure in that it became an individualistic interpretation or response by a dancer to rhythmic accompaniment." That was the idea of hippie dancing (and most social dancing until the disco fad of the seventies): *feel the beat*. Whatever steps or moves you did were just fine.

Scholars of rock-and-roll music dismiss early-sixties dance fever as a commercially manufactured trend, and it was. But you cannot honestly picture the years between 1960 and 1964 without noting that an awful lot of people

—old as well as young—were going "round and around and around and around" (to quote "The Twist"). The frenetic movements that characterized all the foolish dances of the time are a stunning physical rendition of what was happening—and what was about to happen—in social and psychic arenas more momentous than the dance floor. People were breaking loose, feeling free, shedding the old rules of etiquette that had been pounded into their heads during grade-school dance class in the fifties. In other words, if Chubby Checker hadn't loosed the twist in 1960, there would have been no momentum to build the Woodstock Nation that peaked in 1969.

## Party Animals

The surfing and dancing years also happened to be the golden age of partying. The idea of *the party*, like *the beach* and *the twist*, rose up as a great symbol of escape from the button-down demands of modern life.

Surfers were party pioneers. "The ocean-based lifestyle epitomized the age of the Wild Child, and everyone wanted in," Derek Hynd wrote about the surfer scene in Sydney, Australia, around 1966. "Saturday night surf stomps said it all: Surfed-out young men, whacked to the smithereens, brawled with the bikies and lined up at the door of the female rock star in the ladies' dressing room at intermission. The era smacked of sex and rebellion."

The original surf-music sound, created out of the insolent rasp of the Stratocaster guitar and hard-driving drums, with no words to muddy the FEEL of the beat, was the protogenic sixties party music. A 1963 album called *Surfers Pajama Party* by the Centurians of Newport Beach captures the surf-party frame of mind. It contains twelve instrumental Dionysian stompers with titles such as "Intoxica," "Holiday Girl," and "Church Key" (a term for a beer-can opener that caught on in the party years of the early sixties). Liner notes say that the Centurians met while surfing the Balboa Island jetty and now "make playing their pleasure at Pajama Parties, Sorority Parties and Keg Parties, Beach Brawls, and All-Niters."

In addition to beach people, the party pacesetters in the sixties were college kids, fraternity boys in particular. In these years after the restrictive fifties and before the moral licentiousness of the drug culture, as college became the privileged place where society's rules of behavior began to crumble, they perfected a style of blowout that has become a platonic ideal of youthful misconduct.

Wild parties have been the pride of fraternities everywhere and for all time, but there were certain schools in the early sixties, such as the University of Southern California, with its "Rich Row" (where the fraternities were), and the University of Alabama (where the drinking age was nineteen), where the intensity of fraternity parties became the predominant symbol of the schools' campus life. They were known as party schools.

*Six party animals, including one of the authors (second from left)*

The University of Miami—"Suntan U."—was the most notorious of the lot, distinguished by what *The Saturday Evening Post* called its "agreeable program of reading, writing and romping." Students relieved the tensions of their studies (which included courses in fresh- and saltwater fishing) with outrageous fraternity bashes all year long, including theme costume parties such as "Sewers of Paris," "Viking," "Ugly Man," and the classical "Roman Toga." *Post* reporter Jerome Ellison looked in on a U.M. fraternity bash in a Miami Beach hotel in September 1961 and found "boys and girls drinking, dancing, and necking in bathing suits." Midway through the weekend, the merriment got so out of hand that hotel detectives were summoned to kick out the revelers and the fraternity was presented with a five-hundred-dollar bill to cover broken glasses, furniture, and crockery and the theft of a doorman's hat.

The best of the party schools were the big state universities in the Southeast, where Greek societies dominated the social life and after-sports merrymaking was the essential extracurricular activity. It was in Miami and Gainesville (Florida), Oxford (Mississippi), and Athens (Georgia) that students originated the most notorious party dance of the decade, the 'gator. When dancing the 'gator, the male partner made all the allusive sexual moves of ordinary fast dancing explicit by getting prone on the dance floor and humping like a mating reptile. (The female partner, unless she was totally blotto, customarily stayed erect.)

Despite their manifest carnality, fraternity parties were not sex orgies. Sex was still plenty naughty in the early sixties. "By and large on the weekends the boys are 'pigs,' " one coed was quoted in a *Journal of Popular Culture* article about fraternity life. "I mean absolute animals. Not *sex* animals—'pig' animals." Sex was not really the point, and whatever sex went on at a frat party in the early sixties generally happened in the old-fashioned fifties manner—behind closed doors, with a tie or some other warning sign hung on the doorknob to signify that the room was occupied. "In sheer wildness," the Harvard *Crimson* reported in a 1963 story about sex on campus, "today's college students do not compare with their fabled predecessors."

The fundamental purpose of fraternity parties was not to have sex (although sexual adventurism was always an implied theme of the revelry) but to achieve oblivion: via beer chugging or wine, or convulsive recklessness, or simply by abandoning all rules of decorum, etiquette, and tact. The party was a way of temporarily dropping out. You partied on weekends or during spring break. Then it was back to the old grind.

The important makings of an excellent frat party were these: turn the lights low (or replace the bulbs with blue and red ones); cover the entire floor of one room with mattresses; hire a screaming dance band or put hard-driving music on the record player; fill the bathtub with ice and beer or—for special-occasion parties, such as a Roman Ball—mix a batch of purple passions (vodka and grape juice); chug-a-lug enough to get very drunk; dance until you are soaked with sweat; break furniture and windows and punch holes in the wall; pee out the window; spill enough stuff on the rug and mattresses so that they squish; take off some or all of your clothes; make out in the mattress room and/or dry hump while slow dancing (but going all the way in an upstairs room was unlikely); and vomit at least once (purple passions, of course, were the best drink because they produced purple puke). If it was a really good party, the cops would come and tell you to be quiet or, better yet, break it up.

You couldn't have such a party without party songs. A good party song set you moving. It had an almighty beat with a melody monotonous enough to not intrude; it encouraged orgiastic, tribal-style group dancing. It had either no lyrics (such as the Surfaris' "Wipe Out" or Lonnie Mack's "Wham!"), minimal lyrics in the form of exhortations to keep partying (the Isley Brothers' "Shout!" and the Gentrys' "Keep on Dancing"), or obscure lyrics that encouraged cabalistic interpretation (Sam the Sham and the Pharaohs' "Wooly Bully" and Mitch Ryder's version of "Little Latin Lupe Lu").

The most famous and most relentlessly interpreted of all party songs is "Louie Louie," written and first recorded by Richard Berry in 1956 (as the B side of "You Are My Sunshine"), then enshrined in frat-house heaven because of a tinny, amateurish, but incendiary version by a then-obscure Portland, Oregon, group called the Kingsmen. The Kingsmen speeded up the pace of the song (which originally had a lolling calypso beat); and one night in 1963 while performing live, they decided just for fun to perform "Louie Louie" over and over again for forty-five minutes straight. It was an amazing moment: the audience, rather than getting bored, *kept on dancing;* so the Kingsmen decided to try to turn "Louie Louie" into their first record. Because they cut it in a crude studio (they paid fifty dollars for a two-hour session), yelling the lyrics into a single microphone hanging from the ceiling, the recording had a blurry, indistinct sound.

Nonetheless, "Louie Louie" was on the *Billboard* charts by September, and eventually sold more than 8 million copies. It was a great dance song. But what put it in the spotlight were the lyrics, which were so incomprehensible that rumors began to spread that they were dirty. The Jamaican-dialect

*The Kingsmen's provocative recording of "Louie Louie" has set the beat for millions of fraternity parties.*

line, "Me tell her I never leave again," when sung by the Kingsmen and filtered through the crummy studio equipment, then pressed into the grooves of a 45, could almost sound like "Tell her I'll never lay her again." The song was banned from air play in Indiana. The FCC investigated, interrogating Richard Berry and Kingsmen lead singer Jack Ely, finally announcing, "We found the record to be unintelligible at any speed we played it."

"Louie Louie" became the first of many sixties songs to gain fame for their alleged hidden revelations. By weaving its "dirty message" into a pulsating rhythm, it became a precipitant symbol of dancing and partying as provocative ways to be rebellious.

Among the most widespread party-years apocrypha was the rate card sent out by party band Doug Clark and the Hot Nuts. For $2,500, they performed in dinner jackets. For $5,000, they stripped to their jock straps. For $10,000, you got them in the buff. (There really was a Doug Clark and the Hot Nuts, whose albums were recorded for the Gross label; and they really did specialize in raunchy party music for fraternity blowouts—in particular, dirty versions of popular songs, such as "Big Jugs" instead of "Big John." Dirty as they were, however, they were only suggestive. They did not use the F word; and we found no substantiated reports of them performing naked or in athletic supporters.)

Spring has always been the season for college students to stir up
trouble: panty raids, Paddy Murphy
Day (named for the barroom ballad
in which "all the boys got stinking
drunk and some ain't sober yet"),
Mardi Gras, etc. Even students in
the most prestigious schools acted
uncivilized, as reported in a 1963
*Time* article about the "Intercolle-
giate Spring Riot Season": At
Princeton, they burned benches,
smashed railroad cars, upended
Volkswagens, and raided Westminster Choir College, where the
girls defended themselves by tossing
panties and potted plants out the windows. At Yale, when freshmen were
locked inside the Old Campus to prevent them from running amok, they
broke through the barricades and headed for a women graduate students'
dorm, chanting, "We want sex! We want sex!" In Providence, "It's the first
time in sixteen years that a horde of Brown men has managed to reach the
upper floors of a Pembroke dormitory," gasped Dean Rosemary Pierell. It
took police with dogs to get the boys out. "It's spring, and the sap begins to
run," commented New Jersey governor Richard Hughes about the Princeton
fracas.

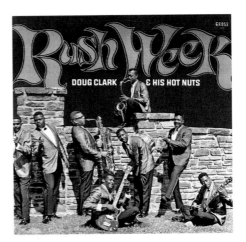

In the early sixties, "spring break" came to mean ultimate party time,
especially on the Florida beach. Since 1938, when the Fort Lauderdale
Chamber of Commerce staged a "Swimming Forum" to attract collegians
during Easter vacation, the pleasant resort community had been a favorite
place for students to let off a little steam. By the late fifties, the steam letting
was starting to get gross. In 1959, a bar named Porky's advertised a bargain
rate for college customers: $1.50 for all the beer you could drink in three
hours. Porky ran out of beer; the students threw his furniture out the window.
The next day, an airplane flew above the beach with a banner announcing
that Porky had replenished his supply.

Twenty thousand students descended on the town of sixty-three thousand
in 1959, making noise all night long and dumping sand sharks and alligators
into local swimming pools. "Not too surprisingly, little that is really calami-
tous happens to Fort Lauderdale," *Time* reported. "The townspeople regard
the invasion with edgy amusement: student-watching has become a local
sport." *Time* concluded its article with a quote from a coed who explained
why she made the migration to the beach: "This is where the boys are."

Glendon Swarthout used the girl's quote as the title of a loopy novel he
wrote in 1959 that described the thrill-seeking frenzy of uninhibited, unchap-

eroned collegians on spring break. The movie made from *Where the Boys Are*, released in 1960, created such an alluring image of the merriment to be had on the Florida beach that the number of partying pilgrims doubled. "What began 25 years ago as a pleasant interlude for a few hundred students during the Easter vacation has turned into a folk ritual that could be better described by anthropologist Margaret Mead," *Newsweek* reported in 1961, describing dozens of students packed into hotel rooms "like shad roe, living on beer and hamburgers and drenched in sun tan oil." Fearing trouble, authorities closed the bars and beaches. They got trouble. Students rioted, chanting "We want beer!" Eight hundred people were arrested, including "one sport clad in snappy shorts who turned out to be 56." The next year, Daytona Beach, two hundred miles north, welcomed the students Fort Lauderdale didn't want. The estimated

*Above, this Indiana college senior was immortalized by the roving campus photographer during a panty raid. Opposite page, his classmates practice male bonding, fraternity-style.*

average daily beer consumption was three cans per girl, nine per boy.

"Parties in Lauderdale are apt to happen whenever you have two kids and three cans of beer," says Merrit, the "well-stacked midwest co-ed" who narrates Swarthout's novel. She takes readers to a blast that epitomizes the ideal:

> The apartment was a mob scene of six-packs and kids in swim suits and Bermudas and sweatshirts, most of whom I did not even know. A portable record player operated in the kitchen by itself and a couple of couples were dancing out on the veranda even though the music was unknown to them. Mostly, though, kids were sitting on the floor boozing and smoking [cigarettes] and playing stockrades, a new game patterned after charades.

From stockrades (in which contestants act out the names of companies on the Big Board), the party gets wilder: two boys dive into the pool from a second-floor veranda. Three couples go into the bedroom and lock the door. Someone starts breaking records and feeding them to the disposal. When the party's over, Merrit collapses into a cairn of beer cans and smoldering butts. "It had been a fine blast," she concludes.

The movie of *Where the Boys Are* imposed severe penalties on the free-wheeling characters in the Swarthout novel: sexual promiscuity leads Yvette Mimieux to a mental breakdown; Dolores Hart as Merrit resists the advances of sleazy Ivy League cad George Hamilton and thereby wins his respect— unlike the character in the novel, who nonchalantly gets pregnant.

Despite its moralistic overlay, *Where the Boys Are* was an inspiration to millions of restless American students, who embraced it as a sympathetic image of young people having fun; Connie Francis's moaning rendition of the title song became an anthem of youth's vague, still-unfocused longing for liberation, sex, and euphoria.

As much as they craved fun and oblivion, and as severely as they tested morality, party animals were not yet ready to be dropouts or rebels. They simply went berserk when and where they had the chance to escape the grind —on weekends, in the summer, or during spring vacation; on the beach and to the beat of the twist.

"Obscene, exciting, erotic, wild, athletic, silly, frenetic, animal, frenzied, relaxing—and a wonderful way to unleash hostilities" is how the twist is written up in promotional material for the movie *Hey, Let's Twist*. It's a pretty good description of the whole decade, don't you think?

# FOLKNIKS

APRIL 9, 1961, was a warm spring Sunday in New York. In Greenwich Village's Washington Square Park, war began at two o'clock in the afternoon.

Police were stationed in the park with orders to silence all folk singers. The parks commissioner said he was worried that the crowds of singers and listeners were trampling the grass, so the hootenannies had to stop. The real reason for the interdiction was the neighborhood residents were peeved: every Sunday, hordes of singers armed with guitars, banjos, bongo drums, autoharps, and dulcimers had been flocking to the square to sing, and hundreds of shaggy-haired oddballs and NYU students crowded in with them to listen. It was becoming an unruly scene. A patrolman on the Greenwich Village beat noted that folk singing attracts hoodlums, perverts, and communists.

At the fountain in the center of the park, known as the cement circle, the folk singers launched their heavy artillery. They sang, "We Shall Not Be Moved." Police charged (nightsticks left behind in their patrol wagon). Folk singers resisted. Shin kicking, wrestling, and screaming ensued. Eleven folk singers were arrested. The next day the New York *Mirror* described the melee as a "3,000 beatnik riot."

The *Mirror* was wrong. Despite their arty look, these people were not the despairing beatniks who had made Greenwich Village home in the late fifties. They were a new breed of nonconformist: folkniks. They were mostly white, mostly middle-class, mostly urban youth enraptured by old-time ballads and new-style talkin' blues.

Folkniks were in no way limited to musicians who sang folk songs for a living or even as a hobby. Folkniks were also ardent listeners, hangers-on, sympathetic souls who affected the manner and attitudes of the folky set, those who carried empty guitar cases to look cool, and many who didn't really give a damn about the music but liked the earthy, work-shirted style that evolved out of the songs and their practitioners.

Folkniks maintained a fundamental belief that honest songs had the power to cut through commercialism, hypocrisy, injustice, inequality, war, and man's inhumanity to man. Their music was the music of hope in a veil of wrongs. As the inscription on Woody Guthrie's guitar read during World War II, THIS MACHINE KILLS FASCISTS.

For those who heard the call of folk music in Greenwich Village or Harvard Square, or even at such far-flung outposts of folkdom as the Know Where Coffee House in Joliet, Illinois, or the Crooked Ear in Omaha, it was a thrilling time in history. Folkniks were certain they were on the verge of something dramatic. Like other groups of early-sixties people, they rejoiced in the notion that the times were a-changin'; and they believed that folk songs were the best way to spread the word.

In the tradition of the ramblers and hoboes they romanticized, folkniks liked to see themselves as outsiders. They wanted to feel alienated from a world they regarded as phony. They drifted to Greenwich Village, to Cambridge, Massachusetts, and to other collegiate and urban crossroads from throughout the land, and when they arrived on the gray streets of the city, they savored being in the street, in the cold; they wanted to *feel* life and to put that lost, lonesome feeling into their songs (or if they didn't perform themselves, into their listening to the songs of others). "Sister mystic and fellow outlaw," Joan Baez called herself and Bob Dylan, referring to their Greenwich Village days. Both had come from comfortable circumstances, but "we were living out a myth, slumming it together in the Village. We walked around the windy streets and had afternoon breakfast on MacDougal Street."

The vision of living outside the luxury of conformist society was rendered in a riveting image on the cover of Bob Dylan's second album, *The Freewheelin' Bob Dylan* (his first big seller), in 1963. Bob Dylan is walking along West Fourth Street with his girlfriend, Susan Rotolo. Gray and brown tenement buildings rise up on either side, nearly blocking the sky, leaving only enough for a halo of light behind them. The street is lined with battered cars, a VW van, a moving truck. There is dirty snow on the pavement, and it is bitter cold. It could be an early Desolation Row.

Dylan's shoulders are hunched up, his hands pushed deep into his jeans pockets, his rumpled brown jacket gathered with a workshirt collar close around his neck. This is not the kind of boy who indulges himself with a comfortable winter coat. He is country simple, and country poor. Suze clings tightly to him, pressing her cheek to his shoulder, her long hair trailing back as they stride towards the camera. They are dressed in dingy city colors, too: dark green, brown, denim, black boots. They are cold.

But they glow. She is looking at the camera, safe in Dylan's warmth. He is looking down, introspectively, with a hint of a smile on his face. You can almost see him making a Woody Guthrie–style talking blues song out of the scene.

The enchantment of these two youth urban freewheelers surrounded by the bitter cold and the looming city, suffering for their art and loving it, made them a mesmerizing romantic effigy. This was an album cover that got propped against a million record players in the early sixties. All folkniks craved to walk that same Village street, in the same bitter-cold winter, arm in arm with their true love. "That cover was a symbol of my generation," wrote

Carol Belsky in a book of folknik reminiscences called *Bringing It All Back Home*. "The cover is the most important part of the album," Bob Dylan told his friends when he saw the first copy.

Folkniks came to Greenwich Village from uptown and the boroughs, from New Jersey and beyond. They were college kids, wandering poets, radical firebrands, curiosity seekers, ethnomusicologists, freeloaders, guys looking for girls, and girls looking for guys—all eager to see and be seen.

Village streets were thronged with bare-faced girls in black leotards and blue jeans, navy-surplus pea coats, Fred Braun sandals over woolen socks, and ornate ethnic earrings clattering from newly pierced ears. The boys dressed in unpressed chambray work shirts with rumpled brown corduroy pants and faded blue-jean jackets with the collar turned up against the fabled cruel winds.

Slung over shoulders of both guys and girls were guitars hung on wide sashes festooned with third-world embroidery that signified their owners' appreciation of honest peasant craftsmanship. As primary symbol of its owner, the guitar warranted extreme care in its selection. Fancy-pants folkniks might flaunt a Martin, the Rolls-Royce of acoustical guitars; and an old Martin had far more panache than a new one. A twelve-string guitar earned instant respect, because that's what Leadbelly had used; and it was cumbersome and hard to play. A weird instrument such as a Dobro was a way to make a quick impression, as was the reverse chic of a really ratty guitar that looked like it had seen some hard traveling, or like it might be a hand-me-down from an old bluesman whose name was Blind Lemon Whatever.

Steel finger picks were sure signs of a serious picker, as was intricate fretting, the use of a capo on the neck of the guitar, and a facility with arcane licks—picking your way through "Nine Pound Hammer" like Merle Travis instead of just strumming the chords. A nice effect was achieved by taping an index card to the top of the guitar, listing all the songs in your repertoire. This implied that your body of songs was so vast you might just forget some without the crib card. Serious folk singers cultivated monstrously thick finger calluses and boasted about frustrated doctors who couldn't prick their fingers to get blood.

You only had to look around Greenwich Village any weekend to know that the Washington Square riot of April 9 (which became known in the community as Black Sunday) wasn't going to put an end

*Joan Baez began her singing career in coffeehouses around Harvard University.*

to the music. The wronged ballad-eers formed the Right-to-Sing Committee and insisted that they would continue to exercise the God-given freedom to lift their voices in public. They returned to sing again on May 7, this time a capella, thereby circumventing the ordinance against playing instruments without a permit. The next week, Mayor Wagner ordered folk singing returned to the park. If anything, the riot had drawn more attention to the burgeoning scene. The oppression that many folkniks liked to sing about had come true, and they looked like seers because of it.

The folknik movement had begun gathering strength in 1957 when Israel Young opened the Folklore Center at 110 MacDougal Street in Greenwich Village. The Center was not just a record and music store: it staged concerts; it hosted cider-and-cheese parties at which those who craved to be part of the scene could meet real folk singers; it became a mecca of folk singers, listeners, and hangers-on from all over America and eventually the world. The record bins were filled with treasures Sam Goody never dreamt of: arcane ballads by seal hunters from Lapland, thirteenth-century Irish ballads, work songs by chain gangs from Mississippi. For many of the most zealous folkniks, the more obscure the tune, the better.

The Center's newsletter was the folknik world's hotline. It was mimeographed, ragged-edged, blemished with typos and misspelled words: just the kind of homespun honesty its readers treasured. In autumn 1961, it noted:

> Odetta goes to Europe to do TV in Holland, Sweden, France. . . . You must get Alan Lomax's new LPs of English Folk music. . . . Alice Conklin, Theo Bikel's new secretary, was seen at Feenjon's recently, enjoying herself to the guitar work of Steve Knight. . . . Jack Ballard works full time, seven days a week at the store now. Please do not ask him to sing every time you come into the store.

The same issue had a one-page announcement for "Bob Dylan in his First New York Concert: Saturday, November 4." Dylan had arrived in New York earlier that year at the age of nineteen, embellishing his autobiography with the kind of vernacular romance folkniks relished. In a newsletter interview, he tells Izzy Young he learned the blues from a Chicago street singer; he played backup for Carl Perkins in Nashville; he spent his childhood as a carnival roustabout, adventuring on the open road. Perhaps most important of all, the rompin', rovin' boy explained, "I dress the way I do because I want to dress this way and not because it is cheaper and easier."

Dylan perfected the attitude and ensemble of the ramblin' man and was soon copied by nearly every boy who wanted to be a folknik: blue jeans, work shirt, beat-up old brown leather jacket, a railroad man's striped hat, and engineer boots with steel toes (for stompin' gears on a motorcycle or travelin' by foot along a dusty highway). Ramblin' men had few possessions, but they all had their guitar and a Hohner Blues Harp (an extra-rugged harmonica made to take the punishment of blues wailing), which they could be counted on to whip out at a moment's notice to blow the gutsy riff. These hard-knock nomads didn't much cotton to personal hygiene; they preferred to smell honest. And it was de rigueur among them to drop *g*'s from the ends of words.

Early Dylan was the best known, patterning himself after Woody Guthrie, Cisco Houston, and Ramblin' Jack Elliott (né Elliott Adnopoz), but other ramblin' man stylesetters of the folknik scene included John Hammond, Jr., Geoff Muldaur (who when he turned eighteen traveled to Texas to sweep the leaves off Blind Lemon Jefferson's grave), and Dylan's fellow middle-class Minnesotans Dave "Snaker" Ray, Tony "Little Sun" Glover, and "Spider" John Koerner—all of whom selected their chain-gang names as teenagers while hanging around Minneapolis's Dinkytown, where the coffeehouse scene made nice boys into ramblin' men.

Girls had Joan Baez to emulate. Her image was not that of a hobo but of a pure-souled, long-suffering madonna in a burlap shmatte and bare feet. Following her lead, folknik girls parted their hair in the middle, scrubbed their faces of all makeup, and perfected melancholy moping. Rough-textured ethnic clothes, the antithesis of perkiness, were cherished: Mexican embroidered blouses, peasant skirts, serapes, and shawls, along with leotards or black

tights and wraparound corduroy skirts in drab colors and—no matter what the weather—sandals. Folknik girls were usually too sad to eat; they subsisted on black coffee and cigarettes. In their knapsacks they carried books of verse or a dog-eared copy of *The Bell Jar*.

Whether they sang or just listened, folknik girls tended to be far more wistful in their musical taste than ramblin', rompin', rovin' boys. Their songs were about white-winged doves, graves dug "long and narrow," and heavy-hearted pilgrims who "travel this world alone."

There was one other look prominent in the folknik scene: the elders. These were mostly guys who were veterans of forties and fifties hootenannies with the Weavers and Pete Seeger. They tended to be professors or artistic types, more sedate than the nomadic youngsters at the vanguard of the folk movement. Instead of leather, they favored rumpled sports jackets (corduroy) with jeans or matching corduroy pants, dark-colored (never white!) shirts with nubby-knit, square-bottomed Rooster ties, brown suede chukka boots, and a big loden green duffel coat worn over the whole affair. Their wives, like folknik girls, favored peasant getup, but were generally able to afford more impressive chunks of turquoise and silver jewelry and elongated Giacometti-esque earrings.

The habitat of folkniks were coffeehouses, ideal havens for philosophizing nomads. "The coffeehouse has become a meeting place for artists and intellectuals," wrote Irwin Silber, publisher of *The Coffee House Songbook*, who credited coffeehouses with making folk music popular in the sixties. Many of the places in Greenwich Village were known as "basket houses" because the folk singers who performed there passed a basket to supplement their wages.

Older coffeehouses in the Village, such as Cafe Reggio and Cafe Rienzi, allowed no live performances at all; they had hi-fi equipment that played the cerebral kind of music beatniks and chess players liked: jazz and classical, never folk. Beatniks, with their bale of A-bomb angst and nihilistic despair, hated folk music, which was so warm and fuzzy and committed to the essential goodness of the human spirit. Beatnik coffeehouses were *cool*, not warm; laid back rather than resolute. Folknik coffeehouses rang with the tidings of jug bands, bluegrass pickers, revolutionary Irish bards, and hootenannies of every persuasion.

"The word spread among the folk singing fraternity," Oscar Brand wrote in *The Ballad Mongers*.

A perfect platform for new songs and new singers had been discovered. In Sausalito, Pasadena, San Francisco, and Los Angeles new establishments appeared bearing such names as the Unicorn, the Garret, the Ash Grove, the Troubadour. In Philadelphia the Second Fret; the Exodus, the Tarot and the Spider in Denver; the White Horse and the Door in Seattle; the House of Seven Sorrows in Dallas. They were springing up like dragon's teeth near colleges and universities everywhere on the American continent, each complete with appended folk singers and their audiences.

The Boston area was especially well endowed with folkniks, because of folk singing's rising popularity on campuses. On what Bob Dylan jokingly called "the green hills of Harvard University," in Harvard Square, the coffee shops were havens for folk singers and those who craved to live the folknik life. *Time* described them as "the Harvard underworld—drifters, somewhat beat, with Penguin classics protruding from their blue jeans and no official standing at Harvard or anywhere else." Best known among the hangouts was Club Mt. Auburn 47, a jazz joint that turned Tuesdays and Fridays into folk nights and paid Joan Baez ten dollars for her first public performance in 1958. (She sang "Black Is the Color of My True Love's Hair.")

In Greenwich Village (home of New York University), they congregated at Cafe Wha?, the Lion's Head, the Fat Black Pussy Cat, and the Figaro. The foremost Village attraction was Gerdes' Folk City—a small, simply furnished bar with a few tables, a stage, and virtually no decor except pictures of performers who played there. Gerdes' attracted no hard-drinking big spenders. It was the folk purists' club. When Mike Porco opened it in 1960, he originally tried to have dance nights and bongo parties; but he came to prefer the folknik audiences. They spent less but were well-behaved and respectful of the performers.

Monday was hoot night at Gerdes'. Admission was a dollar. Established folk singers Josh White, Jean Ritchie, and the Weavers took turns with newcomers Judy Collins, Phil Ochs, José Feliciano, as well as innumerable NYU bluegrass groups whose names are long forgotten. Bob Dylan got his start at Gerdes'; true to his ramblin'-man style, he told the press that he first dropped into the place in the winter of 1960–61 "to keep off the streets and keep warm." When they weren't performing, the newcomers hung around together, trading songs, listening, and wondering which of them would get a record contract and when.

The first folk singers to make it really big did not emerge from the Village scene at all. Folk music's decisive breakthrough came out of San Francisco, where Dave Guard, Bob Shane, and Nick Reynolds—the Kingston Trio—went to college. Like many collegians at the time, the three musicians didn't much appreciate the gummy, adolescent pop music that had come to dominate the record charts in the late fifties. They weren't adolescents anymore, and they wanted to make music with a more mature sound and thought-provoking lyrics. Folk music provided exactly those things. They began performing as Dave Guard and the Calypsonians, but realizing that they needed a slightly more collegiate name to reach their intended audience, they became the Kingston Trio. They liked the name because of its calypso feel; at the time, thanks mostly to Harry Belafonte's "Banana Boat" ("Day-O"), calypso was big.

The trio's genius was to exploit the exuberance of folk music. Performing in nightclubs such as San Francisco's hungry i, they transformed a hoary repertoire of protest songs and anguished ballads into happy-time music. Their folk songs were for shouting out loud in the dormitory, or on the green grass of the college quad, or gathered round the tables in the cafeteria. Theirs was music to imbibe with flagons of beer and bowls of pretzels, in the company of merry maids, at wholesome fraternity shindigs and after-football blowouts on Saturday night. The trio did not pretend to be smelly hoboes or out-of-work laborers. They were crew-cut college boys in short-sleeve pink-and-white-striped shirts and neatly pressed hopsack trousers.

In fact, most of what the Kingston Trio sang did not deviate from the work of more "serious" folk singers. What made them different was the *way* they sang. They launched into every verse with gusto. They bedecked each song with footloose harmonies and gave the impression you were listening to three light-hearted drinking buddies letting loose round a table at their favorite tavern. In 1958, they took a sorrowful, ninety-year-old Blue Ridge Mountain ballad about a man condemned to be hanged originally titled "Tom Dula" and belted it out with all the vim of a half-time march. It hit number one on the pop charts and became so popular that Tom Dula's grave in North Carolina was spruced up by the state and he got an official, if belated, pardon for his 1868 murder.

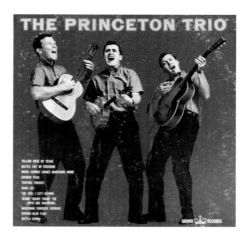

The trio's spirit fit their times. Their optimistic approach to even the direst issue songs was a precise musical expression of the early-sixties gung-ho spirit of *getting involved.* They even came out with an album titled *New Frontier,* inspired by JFK's term for the sense of re-

newal and commitment with which he thought America ought to face the sixties. The album was dedicated to the unselfish volunteers of the Peace Corps.

The Kingston Trio were the catalysts for a giant campus craze. In their shadow came such sound-alikes as the Princeton Trio, the Chad Mitchell Trio, the Dauphin Trio, the Brothers Four, the Cumberland Three, and dozens of ensembles of short-haired, clean-cut minstrels. In a dramatic turnabout, folk singing became a respectable collegiate activity, and folk singers were no longer viewed as suspicious nonconformists. Folk music was still considered more intellectual than pop, and even a bit topical, but its heritage as the voice of railroad tramps, union agitators, and left-wingers was readily tenderized into good-time music for nice people.

Clean-cut collegians and young executives attracted by the folk-music scene had no interest in cultivating the unwashed ramblin'-man look of Dylan and his ilk. They went to nightclubs in their weekend go-to-hell PermaPrest hopsack slacks and neatly ironed short-sleeve shirts. They, too, bought guitars and banjos; but instead of hitchhiking to New York to join the mussed-hair crowd, they sat with their friends in front of fireplaces in comfortable suburban homes around America singing "Michael row the boat ashore" and "Go Tell Aunt Rhody (the old grey goose is dead)." Folk music had become so upbeat that ministers brought guitars to the pulpit and led their congregations in rousing choruses of "This Land Is Your Land," oblivious to its author Woody Guthrie's left-of-center politics. Community centers in small towns opened "coffeehouses" where teens could bring their guitars and drink hot cocoa after school.

No fad can be so big without attracting big money. *Beautiful Hair Breck Presents a Hootenanny*, sponsored by the Breck shampoo company, offered record buyers an album full of real folk songs, including even the once-blacklisted Weavers singing "Fight On" and Theodore Bikel performing "Follow the Drinking Gourd." More typical of corporate America's appreciation of early-sixties folk singing was ABC-TV's "Hootenanny" show, which made its debut in April 1963 and lasted a year and a half on Saturday nights. "Hootenanny" was taped on a different college campus each week. When the show banned Pete Seeger from appearing because of his run-in with the House Committee on Un-American Activities, Joan Baez also refused to go on; so did other militant folk singers. "Hootenanny" featured performers who were more fun than polemical: the Limeliters, the Chad Mitchell Trio, and (in their precontroversial days) the Smothers Brothers.

"Never before have the songs of the shoeless enjoyed so much popularity with the well shod," *Newsweek* observed in 1961, noting that while many campus folk listeners were "pure beatniks," there were also a sizable number of aficionados who were "typically collegiate, devoted to button-down shirts and J. Press suits as well as peace and equality."

The faddishness of folk music was an ambiguous blessing to hard-core folkniks, for whom folk music, to be real, *had to be* noncommercial. The Kingston Trio and other early popularizers such as Burl Ives and Harry Belafonte were 'buked and scorned by folkier-than-thou purists. "It was as if there had never been a Leadbelly, a Jean Ritchie, a Samantha Baumgartner, or an Aunt Molly Jackson," moaned Oscar Brand after judging a college folk-music talent show in 1961, at which everyone tried to imitate the Kingston Trio.

Although even Joan Baez admitted that it was the Kingston Trio who first interested her in folk music, the popular group was shunned by austere folkniks, who demanded not only musical purity but a politically correct attitude from their singers. The trio were branded "folkum" and condemned as dilettantes only in it for the money—guilty of ostentatious harmonizing and of being too popular ("applauded by everyone from Bing Crosby to Admiral Chester W. Nimitz," according to the liner notes on their first album). When they sang about the ills of the world, they sounded like rich kids having a clothing drive for the underprivileged. When the Limeliters sang "The Hammer Song," it came out as melodious as a Mitch Miller sing-along. These too-famous folk singers committed a supreme crime in the folknik world: they acted like people who hadn't paid—and didn't even want to pay—their dues.

High on the list of dubious achievers were Peter, Paul and Mary. Known in the business as "Two Beards and a Blonde," Peter, Paul and Mary were

FIRST BIG ISSUE!!! SPECIAL PULL-OUT SECTION
LYRICS OF ALL-TIME FOLK SONG FAVORITES

HOOTENANNY
THE NATIONAL FOLK SINGING MAGAZINE □ DECEMBER 50¢ IND.

GOSPEL
BLUES·BLUEGRASS
RAGTIME JUG
CRAZE
Campus Reports

CANDID TALKS WITH PETER, PAUL & MARY AND ODETTA; BOB DYLAN SPEAKS;
PETE SEEGER'S FAREWELL; HUMOR BY LOU GOTTLIEB; ERIK DARLING ON GUITAR

assembled in 1961 as a commercial venture by astute manager Albert Grossman, who sensed the record world was ready for a new pop-folk sound (at the same time, Grossman signed newcomer Bob Dylan). Peter, Paul and Mary's luscious harmonies, however, committed the unpardonable sin of being too pretty. And they were suspiciously well groomed. Despite the liner notes of their first album, which announce that "honesty is back," cynics had only to look at the front cover to see Peter and Paul dressed in their jackets and ties, and Mary, with blond hair (another sin), posed holding a dozen roses like a homecoming queen.

Like the Kingston Trio, Peter, Paul and Mary were enormously successful. Their lyrical versions of "The Hammer Song" and "Where Have All the Flowers Gone" pleased the impure ears of Mr. and Mrs. Average, who discovered that they actually liked folk music fine, just so long as it was pretty. Despite their real commitment to noble causes, their right-thinking stand for civil rights and against war, Peter, Paul and Mary never developed a cachet among the folknik elite.

Joan Baez was a commercially successful singer who pleased the most demanding purists. With her crystalline voice and gravity of purpose, Baez was worshiped by the most uncompromising folkniks for her commitment to the traditional songs and also for her commitment to commitment. She was sincerely political—marching in peace marches, joining in ban-the-bomb demonstrations, leading protesters in the singing of "We Shall Overcome" (adapted from a black church hymn called "I'll Overcome Someday"). Furthermore, she didn't give a damn about the greenback dollar, telling a reporter from *Newsweek* that it was "just an excuse for a guilt complex. The minute you start thinking about making money, you lose the spirit."

Baez could never have been criticized for tampering with songs' authenticity. Her ascetic repertoire in 1962 was almost entirely classic ballads, performed without frills or harmonizing. She sang mournful old dirges such as "Barbara Allen," "All My Trials," and "Lonesome Road"—a selection so sorrowful that *Time* observed they "would not be out of place at a funeral." She disdained nightclubs as too crass; her performances were on college campuses. As she had done since her early days at Club 47 in Harvard Square, she sang barefooted and dressed in black or an Oriental-style burlap muumuu, her grieved brown eyes and almond-shaped face (without makeup) circled about by long, straight hair parted in the middle and falling like two somber curtains to her shoulders. "The effect was biblical but gloomy," she recalled in her autobiography. When she went to perform at the Newport Folk Festival in 1960, she arrived in a hearse.

Folk singing was such a big deal by 1962, and so many of its practitioners took the calling so seriously, that it was ripe for parody, which was supplied by shtick comedian Allan Sherman. His album *My Son the Folksinger*, featuring such songs as "Sir Greenbaum's Madrigal" and "Seltzer Boy," went platinum in 1962. The same year, *Life* magazine did a goofy photo essay about "the brightest of the new folk singers," for which each folk group posed in a scene that illustrated its latest record. Peter, Paul and Mary were photographed with a basset hound for "Ole Blue"; the Kingston Trio gathered around a candle for "This Little Light"; and the Smothers Brothers, who had just launched their career as jokester folk singers, posed as drunken riverboat men to depict "Dance, Boatman, Dance."

This kind of daft approach presented folk singing as yet another quirky musical craze, like the twist. No question, it *was* a craze: a record four hundred thousand guitars had been sold in 1961. But the folk spirit's hold on young imaginations was strong. Its call to *give a damn* and *get involved* seemed to grow more urgent as the sixties built a head of steam. Rather than roll away like another hula hoop, folk music stuck around. It metamorphosed.

Leaving behind its image as a campus and coffeehouse fad confined to happy hootenannies and sad songs about gypsy laddies, folk music became the conscience of the protest movement.

The struggle for desegregation in the South in the early sixties—in schools, at lunch counters, at the voting booth—electrified the folk scene. Suddenly those who sang songs of freedom and justice had something that had been conspicuously missing: an urgent issue that was all about freedom and justice. It no longer made sense to revel in America's grass-roots glories when southern blacks were getting chewed by police dogs and beaten by angry mobs. Old slave songs and blues that were the bedrock of the folk repertoire suddenly took on new meaning. Now there were real current-events principles to champion, living evil villains to decry, and a fight that required that big

*As the civil-rights movement grew, folk music found a topical voice.*

storehouse of early-sixties energy which yearned to make the world a better place.

Before the civil-rights surge of the sixties, most folkniks, who were white and middle-class, had perceived American blacks in a curiously romantic way. They were seen as noble founts of folk wisdom and song. The civil-rights movement removed them from the pedestal. As so many of the folkniks joined the protest marches, went south, and experienced oppression firsthand, arm in arm with black brothers and sisters, the meaning of the music changed. The reality of what was happening eliminated the gauzy, unreal aura of slave songs and spirituals.

So many accounts by northerners who went south to help the cause are filled with telling details that describe the shock of trading romantic notions for gritty reality. Urban white kids wrote home not only about their high-minded mission but about the body odor that arises when one toils all day in the Mississippi sun without benefit of air conditioning; about the chigger bites and rickety cots in bug-infested cabins. For the first time, many folkniks were face to face with the real stuff of which the blues are made.

There was a heavy spiritual bond between the civil-rights crusaders and the folkniks. "Songs are the *soul* of a movement," Martin Luther King, Jr., said in 1965. "For the same reasons the slaves sang, Negroes today sing freedom songs, for we, too, are in bondage. We sing out our determination that 'we shall overcome, black and white together, we shall overcome someday.'"

Two hundred thousand people sang "We Shall Overcome" together on August 28, 1963, in Washington, D.C., led by Joan Baez. This was the day of the great March on Washington to commemorate the hundredth anniversary of the Emancipation Proclamation, and of Martin Luther King, Jr.'s history-making "I Have a Dream" speech. In her autobiography, *Movin' On Up*, gospel singer Mahalia Jackson remembered it as a moment of

> happy joyous celebration as if the day of Jubilee had come. . . . All
> through the throngs of people you could hear the stirring melodies of
> old spirituals and church hymns and the new Freedom songs. People
> gathered in groups to sing "We Shall Overcome," and "We Shall Not
> Be Moved," and "Before I'll Be a Slave I'll Be Buried in My Grave and
> Go Home to My Lord and Be Free," and "Blowin' in the Wind."

Fortified with newfound urgency, folk music was in the trenches of a great and noble fight.

The next year, the crusade for civil rights became a virtual civil war. The Student Non-Violent Coordinating Committee (SNCC) declared a Mississippi "Freedom Summer," with the goal of registering voters and creating an integrated Democratic party to challenge the old guard at the fall convention. To folk singers—particularly those who wrote the songs—the assault on Mississippi was a call to arms. During Freedom Summer, Judy Collins, Phil Ochs, Barbara Dane, and Peter La Farge created a Mississippi Caravan of Music to teach and sing in Freedom Schools and help register black voters.

Phil Ochs expressed how the image of folk singer was changing from coffeehouse minstrel or carefree college swain to battler on the fields of injustice in an ode he wrote to folk singer/activist Guy Carawan: "He not only writes songs, but devotes his full time to the civil rights movement in the South, actively working in a real struggle, promoting workshops on how to use music in the movement, and getting his banjo broken over his head on a picket line."

It was Bob Dylan who signified the evolution of the folknik image into that of a seriously political character. The original ramblin'-man pose, which he had adopted as a living homage to his hero Woody Guthrie and which thousands of folkniks had adopted as their odes to Dylan, seemed to naturally evolve into the image of an angry agitator. In a flurry of furious protest songs such as "Hollis Brown," "Who Killed Davey Moore," "Talkin' World War III Blues," and "With God on Our Side," he established himself where no folk singer, no popular singer of any kind, had been. Dylan wasn't just reflecting people's feelings. "He gave character to the sensibilities of the Movement," SDS president Carl Ogelsby declared. "He seemed to be a part of it." He was leading. He was heralding and teaching, instigating and even exhorting his listeners about civil rights, war, and defiance.

It was in this new role as conscience of "the movement" that many collegians outside the folk scene first encountered Bob Dylan and began to feel a powerful sense of destiny—not only about his inevitable success but about where the folk movement was headed. Songwriter Eric Andersen recalled, "The whole scene was generating a lot of vibes, and Dylan had the heaviest vibes of them all. Dylan was sowing the seeds of the decade."

To many folkniks, Bob Dylan was what the movement had been waiting for. "Bob's songs seemed to update the concepts of justice and injustice," Joan Baez wrote. "And if the songs were not about justice, he made you think they were, because of his image, his rejection of the status quo." Few of those who adored him at the Newport Folk Festival of 1963, when he led a group sing of his "Blowin' in the Wind," could have predicted that he would soon abandon protest singing to become a rock-and-rolling sex symbol.

From the beginning of his career, Dylan had been a strange character, never at ease with the images he created for himself. With his scarified voice, odd looks, and peculiar delivery, he was a reporter's dream—always a colorful story. *Time* made fun of him in May 1963, describing him as "faintly ridiculous" because of his citybilly idiosyncrasies and a voice that "sounds as if it were drifting over the walls of a tuberculosis sanitarium."

What critics miss, little girls understand. Unlike his mentor Woody, and unlike any of the other gravel-voiced shouters and pickers, Bob Dylan had fans—*fans*, not aficionados: squealy fourteen-year-olds who came to Dylan concerts and behaved like he was Fabian or Frankie Avalon. They didn't listen to his lyrics thoughtfully. They came to see Bob Dylan the heartthrob.

As early as September 1962, *Seventeen* magazine had profiled the baby-faced Dylan in a report about "The Teen Scene from Coast to Coast," picturing him opposite TV glamour puss Richard Chamberlain. Serious folkniks did *not* consider themselves part of a teen scene; and it was disturbing to find their most gifted singer-songwriter there.

*Teen* magazine wrote a swoony piece about "Dream Dates" with idols such as Peter Noone of Herman's Hermits and Barry Sadler, the singing Green Beret. Included among them was dreamy Bob Dylan, about whom *Teen* gave its readers these tips:

> If you had a date with Bob, he would take you in your poor boy shell and bellbottoms to some joint for a bite to eat. No fancy dinners or lavish restaurants. Then you and the gang would follow him along to some Greenwich Village coffee house. Bob would not ask you what you wanted to do, as many teen fellows do. In conversations, you would have to put up with Bob's put-ons. It's sometimes difficult to tell when he's serious and when he's putting you on. When you make the fatal mistake of falling for one of his subtle scams, you can tell by the mischievous gleam in his eye that he is silently laughing at you. After the show ends and you and the crowd have had another snack at another joint, all of you go to his pad for a bull session until dawn. That's what Dylan digs—a hazy dark room with a group of people just talking.

Dylan was one of the few folk singers ever to be pursued by *Photo Screen* magazine. His cockeyed poetical responses to *Photo Screen*'s questions were as recondite as Murray the K's secret teen language, and his fans ate it up: "Folk music is the only music where it isn't simple. It's weird, it's full of ghosts and yeah, chaos—watermelons, clocks, and everything." Dylan's sly idiosyncrasies had a magical appeal to teenage girls looking for a ragtag poet to sweep them away.

It seemed impossible for Bob Dylan to say anything that didn't add to the oracular mystique. When *Photo Screen* asked him what type of friends he had, he answered, "Horrible people. A lot of my friends are thugs, midgets." Asked what kind of girl he was looking for, he said, "I want my woman dirty-looking, as though I'd just found her in some alley."

The more defiantly enigmatic his behavior, the more Bob Dylan spawned a new style of folknik. It wasn't just girls who were smitten. White boys, no matter how hard they tried, could never look like Sonny Terry or Howlin' Wolf; but they sure as hell could imitate Bob Dylan—the coolest middle-class white Jewish boy who ever picked up a guitar.

By 1965, Dylan's style had radically changed. The cloth cap was replaced with a wacky top hat. His curls cascaded to his shoulders. His work boots

were exchanged for winklepicker shoes like the mods wore. With Dylan in the lead, losing all his circa-1961 baby fat, the archetypical folk-singer look shrunk from brawny troubadour towards pained and scrawny psychedelic aesthete.

The earnestness of his protest ballads gave way to an I-don't-give-a-fuck attitude that was about to knock the folknik community on its ass. Lily-livered purists would never recover from the blow, but those who did were about to boogie to a new and different beat—folk rock.

The infamous moment of disconnection was July 25, 1965, when Bob Dylan ran onto the stage of the Newport Folk Festival wearing a black leather jacket, tight black pants, a polka-dot shirt with cuff links, and pointy-toed, high-heel Beatle boots. The rumpled work clothes were gone. So was his ingratiatingly bumbling stage demeanor. So was his folk guitar. He toted a solid-body electric Fender Stratocaster, and amplifiers were marshaled across the stage. Backed by the high-powered Paul Butterfield Blues Band, he sang "Maggie's Farm," a tightly coded allegory about quitting social protest, then launched into "Like a Rolling Stone."

The audience was aghast. You could scarcely hear Dylan singing above the din of the electric instruments. "Go back to the Sullivan show!" someone shouted. "Get them off the stage," cried a contingent Eric Von Schmidt called "the folk mafia" in his memoir, *Baby, Let Me Follow You Down.* "Pete Seeger was livid," Von Schmidt recalled. "He ran back somewhere and came back with an axe and he said, 'I am going to chop the power cables if you don't take them off stage right now!' Theodore Bikel, who was on the board of directors, said, 'You can't do that! Pete, you can't stop the future.' "

Dylan set off on a worldwide tour backed by Levon and the Hawks (later renamed the Band). During these concerts in 1965 and 1966, the image of folk music was revolutionized. Rock music was transformed. *Billboard* coined the term "folk-rock" to describe what was happening. Folk singer Tom Paxton called it "folk rot." It didn't always go down smoothly: "Judas!" called the folkniks in Royal Albert Hall. "You're a liar!" Dylan spat back. "I can just imagine some of the cops at Newport who happened to be folk purists reaching for their holsters muttering, 'That's not folk music,' " Phil Ochs wrote to *The Village Voice* in August 1965, defending Dylan's evolution against a critic who had called him a traitor. " 'Just wait and see if we invite you again next year, Bobby Teenybopper,' " Ochs wrote facetiously. Bob Dylan was *not* invited to the Newport Folk Festival in 1966.

In a wrought-up story about the "latest mutation in the biology of the big beat," in September 1965, *Newsweek* gulped that "even Joan Baez, the stern Cassandra of folk whose singing style is as pure as her anti-establishment stand, will enlist the bass and electric guitar in her new album, *Farewell, Angelina.*" *Newsweek* called Dylan "the Patrick Henry of the folk-rock revolution," then listed its other main partisans: the Byrds (who started the trend by giving Dylan's "Mr. Tambourine Man" the high-volume electric treatment), the Animals (who turned the antique "House of the Rising Sun" into a rocker), Donovan ("Dylan's work-shirted cloth-capped English counterpart"), and a duo formerly known as Caesar and Cleo, now going by the name Sonny and Cher (who "have risen from rags to custom-made rags").

Although immense numbers of folknik types who had been part of the scene in the first years of the sixties got swept into the torrent of folk rock, many in the old guard stayed loyal to tradition. "Pious love-doves!" wrote Josh Dunson about Sonny and Cher in *Sing Out!* magazine. "Folk rock is pretty much a dither cooked up in a vacuum by a bunch of hip city kids," scolded Izzy Young of the Folk Center. "It can't last long because it does not have its feet on the ground." Defenders of the new fusion countered by saying

*Folk purists were horrified when Bob Dylan traded his work shirt and acoustic guitar for the look and sound of a rock singer.*

*The folk-rock look: Sonny and Cher*

that old folkniks' complaints sounded like "a prissy virgin who had just lost her virginity."

In fact, folk music had not been raped by rock and roll. In some significant way, the opposite was true. Folk had gotten inside rock and roll and used it like a Trojan horse to infiltrate the Top 40. The new folk-rock sound appealed not only to the "somewhat beat college underworld" *Time* had described in 1962 but to what trade magazines now called "nubies," the nine-to-twelve-year-old girls who bought records by the millions.

Pure-souled folkniks died a thousand deaths when their sanctified ballads were described by *Photo Screen* as having "messages that are a little anti-establishment and give the kids a kick." These days, *Photo Screen* explained in 1965, "everything is a song-word: Vietnam, Selma, the bomb, the FBI. But it's all for fun, we guess. Songs never changed the world." Sonny and Cher, who signified the new folk-rock style, "dig message songs," *Photo Screen* advised. "They are happyweds."

Cher told *Teen* magazine that politics and pop music don't mix. "If you want my honest opinion, does Barry McGuire [singer of the number-one protest song "Eve of Destruction"] have the qualifications to talk about politics? Sonny would never write about something he didn't know about. Anyway, I think there has been just too much protesting. Maybe there are a lot of problems in the world, but it seems like an okay place to me."

Sonny and Cher's fans were more interested in the way their idols dressed than in the messages of their songs. If the medium was the message, Cher was telling listeners to invest heavily in big furry vests, to wear groovy striped bellbottoms, and to find a cute boyfriend. Sonny and Cher had new issues to deal with, considerably less global than the bomb or civil rights. Hair, for example. Their number-one hit from August 1965, "I Got You Babe," was a lilting refrain that pledged mutual eternal devotion despite the fact that people say Sonny's hair is too long.

"I Got You Babe" is a love song. It's about a young couple who don't have the money to pay the rent but have each other, so things are fine. In a circuitous way, it conjures up the image on the cover of *The Freewheelin' Bob Dylan*, on which Dylan—poor but happy—walks arm in arm with his girlfriend. But the similar theme underscores how far folkniks had come in a few years. Listening to Sonny and Cher, one thinks not of the gray streets of Greenwich Village but of groovy California, of bright sun and lazy days without a care in the world. The new folknik sensibility was meshing smoothly with that of the hippies, who burst upon the scene at the same time, with this message: kick back and relax. Love will solve all problems.

By the late sixties, coffeehouses and folk clubs were scarce. People still congregated in Washington Square Park, but it was a different crowd. Nobody sang earnest laments about Appalachia anymore. Jolly jug bands played cute tunes, mimes juggled, and people in furry vests and cowboy boots smoked joints. The lonesome sound of the few remaining acoustic guitars provided only background music to the new scene.

# I'M ENGLISH

IN DES MOINES, IOWA, on a Friday night in the fall of 1966, Randy "Ringo" Babirusa is looking in his bathroom mirror, and he is frustrated by what he sees. Even when wetted with official Beatles Yeah! Yeah! Yeah! Hair Spray and brushed straight ahead, Randy's bangs barely reach halfway to his eyebrows. They look like a wet crew cut. Hey, luv, that's exactly what they are, because the ruddy bank where Randy works as a teller since he came to Des Moines from the family farm in Walnut has a firm rule: no Beatle-length hair! Every Friday, male employees face sideburn inspection, at which they must demonstrate clean-cut space between ear and sidewall, and an exposed hairline up front.

It is just too humiliating to be going to the fab new night spot in Des Moines, the Westminster Disco, looking so bloody *American;* so Randy considers . . . the wig. Advertised as "the only authentic Beatle wig," it arrived by mail wrapped in a clear plastic bag, with a cardboard label that features cameos of the four Beatles and an exclamation: *WOW! the Beatles are here!* Randy rips open the bag and pulls out what looks like a deflated wad of black cotton candy. It was guaranteed to fit all size heads, but it looks like a diminutive chignon on top of Randy's hedgehog hair.

There is another solution: the Beatle-style Dutch-boy cap Randy bought from the Montgomery Ward mail-order catalog Carnaby Street Boutique. The circular gray-flannel hat has a tall band and low-slung visor, so if it's pulled down and kept low all night, none of the blokes at the Westminster, not even the birds who hully-gully with him, will notice his embarrassing secret.

If the humiliation of short hair can be camouflaged, the rest of Randy's outfit is gloriously, undeniably gear! From the Brolly Male collection by McGregor ("Edwardian updated to fit the brawny American"), he wears angled-pocket, Liverpool Flame low-riding bell-bottoms—so low that the "waist" measurement is taken at the hips and the rise is guaranteed less than four inches. The slacks skim across the tops of pointy-toed black shoes fastened with buckles instead of laces, like boots that might have trod London's cobblestone streets a century ago. The kinky thing about them is that their buckles match the pilgrim gilt buckle on his belt, a two-inch-wide roughed-up-cowhide sash with corduroy edging. Now, that's fab!

Randy's Fleur-du-Jour shirt is olive green with a pale blue daisy pattern and a white highboy collar with matching white curved-barrel cuffs. One potential problem here: the shirt has a drastic eight-inch taper to hug the torso, which means that Randy will have to suck in his stomach all night to keep the buttons from popping. The straining gaps between the buttons are no problem at all: they will be fully covered by the grottiest element of the wardrobe—Randy's four-inch-wide blue-on-yellow polka-dot wool taffeta mod necktie.

Randy pats Margo of Mayfair Beatles Talc on his neck, swabs a few palm-fuls of English Leather cologne on his cheeks, then tops off the London-look ensemble with nautical outerwear straight from Her Majesty's Navy, in the form of a double-breasted eight-brass-button navy pea coat with shoulder epaulets and full paisley lining.

Unfortunately, he has no fab British Racing Green sports car in which to drive to the Westminster Disco, but he does steer his Ford Falcon wearing open-knuckle action driving gloves with rampant lion crests on their straps. From the parking lot, he can hear the happy trills and yeah-yeah-yeahs of Des Moines's own up-and-coming quartet, Wide Wail and the Mersey Lads (who last year used to be Cowabunga and the Surfin' Hodads).

The doorman asks, "Hey, aren't you Randy Babirusa?"

"Very fooney, mate," Randy says in his best imitation Liverpool accent, pulling the visor of his cap down low. "The name is Ringo."

"From the bank?"

"Not tonight," Randy says, opening his jacket and waving his fat polka-dot tie in the Nurk's face. "Can't you see—I'm English!"

For a few crazed years at the height of a crazed decade, being English was the coolest—pardon, fabbest—thing anyone could be. From Motown singing groups and French haute couturiers to vast numbers of fidgety Americans, old and young, the image of England was a bright and shining beacon of modernity. Anything and everyone under the dominion of the Union

Jack was the epitome of style. In 1966, just about anywhere in the Western world, the one and only thing to say if you wanted to prove you were supremely hip was "I'm English!"

England was free, it was young, it was full of peppy little Mini-Moke runabouts and blossoming anemones. It was the home of James Bond and the Beatles, of carnival stripes and houndstooth checks and polka dots, of ultrachic geometric hairdos, of high-contrast photography and hard-edge op art, of swinging discotheques and crazy-named boutiques such as Granny Takes a Trip and Hung on You. Here was the climax of the great myth that had been gathering momentum since the sixties began: the world was being reborn! The time had come to sweep away all things fusty and *be modern.* All eyes turned to England to watch the faded world power rediscover the lust for life.

This was a miracle! A Technicolor butterfly was emerging out of the drab old Britannic cocoon. Vanished was the abstemious land of pinstriped prigs ruled by a dowdy queen garbed in acres of itchy tweeds and chiffon. Long live the new queen: Twiggy, a ninety-pound "cockney dowsing rod" with an accent as coarse as a crow's croak. A country once known for rumpled gabardine raincoats and black umbrellas had become the land of loverly rainbow-colored polyvinylchloride wide-striped slickers and short, short miniskirts. Like perky girls, mod England was giddy; but beneath the delirium bubbled a cultural revolution.

Along with the Beatles, miniskirts were the banner of the whole dazzling metamorphosis. Seeing London's birds (girls) parade along the King's Road wearing their scanty minis (made by Mary Quant beginning in 1965) was hardly less startling than seeing them in the altogether! Londoners, then soon the whole world, gasped at the profusion of knees, thighs, and more thigh—more thigh than any presixties girlwatcher could ever have hoped to see in public. Miniskirts were banned in Vatican City and in Greece. American and British schoolgirls who couldn't pass the kneeling test (does your hem touch the floor when you kneel?) were expelled. To the wearer, miniskirts presented major problems: women had to learn how to sit down all over again. (In Rio, a sixty-three-year-old man was so unhinged when a miniskirted woman sat close to him on a bus and crossed her legs, he bit her on the thigh and got three days in jail for it.) And woe to her whose gams were fat or scrawny or too short. But oh my—for dancing, there was nothing like a mini! And reborn England loved to dance.

The most amazing thing about England mid-decade is that it seemed to have an entirely new population: people who simply did not exist ten years earlier! In April 1966, *Time* editors were so inspired by the miniskirt that they declared London "the city of the decade." The epochal cover story marveled at a brash new social order it called the "swinging meritocracy": artists, television executives, university professors, fashion photographers, singers, proud arrivistes from the North Country and the Midlands, and scrappy East

This Christmas GO-GO MOD
Designs by Jonathan Burn and John Steiner

CARNABY ST.

Young Mod Classics    Nautical Mod Look

End rogues with as much clout as the old aristocracy. They were all busily engaged in nothing less than remaking not only English culture but the Western world's.

The Beatles set the beat: happy young lads from working-class Liverpool, bursting with irreverence, wit, style, artistry, and a complete confidence that the world was theirs. After their royal command performance of November 1963, at which it was reported that in their royal box the queen mother stomped her feet and Princess Margaret clapped with the beat to "Twist and Shout," the *Daily Mirror* proclaimed that "Beatle people were everywhere. From Wapping to Windsor. Aged seven to seventy. And it's plain to see why these four cheeky, energetic lads from Liverpool go down so big. They're young, new. They're high-spirited, cheerful." The headline for the editorial read, BEATLEMANIA! YEAH! YEAH! YEAH!

James Bond movies in 1962 and '63 had paved a devotional path to England, but Bond was English in a familiar, untouchable sort of way. The Beatles were cuddly. When fans fell in love with them, they were also falling in love with England. Mop-top hair, lapel-less jackets, Beatle boots, slang words like "fab" and "gear" and that kicky accent: these were Beatles things, but they were English things, too; and if you loved the Beatles, you loved everything English about them.

To most Yanks, the Beatles' status as working-class boys from Liverpool meant nothing. They were simply and entirely English, and all the subtle variations of what that could mean were lost in translation. The average American Beatle-lover couldn't tell a Liverpool accent from an Oxford one. When the Beatles talked, it sounded basically like a BBC announcer or Harold Macmillan, only funnier. And it was so easy to imitate an English accent.

Jonathan Burn and John Steiner

CARNABY ST.

Even the worst attempts by radio deejays and Beatlemaniacs, if sprinkled with plenty of "I say, old chap"'s and "cheerio"'s, got the point across.

Thanks to the Beatles, being English came to mean being zany and hyperkinetic, dressing in madcap clothes, and being wildly rich and famous. Their image of what it was like to be English was sheer happiness. Is it any wonder, with the Beatles as the best-known envoys of the new sensibility, that so many people craved to tell the world "I'm English!"?

Music critics have looked long and hard into the Beatles' importance and have drawn exhaustive grids of cultural cross-pollenization between American rhythm and blues, skiffle, and country and western, explaining how it all came together in a wonderful volley across the Atlantic in the mid-sixties, creating, after Elvis, the second big wave of rock and roll. Whatever their musicological significance, the Beatles had a stunning impact on the way people lived. The British music explosion was the sound of a new lifestyle—*mod*—upon which the myth of swinging England was built. It was a lifestyle that the Fab Four epitomized.

To Americans who wanted to look and act like the Beatles, mod meant little more than modern, up to date, with it—in this case, British. But to the Beatles' English followers, the term "mod" had begun with a very different connotation.

Mods evolved in the late fifties as a small group of British teens who had glimpsed sophistication in the form of Italian and French New Wave movies. They wanted to be continental, too. As described in Colin MacInnes's novel

The MOD Set

For the Modern Look

*Fits all ages*

*Absolute Beginners*, they listened to modern jazz, carried around (but didn't necessarily read) books of beat poetry, and expressed themselves with an impeccably streamlined wardrobe. They called themselves modernists; and although they aimed for an image of impassive finesse, they never quite shed their tough-guy hustle.

Mod boys favored a meticulous hairdo, a high-collared, lapel-less jacket or a sports coat made of black leather, a shirt with a small, tight collar pin, a skinny black tie, a stingy-brimmed high-peaked trilby or porkpie hat, tight stovepipe pants, and black ankle-high, pointy-toed boots. Girl mods sported starchy high-rise hairdos, sickly pale-white makeup with coal-black eyes, tight leather skirts and fishnet stockings or skin-hugging ski pants, and high "Tom Jones" boots or Italian shoes with lethal stiletto heels. They hung out at mean night spots such as the Ska Bar and the A-Train in London, and because they darted about town on Vespas or Lambrettas, they were sometimes known as scooter boys.

It was from this same gritty youthful underclass that the Beatles came. When they began performing in a Liverpool strip club as the Silver Beatles in 1960, they were greasers. John Lennon had long sideburns and slicked-back Crisco hair; they wore jeans and leather, they made a point of swearing and talking mean, and they affected the crude belligerence of Liverpool street bullies.

In early 1962, after signing the Beatles to a management contract (which Paul McCartney's and George Harrison's fathers had to witness, as they were both under twenty-one), Brian Epstein dramatically refashioned their image.

To John's dismay, he made them exchange their leathers for shiny gray lounge suits with skinny lapels. He made them stop smoking Woodbines (the working man's cigarette) and take up the classier Senior Service brand. Under Epstein's tutelage, they no longer burped into the microphone or drank beer onstage, and they weren't allowed to give the finger to members of the audience they didn't like. By the time they appeared on the English Saturday-night pop television show "Thank Your Lucky Stars," in January 1963, singing "Please Please Me" in front of four metal hearts, shaking their long (but greaseless) hair as all of England watched in rapt amazement, their transformation was complete. The Beatles had gone from obnoxious to adorable.

America developed Beatle awareness in late 1963; when the lads first arrived to conquer the U.S. in February 1964, the term "mod" arrived with them, carrying nothing but happy connotations. As it applied to the Beatles, mod meant four smiling boys—a little sassy, but well shampooed, dapper, and cheerful. The sullen, fetishistic foppery that had been the mark of the low-rent, amoral early mods had been left far behind. To Americans, anyone with an English accent and a tie and jacket had a leg up on being a gentleman.

Thanks to the immense popularity of the Beatles, and a craving to find some label to describe the swirl of values and attitudes inferred from their music, mod became synonymous with England, at least with the new, swinging England that dominated the mid-decade.

The single most important sign of being mod was hair. Long hair became the quintessential symbol not only of Englishness but of youth, modernity, and all forward-looking people on the planet earth. There had been long hair before the mod invasion: on young vulgarians (but it was greasy); on surfers (but it was bleached blond); on folkniks (but it was scraggly and unkempt); on Hell's Angels (but it was filthy). England's great contribution to the history of postwar hair was to make long hair into an avant-garde fashion statement for men.

On man or boy, Beatle-cut hair was the only truly convincing way to say "I'm English!" Boys whose parents made them cut it short brushed it down over their foreheads as soon as they left the house. High-school principals retaliated with Byzantine regulations spelling out the length of hair and how it could be combed. Balding men with only a few-dozen strands remaining around the edge let them grow over their ears as a token gesture of solidarity with the free-swinging values of the long-hair set.

No one was immune to the Beatles' bushy-headed spell. Prince Charles, aged sixteen in 1965, affected a modified Beatle bob and gave teenage parties at Windsor Castle, where he played Beatles and Rolling Stones records for the guests. When the press accused him of wearing his hair Beatle-style, he boasted that he had worn a Beatle cut since he was two years old.

As head-hair pioneers, the Beatles must share honors with various bohe-

*Inspired by the Beatles, men
and boys affected long hair
and acted irreverent. Even
Prince Charles temporarily
hid his royal locks under a
mop top.*

mians, beatniks, and early hippies; but they alone deserve credit for resuscitating mustaches. Prior to the Beatles, mustaches were symbols of dapper old gents such as David Niven and Errol Flynn. But according to publicist Derek Taylor, in 1966, while visiting Los Angeles, the Beatles were inspired by an obscure musician named Danny Hutton, who had grown a mustache as a gimmick to attract attention. The next year, *Daily Mirror* reporter Christopher Ward noticed "this shaggy rash spreading over the face of Britain. . . . You're nobody in England these days if you haven't got half an inch of nicotine-stained hair hanging from your stiff upper lip." Ward attributed the rash to the Beatles, all of whom had mustaches by 1967, and noted that ready-made ones, like Beatle wigs, were now on sale in London for thirty shillings. Although far less fuss was made over the Beatles' facial hair than over their head hair, mustaches have far outlasted mop tops as an acceptable male fashion statement.

Other than parading hair around the world, the Beatles' greatest contribution to the concept of mod was their special brand of male perkiness. After Brian Epstein's makeover in 1962 and before the Maharishi metamorphosis in 1967, the Beatles were *perky boys*—like perky girls except even more animated. If perky girls were exclamation points, the early Beatles were human ejaculations. They didn't walk or move; they *spurted*. The lovable mop tops were never without a rapier quip, a wacky pose, or a dizzy shake of their famous hairdos. Onstage, they hopped and bounced, their legs jiggled, and their heads bobbed. Offstage, they were always racing in and out of limos and recording studios, escaping from fans, skipping, running, jumping.

The director they chose for their first movie was Richard Lester, whose main claim to fame, other than American television commercials, was as director of the Mack Sennett–like *The Running, Jumping, Standing Still Film.* Lester's *A Hard Day's Night* (originally titled "Beatlemania") was far too frantic to contain a story. Its premise was: here are the Beatles being Beatles. Watch them sprint, hop, gambol, scurry, disappear, and reappear all over the screen. Beatle heads pop out of car windows, Beatle legs run down hills, Beatle bodies hurdle over bushes and roll down precipitous lawns. They don't just move, they move cute. They do goofy walks in slow and fast motion, they pose with silly glasses and hats, they make faces at the camera.

This jittery bustle summarized the world's new image of England, not only in Richard Lester's Beatles film. The England of *Time*'s cover story is "a sparkling, slapdash comedy . . . switched on . . . a dazzling blur . . . buzzing

*Before they learned to be sullen, even the Rolling Stones engaged in cheeky Beatles-like antics.*

. . . pulsing . . . spinning." *Teen* magazine marveled that Britain's mod girls were so hyperactive that they washed their faces three times a day. Piri Halasz's *Swinger's Guide to London* described London as "the gayest city in the world"; and it promised readers an answer to the frantic question "Where's the action and how do I get in on it?"

London was the primary magnet on this planet for all people looking to get in on the action in 1966. *Time*'s story (abetted by similarly swooning coverage in *Life, Esquire*, and *The Saturday Evening Post*) became one of the greatest feats of salesmanship in the history of modern tourism. What young person, smitten with the notion of a city where everything is "new, uninhibited, and kinky," wouldn't immediately pack his or her bags and buy a youth-fare ticket to London in hopes of catching a glimpse of Mick Jagger sipping espresso at the Guys and Dolls Coffee House in Chelsea (as *Time* assures readers he does) or stopping in at Robert Fraser's art gallery to see "starlet Sue Kingsford in a two-piece pink trouser suit with a lovely stretch of naked tum"?

There was a new breed of tourists who descended on London, not only from America but from Yorkshire and Birmingham, even from Rome and Paris: young people looking to get in on the action. Inspired by the music and the miniskirts, they surged into the King's Road and Carnaby Street with knapsacks on their backs and transistor radios tuned to pirate stations such as Radio Caroline and Radio Luxembourg, which played Little Richard, Stones, and Beatles songs too hot for the BBC. They bought Aubrey Beardsley posters from Nigel Waymouth (who opened the Granny Takes a Trip boutique) and Michael English, operating as a firm named Hapshash and the Coloured Coat.

The city's makeover was so fundamental that its very physical shape went mod. Centre-Point, deemed London's "first pop-art office block" (for no apparent architectural reasons), marked the peak of a building boom that changed the skyline from slate and chimney pots to glass and chrome. The eighteenth-century-village atmosphere of Chelsea was transformed into a mod bazaar by boutiques, secondhand stores, and poster shops along the King's Road. Here you could buy eccentric antique garments such as silk and lace tea dresses, ostrich-feather hats, and genuine "granny" shoes.

Chelsea's most famous place to shop was Bazaar, a boutique opened in 1955 by Mary Quant and her husband, Alexander Plunket Greene. Here was the beginning of the swinging London look, in the form of amusing handbags and Butterick-pattern dresses that Mary cut and snipped to make her own. Next to the Beatles, no one did more to create and sell the image of a reborn England than Quant, known in the annals of fashion history as "Mother of the Miniskirt." (She received the Order of the British Empire in 1966, a year after the Beatles were invested—and she wore Quant putty-colored tights and schoolgirl beret to the ceremony.)

Quant didn't like what other manufacturers were making, so she began designing her own: cheap-to-make (and to buy), ready-to-wear, exuberant outfits made for the irreverent, the young, and the slim. Her fashions combined severe tweeds with laces, riotous stripes with bold checks; she designed rib-tight poor-boy sweaters and vests made out of knotted string, shiny plastic raincoats, fishnet gloves, foolish patterned stockings, and great fox-fur hats in the style of the cossacks. In a country where fashion had always been either the work of exclusive private tailors or imports from France, Mary Quant was an original: an English designer mass-producing the dernier cri.

Bazaar was as much a happening as it was a dress shop. "Like a youth club," wrote Marilyn Bender of *The New York Times*, "where the customer could find friendly advice, a congenial atmosphere, as well as realistic clothes at cheap prices." Window mannequins at Bazaar did not stand demurely with one foot posed in front of the other. Quant mannequins were thinner than all others; they had angular faces and long legs modeled after cover girl Jean Shrimpton's. They posed in riotously gawky ways with legs kicking, bending, and jumping. On occasion, they floated midair at outrageous angles; other times, they held fishing rods and reels with filament lines ending in a small, round tank of live goldfish. Bald mannequins wore goggles and played musical instruments, walking live lobsters on a chain. In the early sixties, these window displays were emblems of a fashion revolution.

In 1961, *Seventeen*'s spring fashion issue introduced Quant clothes to America, and in 1962 her designs were marketed by J. C. Penney stores in order to give the chain a youthful image. By 1966, when the myth of swinging England peaked, Mary Quant fashions were at the heart of it, and she had the world in a dither all over again with a new concept, the pantsuit (originally presented in 1962 as the trouser suit).

Quant spun out fashion fantasies like fireworks. She produced underwear specially imbued with the scent of Harris tweed, or cotton, or linen. During the great topless years of 1964 and '65, she suggested women go to the beach wearing nothing but body paint and stenciled patterns. She declared pubic hair to be the great forthcoming fashion accessory.

What was truly revolutionary about Quant fashions is that they were bought (in her words) "by the daughters of dukes and the daughters of dock workers." For the first time in British fashion history, and subsequently in the rest of the world, clothes were designed to signify not the gap between rich and poor but that between young and old. "Many items shouldn't be worn by people over twenty-eight," announced Quant's husband, Mr. Greene, in 1967 (he was thirty-three). *The New York Times* called him "an elder statesman of the Mod movement."

Mary Quant wasn't just selling clothes. She was selling youth. She observed:

There was a time when every girl under twenty yearned to look like an experienced, sophisticated thirty; when round-faced teenagers practiced sucking in their cheeks to achieve interesting hollows; when every girl dreamed of a slinky black dress worn with high heels. All this is in reverse now. Suddenly, every girl with a hope of getting away with it is aiming to look not only under voting age but under the age of consent. . . . Their aim is to look childishly young, naively unsophisticated.

In record time, American manufacturers tooled up to produce products in the Quant spirit. Even Scotch tape went mod with ad campaigns showing British birds modeling short slicker raincoats onto which they applied colored plastic raindrops made from Scotch tape, and wearing sunglasses with Scotch tape–appliquéd eyelashes. The mod mystique was used to sell even sanitary napkins. Kotex ads showed a gear-looking girl with the caption "Be a bird, be a beat, be a blitz, be sure."

One of the most shocking things about the mod revolution was that it detonated men's as well as ladies' clothes. The revolution in menswear began on an obscure alley behind Regent Street in Soho, where in 1962, twenty-four-year-old John Stephen opened a small shop selling tight, hip-hugging trousers inspired by blue jeans but not so déclassé. The pants, worn with a turtleneck sweater and a Dutch-boy cap, were the foundation for the mod look in men's fashions. And the site of John Stephen's shop—Carnaby Street —became a worldwide symbol of swinging England's youthful audacity. By the mid-sixties, the grubby lane was lined with boutiques specializing in screaming flower-patterned shirts, epauleted jackets, suits emblazoned with gigantic prison-uniform stripes, paisley ties as wide as lobster bibs, and fat vinyl belts. Like Mary Quant's Bazaar, they were fun places to shop—pulsing with rock and roll, offering striped plastic tents for fitting rooms.

Carnaby Street fashions were even more fickle than women's. Mod style for men omnivorously grew to include a dandyish Lord Fauntleroy look in the form of Edwardian suits and shirts cascading with lace at the collars and cuffs, or floppy bows tied at the throat. Mod came to mean almost anything op, pop, or foppish, from Regency ruffles and nineteenth-century frock coats to silver lamé capes and gorillalike fur vests. *Life* proclaimed that "the latest in London" was "elegance from the past" and showed a picture of English-man Michael Williams at the Salisbury Pub modeling his long velvet-collared jacket and patterned trousers—his tribute to the nineteenth century. "I live only for my car and my clothes," Mr. Williams boasted. *Life* advised its readers that visits to Carnaby Street were "so much a part of the routine of England's youth that they have a special word for it—Carnabying."

In America, when Stern Brothers department store in New York City offered a show of John Stephen's Carnaby Street clothes in 1966, a thousand teenagers showed up to buy Beatles caps, polka-dot shirts with white collars and cuffs, low-slung pants, and ankle-high boots. Chicago retailer Cesar Rotondi marveled that schoolboys in the Windy City were paying up to $150 a month to outfit themselves in high-heeled boots, broad belts, and flared-bottom trousers.

By 1966, English style was an unstoppable juggernaut. When Mary Quant

toured the U.S. in 1965 to show her latest fashions, many radio stations played only British music and talked only about British things (often in bogus British accents) the day the Quant Trunk Show came to town. If the deejays didn't know how to do it, Alexander Plunket Greene did; and in Kansas City, Chicago, and other cities across the U.S.A., as Quant fashions were displayed, he commandeered the microphone and turntable, playing Beatles hits and speaking in an exaggerated accent about the glories of life in swinging London.

Although Quant's importance as a women's fashion oracle endured, Carnaby Street was almost instantly consumed by its own fame. By 1967, British fashion savants had dismissed it as a tourist trap selling dish towels made out of the Union Jack and overpriced cravats of last season's design. The mod look, because it was by definition "instant and disposable" and therefore cheap and mass-produced, was all too easy to imitate badly. For American mods on a tight budget, dime stores offered novel ways of achieving the English look. When knee-high boots became the rage, out came a product called Insta-Gators: black vinyl tubes designed to be pulled onto the leg just above one's shoes, thereby miraculously turning shoes into instant boots.

*Carnaby Street (opposite page) was where mod males, such as this miniskirted bloke (above), shopped for the latest fashions.*

*Vidal Sassoon demonstrates the haircut that made him famous.*

Desperate would-be teen modsters bought ankle-high Totes galoshes, convinced by conniving parents that they were dead ringers for the go-go boots
that all the British birds were wearing.

Even at the high end of the fashion scale, and even in France, shameless
Anglophilia inspired Pierre Cardin to offer Gallicized versions of Carnaby
Street clothes at his Adam and Eve boutiques. Cardin sold double-breasted
blazers, regimental ties, tweeds, and Shetland pullovers to French boys whose
mid-sixties sartorial hero, curiously enough, was the Duke of Windsor. The
famous Cardin look—long, slender jacket with a nipped-in waist and pro-
nounced flare at the bottom, worn with tight bell-bottom trousers—was
Monsieur Cardin's homage to earlier, Edwardian England.

As much as miniskirts and bell-bottoms and the mop-top Beatles, hairdresser Vidal Sassoon was a vital element of swinging England. Sassoon's
sculpted, chunky, blunt cut—close to the head, exposing the nape of the neck,
sometimes with points in front of the ears, occasionally asymmetrical (short
and square on one side and long on the other)—was an absolute shock to the
world of hair fashions. He originally devised it not for people but for mannequins, in 1961, when Mary Quant asked him to fix their hair so it wouldn't
interfere with the high collars she was showing in the Bazaar window. "All I

really did was take the pageboy and reverse it, giving an elegance to the neck," Sassoon modestly explained. It was modern hair styling's greatest coup.

The beauty of Sassooning one's hair was that even if you were too dumpy to dare wear a miniskirt, or too poor to afford a constant change of fab clothes, all you needed was a scissors to ally yourself with the mod set. As simple as it appeared, however, the Sassoon look was deceptively difficult to wear. It demanded perfectly straight hair. To advertise it, Sassoon used Oriental models whose thick black tresses fell like shiny blunt-cut curtains around their faces. The weird angles of the haircut also demanded flawless bone structure, or at least unblemished youth. Hair that hangs low on one side and dramatically high on the other calls fatal attention to double chins and sagging jawlines.

Sassoon was more than a haircut. He revolutionized beauty parlors. They used to be women's hushed sanctuaries where attendants scurried about ministering to the rituals of glamour in a manner aimed to unwind clients; Sassoon made them mod, as hip as discos and as sexy. Good-looking male hairdressers in hip-hugger pants toted blow driers from their belts like six-guns. They boogied from chair to chair to the beat of blasting rock music from groups such as the Rolling Stones; they ran their fingers through clients' hair, giving them a kiss on the neck or a squeeze on the thigh. These were not fruity men with foppish manners and names like Mr. Pierre. They were heavily heterosexual kingpins of the mod social scene.

In addition to hairdressers and dress designers, photographers were among the pillars of Anglomania. Antonioni's 1966 film *Blow-Up* featured David Hemmings as a cool, shaggy-haired lensman who worked in a high-tech home studio with blasting rock music and gorgeous models frolicking on rolls of seamless paper. The enigmatic plot about a murder revealing itself in the darkroom was less important to the young audiences who flocked to the film than the idea of the photographer as a superstar. Cameras became a quintessential mod fashion accessory. Everyone wanted a classy Nikon rig with a huge phallic lens; even better were two cameras, or three, slung over shoulders and combined with a khaki photographer's vest with a dozen small pockets for film and lens caps, worn over a sexy turtleneck sweater.

Fashion photography went mod with stunning results. Like so much English-inspired fashion, it went against all known precepts of beauty and taste, using grainy, high-contrast film and wide-angle lenses to warp such images as heavily mascaraed eyelashes in ultra close-up, a nude wearing only go-go boots, or the back of a woman's perfectly tonsured neck.

By 1966, everybody wanted a piece of England, and it was everybody's to be bought. Yardley of London, once known for its little-old-lady scents, retooled such old-fashioned delights as English lavender into a with-it cologne and came up with a new flowery Britannic scent called Oh! de London, a "frisky-frilly fragrance full of tender flowers." Yardley face powders came

*The movie* Blow-Up *established photographers as mod heroes.*

with brushes called "luv puffs"; face masks were marketed in a color called Blimey Blue.

Readers of the Autumn 1966 Montgomery Ward catalog were offered a "Go-Go Mod Christmas" collection of double-breasted pea coats, six-button blazers with removable shoulder epaulets and full paisley lining, and "little swinger" junior-sized Carnaby Street polka-dotted shirts "sure to please a lad's 'Mod' mood." That same year, the Wilton Cake catalog suggested that a sheet cake could "make the generation gap disappear" if it sported a set of "Go-Go Swingers" as a decoration. The Swingers, in lapel-less jackets and bowl haircuts and molded into jaunty postures at their microphones, were dead ringers for the Beatles.

Adoration of England was total in the world of pop music, where in the Beatles' wake came a siege of musical talent known as the British Invasion: Gerry and the Pacemakers (who actually predated the Beatles as a local hit in Liverpool), the Searchers, the Hollies, the Zombies, the Dave Clark Five, Peter and Gordon, Chad and Jeremy, Herman's Hermits, Freddie and the Dreamers, Wayne Fontana and the Mindbenders, the Kinks, the Troggs, the Animals, Manfred Mann, Them, the Who, the Yardbirds, the Swinging Blue Jeans, and, of course, the Rolling Stones. Each group had its own personality.

The Kinks were fierce; the Dave Clark Five was glad; Gerry and the Pace-makers were sentimental; the Rolling Stones were sullen anti-Beatles. What-ever the differences, and however mediocre some of them were, they all possessed the magic: they could say "I'm English!"

If being English was a sure road to musical success, being Beatle-like was even better. *Time*'s swinging-London cover story reported that Czechoslova-kia alone had five hundred rock-and-roll quartets with Beatle-like names. Hundreds, probably thousands, of bands in America formulated around this basic Beatle concept: a quartet of kicky lads with long hair, thumbing their noses at pretension and having a gay time doing it.

For example, the Liverpools: four hopeless studio drones described in the liner notes of their *Beatle Mania!* album as "four *liver*-uppers who have *pooled* their talents." Or the Schoolboys: "Liverpool Moptops, four young men, who with a group of excellent musicians, adopted the style of Beatling, the hottest craze in show business." Or the Liverpool Kids, whose album *Beattle Mash* [*sic*] shows the "Kids" as three middle-aged buggers with thin-ning hair desperately brushed forward to cover the bare spots. Then there were the Buggs, whose album *Beetle Beat* has liner notes screaming "Mersey Beat! The Liverpool Sound!" The weirdest of the bunch were the Beatle Buddies: four tough broads who look only recently paroled from a maximum-security penitentiary. Posed and lit exactly like John, George, Paul, and Ringo on *Meet the Beatles*, the Beatle Buddies are described on their album jacket as "cute and talented," with "looks and sound destined to last long after the Beatles are gone."

The most successful imitators were the Monkees, created by American television executives in the Beatles' image. They neither wrote nor played their hit songs (that was taken care of by studio musicians); but they knew how to act zany whenever a camera was around, and they had cute long hair. And so they had three number-one hits, were mobbed by fan clubs, and sold millions of dollars in souvenirs. In fact, they were so big, there were *Monkees* knockoffs! In 1967, you could buy *The Monkees Song Book* album by the Golden Gate Strings, *The Monkeys A Go-Go* (with a chimpanzee on the cover and songs by a sound-alike group inside), and *The Manhattan Strings Play Instrumental Hits Made Famous by the Monkees*. So successful were the Mon-kees at aping the Beatles' image that when British Monkees fans stormed the U.S. embassy in London to plead that Monkee Davy Jones not be drafted into the United States Army, UPI sent out a story and picture about the protest, describing the manufactured foursome as "a British pop singing group"!

Surely there is no example of Anglomania more painful than the transfor-mation of Sam the Sham and the Pharaohs. Sam, whose real name was Domingo Samudio, led his Hispanic (but Arabian-costumed) singing group to triumph in 1965 with the Tex-Mex party song "Wooly Bully." Sung half in Spanish, half in gibberish English, accompanied by a wild saxophone and a relentless cascade of organ triplets, "Wooly Bully" was a monster hit but

utterly un–Mersey Beat. And by 1965, the British Invasion had to be reck-
oned with; so the next year the Pharaohs' PR firm sent out a press release
headlined LOOK! THEY'VE GONE BRITISH!, explaining how "the Wooly Bully
boys will be making their first appearance in 'New Look' non-Pharaoh hairstyles and costumes." The picture with the press release shows Mr. Samudio
and his band in Dutch-boy cloth caps, Edwardian shirts, and perfectly styled
Beatle bowl-cut hairdos.

The Beatles were the best salesmen of Anglomania, and their trajectory
through the sixties shows how the craze for England faded and died. In
August 1966, at the end of the summer when the myth of swinging England
peaked, the Beatles released *Revolver*—their first "concept album." In his
Beatles biography, *Shout!*, Philip Norman described it as "like no pop album
before it. . . . *Revolver* was London as she flourished in the swinging summer

*The Monkees, manufactured for American television, were even kookier than the
British bands they imitated.*

afterglow. It was hot pavement, open windows, King's Road bistros and England soccer stripes [England won the world cup in '66]. It was the British accent, once again all-conquering." *Revolver* was the end of an era: with its release, the Beatles announced they would never again perform live. No more touring. No more screaming fans. No more yeah-yeah-yeah. The album ended with the song "Tomorrow Never Knows," including John Lennon's enigmatic spoken words, "Turn off your mind, relax and float downstream."

John had borrowed the spiritual incantation of "Tomorrow Never Knows" from Timothy Leary, who had borrowed it from *The Tibetan Book of the Dead* as a chant to help LSD trippers find cosmic consciousness. The Beatles, who had started as mod rock and rollers, were becoming psychedelic mind voyagers. And as they floated downstream, they left their original perkiness far, far behind. They were serious now, deemed deep thinkers rather than madcap lads.

By the time *Sgt. Pepper's Lonely Hearts Club Band* came out in 1967, *The Partisan Review* declared their work "an astounding accomplishment for which no one could have been wholly prepared." Instantly proclaimed by intellectuals and teenyboppers alike to be the greatest rock-and-roll record ever made, *Sgt. Pepper* finally shattered what remained of the image of the Beatles as a lovable Fab Foursome. They had become *important artists,* so important that all the frivolities of their earlier personalities seemed like only "gestations of genius that have now come to fruition" (*The Partisan Review* again). *Newsweek* compared the Beatles to T. S. Eliot. *The New York Review of Books* called *Sgt. Pepper* "a new and golden Renaissance of Song." Abbie Hoffman said the album was the essence of radical politics: "anti-war, anti-racist, anti-bomb." Kenneth Tynan declared it a decisive moment in the history of Western civilization.

In the blinding light of the Beatles' apotheosis, the giddiness and blithe materialism of swinging England began to pale.

No longer were the Beatles symbols of good times in the land of mod. They had become the pacesetters of a vast, seething counterculture that had goals more high-minded than merely swinging. When the Beatles joined in a satellite television broadcast to 200 million people in June 1967, they sang "All You Need Is Love." The love in these lyrics was very different from the joyful feeling of their early hit, in which they sang "She loves you, yeah, yeah, yeah!" This new song was an anthem, and the love they extolled was nothing frivolous; it was a weapon in the youth revolution.

As sixties rock and roll—squired by the Beatles—grew complicated, so pop fashion evolved from mod-pop cheer into aggressive psychedelic anarchy. "We wore fabulous braided, beribboned, rick-racked, gilded, star-spangled, belled and beaded blouses, shirts and tunics over flared hipster trousers or long flowing skirts, with moccasins or laced-up reverse calf boots." So wrote Derek Taylor about post–*Sgt. Pepper* fashions. "Any clothes would do so long as they were dreamlike."

By 1967, the King's Road was blossoming beyond even the maddest mod dazzle. "Any fine Saturday you can see the full psychedelic fancy dress parade," *The Daily Express* reported in July. "The effect is strange, not really horrific if properly done, but the mind boggles at what could happen." In the summer of 1967, it *did* happen, and minds *were* boggling—but not so much in London anymore. A place called Haight-Ashbury had stolen the thunder of the King's Road. In an unprecedented coup, San Francisco had displaced London as the city of the decade.

It was still okay to say "I'm English!" in 1967, but if you really wanted to convince the world you knew what was happening, the way to do it was to say "I'm stoned." The myth of swinging England, in all its material splendor, was overwhelmed by the myth of hippies.

# HIPPIES

You are now entering the largest hippie colony in the world and the very heart and fountainhead of the hippie subculture. You are passing through the Bearded Curtain. Marijuana is a household staple here, enjoyed by the natives to stimulate their senses. Among the favorite pastimes of the hippies, besides taking drugs, are parading and demonstrating; seminars and group discussions about what's wrong with the status quo; malingering; plus the ever present preoccupation with the soul, reality, and self-expression, such as strumming guitars, piping flutes, and banging on bongoes.

S O  S P O K E  the guide on the Gray Line bus that took sightseers through the Haight-Ashbury district of San Francisco in 1967. The excursion was called the Hippie Hop, and was billed as "the only foreign tour within the continental limits of the United States."

Hippies were so the rage that J. C. Penney enrolled its merchandising executives in a two-day crash course titled "Sell It Like It Is." Each participant received a Day-Glo paper bag containing a kaleidoscope, a poster of a nude girl with flowers in her hair, incense, underground newspapers, and a stash to hold grass. It was hoped that exposing the executives to these totems of hippie culture would help them come up with ideas to overcome the store's square image.

Hippies were blowing the world's mind. Sixties style became so completely theirs that twenty-five years later, their favorite words of awe, "Oh, wow," symbolize the times as much as "We Shall Overcome" or "(I Can't Get No) Satisfaction".

The dazzling thing about them was that they were so happy. They did not reject the perkiness that suffused the early sixties. They smiled and danced and got high and loved everybody. They wore flowers in their hair and painted their bodies like freaky Easter eggs. Their program for a better world was one where everyone was mellow.

Most things by which they are remembered, including outrageous hair, running around nude, and mind-bending drugs, were thriving well before they came along. In 1966, all these eccentricities congealed into the sixties' most famous faddish lifestyle.

The first notice of the hippies' birth was in the San Francisco *Examiner* on September 6, 1965, in an article about the Haight-Ashbury area of San Francisco. A NEW PARADISE FOR BEATNIKS was the headline. Reporter Michael Fallon described the "new hip hangout"—a coffeehouse called the Blue Unicorn at 1927 Hayes Street. The Unicorn was headquarters for what one contemporary account called "bearded philosophers, would-be artists, intellectual Negroes, peace workers, and anyone alien to square society."

Haight-Ashbury was different than the old North Beach scene. The beat and offbeat characters who hung out on the Haight didn't get mellow on a pipe of pot, then listen serenely to jazz or poetry. They were post-Beatles hipsters who liked rock and roll, or what was then being called folk rock. Instead of lying supine dreaming about the Xanadu they might write about someday, they *danced all night*. Old beats had looked down on social dancing (with the possible exception of gypsy folk galops) as a phony thing for overly hormonal teenagers on "American Bandstand." These new bohemians loved to dance. They were hot and physical, not cool and cerebral.

In place of the old ascetic look of black berets and tidy goatees, the new denizens of the Haight fancied a riotous getup of thrift-shop Victorian shawls, low-slung mod bell-bottoms, and mind-blowing paisleys. They combined bowler hats, fringe jackets, and western boots; they carried foppish canes.

Their hair was wild and unruly, their beards full instead of neatly trimmed. They swooned about life with hyperbole borrowed from San Francisco's campy underground. Artists among them forsook somber-paletted expressionistic splats for art nouveau à la op in blinding color. These new nonconformists took LSD trips and came back singing of joy and talking about good vibes. Many called themselves acidheads, but reporter Michael Fallon coined a less corrosive term to describe them. It was a merry twist on the old term "hipster": hippie.

In January 1966, one event launched the new subculture. It was a weekend happening in San Francisco's Longshoremen's Hall called the Trips Festival. Designed as a celebration of the LSD experience, the festival was the first major coming together of the acidhead underground.

Advertised as "an LSD experience without LSD," it was in fact an LSD experience saturated with LSD—mixed into punch, ice cream, and cake and given away as tablets from full shopping bags that circulated through the hall. Acidheads who had previously only tripped alone were dazzled by the *vibes*, the *energy* of thousands of like-minded freaks freaking out together! Here was an amazing new world, *their* world: ultraviolet lights; poetic readings of

Beatles lyrics; spontaneous toplessness; Allen Ginsberg chanting to bring about good karma; Marshall McLuhan's pearls of New Age wisdom; Hell's Angels parading about in leather and chains; Ken Kesey's Merry Pranksters in clown regalia; the Grateful Dead; Big Brother and the Holding Company; and Neal Cassady dressed as a gorilla bridegroom in a weirdo wedding ceremony billed as "Neal Cassady vs. Ann Murphy Vaudeville."

Ten thousand acidheads came together, looked at each other and the scene around them, and realized THEY WERE HAPPENING. The underground was erupting aboveground; and surging out along the groovy grapevine went tidings of the new way of life in San Francisco—the way of the acidheads, a.k.a. hippies. Here was a lifestyle that contained all the moment's most provocative gestures of defiance: free sex, daring drugs, aggressively loud music, miniskirted chicks and long-haired guys who dressed in peacock colors.

What made it all so charismatic was the newborn hippies' sense of mission, their conviction that the flashing light shows, happy hallucinations, and farfetched philosophizing were keys to something really big. They weren't just another group of outsiders rejecting straight society. These flower children presented themselves to the world as the dawn of the New Age.

More than anything else they did, hippies were known for their favorite drug, LSD, which had two main champions. In the east, there was Professor Timothy Leary of Harvard. Starting in 1960, he gave students psychedelic lessons in a Psychodrama Room outfitted with mattresses on the floor, candlelight, Buddha posters, and Hindu ragas on the stereo. Leary was so possessed by his drug visions that after he was fired in 1962 because of these controversial teaching methods, he began traveling around the country telling people to "tune in, turn on, drop out." He even started a religion, the League for Spiritual Discovery; its maxim was "You Have to Be Out of Your Mind to Pray."

In the west, Ken Kesey took his first trip as a volunteer in a Menlo Park veterans hospital drug experiment in 1960. Kesey, author of *One Flew Over the Cuckoo's Nest* (1962), was an all-out iconoclast. He irreverently dubbed LSD "acid" (to Professor Leary's dismay). He hit the road in 1964, surrounded by an entourage of proto-hippies energized by fantastic acid visions. They called themselves the Merry Pranksters and traveled in the original psychedelic bus, a rattletrap International Harvester painted in the wildest shades of schizophrenichrome. They wore superhero capes and goggles and American flags and glow-in-the-dark, on-the-warpath uniforms. They declared themselves living works of art. Their goal was to "prank" everyone they saw. For instance, they pulled up in front of (then presidential candidate) Barry Goldwater's department store in Phoenix and waved banners saying, VOTE FOR GOLDWATER—VOTE FOR FUN!

By 1965, Kesey, like Leary, had become an evangelist of enlightenment via LSD. He packed a few tens of thousands of doses of acid (not yet illegal) and began a mind-bending set of "acid tests" during which he and his gang doled it out at antiwar rallies, private and public parties, and campus gatherings throughout the Bay Area. The Grateful Dead joined the fun with a never-before-heard level of amplified rock and roll. The Pranksters snuck LSD into coffee, Pepsi, cake, and Kool-Aid, so no one knew they were going on a trip until they heard the color yellow scream.

1965 was Kesey's glory year, and the generative tide behind hippie culture. His acid tests helped establish the psychedelic lifestyle: throbbing rock music, protoplasmic light projections, body painting, and freaked-out Prankster buffoonery. At the soul of each acid test were mass LSD hallucinations, prized by Kesey and his entourage as the true path towards the rapturous state of mind they sought.

Hordes of vaguely disenchanted, vaguely antiwar and antiestablishment sixties people were encouraged by these acid tests to drop out and embark on the great grope towards a mental condition they called expanded consciousness.

By early 1966, the center of the hippie universe was between 1400 and 1800 Haight Street, where most of San Francisco's acidheads were encamped —and hundreds more were arriving every week from around the nation. They slept on the sidewalk and in doorways. They sat together playing guitars and tambourines and flutes. They sold beads and buttons and panhandled spare change and copped and sold marijuana joints and acid tabs. Hell's Angels hung out in front of Tracy's Doughnut Shop; acidheads made love in the meditation room at the back of the Psychedelic Shop.

In addition to hippies, Haight Street was crowded with hippies' dogs. Like their masters, the dogs were dubious fashion pioneers, known for originating the now-classic counterculture canine costume of a red bandanna in lieu of a collar. Collars (the dog version of a necktie) were so uptight, as were leashes; and so these "free" dogs wandered and pooped wherever they wanted to go. As a result, Haight Street became notoriously filthy. "Several times, I saw barefoot hippie girls squish their toes into a big pile of dog excrement, calmly walk to the curb, and scrape it off like you would from your shoe," wrote Burton Wolfe in *The Hippies*, a contemporary account of the scene. " 'I used to worry about things like that before I took LSD,' one of them told me. 'Now my mind has opened, and I see that it's all part of life: dirt, feces, everything. Feces are groovy!' "

Before they emerged as a provocative public issue, the random congress of ex-beatniks, disenchanted lefties, folk rockers, street people, and dropouts had begun to see themselves as a new tribe. Throughout 1966, after the Trips Festival in January, the hippies' growing sense of community was expressed in street fairs, a summer-solstice festival, acid-rock concerts, a "Love Pageant Rally" in October (called to mark the sixth of the month, the day California's law making LSD illegal went into effect), and climactically, the Human Be-In of January 1967.

The lofty promise of the Be-In, according to the January 12, 1967 press conference at the Print Mint (during which dope-laced cookies were passed around), was that "Berkeley activists and the love generation of the Haight-Ashbury will join together with members of the new nation who will be coming from every state in the nation, every tribe of the young (the emerging soul of the nation) to powwow, celebrate, and prophesy the epoch of liberation, love, peace, compassion, and unity of mankind."

Word of the Be-In had spread across the U.S.A. in a budding network of underground papers; it was legendary before it happened. A local astrologer announced that January 14, the day of the Be-In, would be the day when the earth's population would exactly equal the number of all the dead people in human history. Oh, wow.

It was a joyful day in the annals of hippie history: LSD was given away to all who wanted it. Allen Ginsberg chanted "om." Chocolate George, the lovable, furry-faced Hell's Angel, found children who got lost. Timothy Leary wore flowers in his hair and said, "Whatever you do is beautiful." Ten thousand hippies, dressed in feathers, war paint, buckskin, and holy-man pajamas, made love to an ideal, all at the same time. And when the Be-In was over, they picked up all their litter and left Golden Gate Park clean.

"A great butterfly had emerged and taken wing in the setting sun of the San Francisco Human Be-In," wrote Gene Anthony in the book *The Summer of Love.* "It flew across the land, then on across the sea to other continents. Wherever that psychedelic butterfly touched down to earth, its spirit captured the consciousness of masses of young people. . . . A non-violent revolution had begun." New York hippies staged their own be-in on Easter in the Sheep Meadow in Central Park. When the fuzz showed up, their cars were pelted . . . with flowers. *The Village Voice* breathlessly proclaimed that it seemed "almost a sacred event, harking back to medieval pageants, gypsy gatherings, or the great pow-wows of the American Indians."

The be-ins of early 1967 were confirmation to the world, and to hippies themselves: something important was happening. Maybe they really were the New People; maybe this was the millennium.

As their evangelical spirit swelled, many heavenly-minded hippies began to look the part. While the earliest denizens of Haight-Ashbury had been known for clothes that flaunted worldly splendor, a large faction of the movement began dropping the beads, bangles, and bright clothes for a more ascetic look of saintly whites. The holy hippie sported a Jesus look, complete with pageboy hair, full beard, sandals, and flowing vestments.

Body fashions told the tale. Despite a few fatties among hippie heroes (Mama Cass, Pigpen of the Grateful Dead, and various beer-bellied Hell's Angels and earth-mother types), lean and austere was where it was at. Mortified flesh was evidence that you were on a spiritual trip, and that you were not hogging all the earth's resources. All the well-known hippie diets, including macrobiotics, the brown-rice-and-sprouts regimen, and mucus-liberating fruitarianism, were just barely nutritious; in some cases, they actually starved people to death.

*Meditating in New Mexico*

The culmination of hippie religiosity happened in August 1967, when a relatively obscure holy man named Maharishi Mahesh Yogi came to London to deliver what he declared would be his last lecture before retiring to a life of silence back in India, and the year of the hippie turned into what *Life* magazine called "the year of the guru."

Among the Maharishi's listeners were the Beatles, who were so impressed that without ado or delay, the entire foursome offered themselves to the holy man as disciples. Having these guys as followers was the next-best thing to an endorsement by Shiva himself; so Maharishi postponed his retirement and invited John, Paul, George, and Ringo to come the next day to his course of indoctrination at University College, Bangor, North Wales. Joined by Mick Jagger and Marianne Faithfull, the Beatles spent a "Weekend for the Spiritually Regenerated" . . . at the end of which they declared that drugs were passé and meditation was where it was at.

To understand the momentousness of this event, you must remember that the Beatles of 1967 had already attained maximum hippie signification. John's Rolls-Royce, unveiled in May, was a three-ton acid-rock poster on wheels. Heads around the world were busy discovering drug motifs everywhere in their just-released *Sgt. Pepper* album. Only that summer, Timothy Leary himself had declared the Beatles to be "the wisest, holiest, most effective avatars the human race has ever produced."

*Hippies sought enlightenment in India
(below). Bill Dana, who earlier created
the character José Jimenez, played backup
sitar to the guru on the cover of this record
album spoof of the Maharishi Mahesh
Yogi (left).*

By the next spring, the Maharishi's hippie votaries included Donovan, Mia Farrow, and even Beach Boy Mike Love, who grew a sacerdotal beard to signify his conversion. John and George grew pious whiskers, too, and all four Beatles went to Rishikesh above the Ganges to chant, fast, and pray with their new master. They shed worldly hippie garb such as paisley shirts, bell-bottoms, and buckskin boots in favor of *kurta* tunics and sandals. Word leaked out of the Ashram that the Beatles were having a contest to see who could meditate the longest. (Paul won: four straight hours!)

Some hippies followed the example of the Beatles in their search for Truth via meditation; but the discovery of India had an impact way beyond religion and trippy relaxation exercises. India became the hottest fount of style since London. Anything Indian was chic, from the *Kama Sutra* to the Nehru jacket, to sitar music, hot curry, and the sweet smell of patchouli oil.

Holy men with subcontinental accents suddenly began appearing in movies and in TV variety shows, offering hippielike homilies to everyone from the Beatles (in *Help!*) to Lucille Ball ("The Lucy Show") to Dan Rowan and Dick Martin (whose "Laugh-In" featured Arte Johnson in a regular role as a wise and witty, Nehru-jacketed Indian pundit). *Eye* magazine, which reported that "more and more followers, American as well as English, bow to the east," ran a cartoon strip called "Ravi Duck" (homage to sitar player Ravi Shankar) about a mallard in a Sgt. Pepper tunic who goes to India to visit the Mahayoni Mishi-Mashi, "Guru to the Stars."

Life-Tone Enterprises of Hollywood offered a series of wall posters entitled "The Love of the Guru." Buyers had their choice of the Maharishi alone, the Maharishi with the Beatles and their wives, or the Maharishi with Marianne Faithfull, Donovan, Mia Farrow, the Rolling Stones, Cliff Richard, the Beach Boys, "and many, many more." Life-Tone promised that the posters were so lifelike that "you can actually feel and receive the warmth, kindness, and love of the Maharishi."

Hippie theory, such as it was, made small distinction among a mind-bending acid trip, divine communion, and beautiful scenery; and so it came to be that hippie trippers often complemented neurological voyages and the pontifications of the religious convert with pilgrimages to the mystical-religious-exotic wonders of the world, especially of the East: the beach at Goa, the shrines of the Himalayas, and the holy cities of North Africa. Their grail was double-size—big enough to hold not only the sixth-century wisdom of the Tantrics but also pipeloads of dynamite hash.

Hippie apologists loved comparing the exasperating barefoot longhairs to their biblical and historical progenitors, from Samson to William Blake. "The first hippie, then, is clearly Socrates," wrote Delbert L. Earisman in *Hippies in Our Midst*. He asserts that Saint Francis was a hippie, too: the first holy panhandler. California bishop James Pike likened hippies to early Christians: "There is something about the temper of these people, a gentleness, a quietness, an interest—something good."

Other men of God, less impressed by the hippies' love-and-peace image, saw them as lost souls desperately in need of real religion. But rather than bring them into the ordinary church, they brought the church to them. No one tried harder to make hippies see the Holy Light than Arthur Blessitt, the "minister of Sunset Strip" and proprietor of His Place—the nightclub haven famous for its "toilet services." A toilet service ensued whenever a hippie accepted Christ. He was moved into the bathroom at the back of the club, where he emptied his stash into the commode. The Reverend Mr. Blessitt then assured the convert that he was about to be turned on to "a trip with an everlasting high—Jesus, man. He won't hassle you. He's the greatest trip of all. Be a weirdo for Jesus." And as the swirling water sucked down grass and pills, everybody crowded into the bathroom and sang, "Down, down, down, down—all my dope is gone!"

Carl F. Burke, chaplain of the Erie County Jail in Buffalo, New York, took the idea of idiomatic theology to its outer limit by listening to street kids tell it like it was: the Bible in their own words. The results were collected in a book called *God Is for Real, Man.*

The story of Doubting Thomas begins:

After Jesus busted outa the grave he met two of his gang on the road. Man! Were they ever spooked and surprised. They ran like crazy to the place where the other guys were. And started to tell who they seen. Before they could say much, bingo! Jesus was there, came right through the door, and they couldn't figure that out either. He said, "Peace!"

The first of the Ten Commandments is reworded to read "God is Mr. Big, real big"; the second (about graven images) is translated thus: "No making things that look like God in the craftshop at the settlement house."

Published by the YMCA, *God Is for Real, Man* was so successful it went through six printings in 1966; Sammy Davis, Jr., guesting on "The Mike Douglas Show" (and wearing a Nehru jacket with American Indian beads), said, "I love this book, man."

If spiritual exploration was the hippie's motivation, rock music was his mantra, enshrined as an essential element of hippie life in June 1967 at the Monterey Pop Festival. It was the festival at Monterey that permanently braided hippies with rock music in the world's eyes, introducing Janis Joplin, Jimi Hendrix, and Ravi Shankar as new-sensibility heroes. When *Monterey Pop*, the movie, was released, flower children everywhere were given a feature-length lesson in hippie music, fashion, and trip behavior. "The children danced night and day," Eric Burdon sang. "Religion was being born down in Monterey."

"Extremely typographic people are unable to experience it," Chester Anderson explained in *The Oracle.* "Any artistic activity not allied to rock is doomed to preciousness and sterility." Maybe, maybe not; but this is certain:

acid rock was the current that electrified the hippie grapevine in 1966–67. Listening to key albums was as revealing as astrology and the I Ching. It was a vital means by which hippies shared their tribal vision of the world.

Across America and the world, stoned freaks spent days listening hard to records—played loud, played at 78 rpm instead of 33⅓, played backwards—in order to tune in. In some cases, anyone could hear the revelations. Country Joe and the Fish chanted "L-S-D, L-S-D" in their playout groove. The Jefferson Airplane's "White Rabbit" ("One pill makes you larger, one pill makes you small . . . *Feed your head!*") was a psychedelic update of *Alice in Wonderland.* Donovan's "Mellow Yellow" inspired many a trustful teenybopper to try smoking bananas. For its title alone, the Byrds' "Eight Miles High" was banned on radio stations in 1966.

The message didn't have to be explicit. It was like inverted paranoia: once you got into this *secret* bag, you heard forbidden mysteries in almost any song. "Puff the Magic Dragon," a children's poem written by Lenny Lipton in 1959, then recorded by folk singers Peter, Paul and Mary, was widely thought to be a paean to puffing marijuana.

There was no need to stretch to find the brain benders in most Beatles songs. Starting with *Revolver,* they plunged into a world of musical enigmas by suggesting, "Listen to the color of your dreams," and using tape loops, backwards tracks, and sound effects to undermine rational comprehension. Their lyrics became a lush arbor of hidden footnotes, drug visions, and veiled parables just waiting to be plucked by wide-eyed cognoscenti.

The pinnacle of Beatles baloney was the *Sgt. Pepper* album, a colossal load of signs and messages hiding in between the words. It wasn't only the mnemonic significance of "Lucy in the Sky with Diamonds" that sent heads reeling. It was every word in the song, which was surely meant to invoke a dynamite LSD trip. Then there was "A Day in the Life": the man who *blew his mind* out in a car; the "four thousand holes in Blackburn, Lancashire" (needle marks, right? [wrong; they were potholes in a road]); and the orchestra's crescendo, which was, to every acid-softened mind that heard it, the musical equivalent of the greatest drug rush imaginable. And, hey, man—what about the thirteen-kilocycle whistle on "A Day in the Life"? Humans cannot hear it, but it freaks out dogs!

Hippies didn't invent the concept of recondite record listening; since 1963, "Louie Louie" had provided frat boys partyloads of fun hunting for sexual innuendo in the lyrics. But it was hippies who distilled the concept of music as a secret means of communication among those in the know.

Being tribal and mystical, hippies cultivated an extravagant catalog of giddy folklore beyond their musical apocrypha. All the then-fashionable palaver about the world becoming a global village perfectly fit the way information spread along the white-hot hippie grapevine.

For example, the tall tale of Emmett Grogan. Mr. Grogan was one of the motivators behind the hippie social-service group that called itself the Dig-

*Co-author Michael Stern's parents (above)
hosted a hippie party for friends and relatives
at their home in Winnetka, Illinois.*

gers; he was an original San Francisco street-theater agent provocateur. Or was he? According to *The Hippy's Handbook*, "He doesn't exist; he was invented to satisfy the curiosity of journalists who kept asking San Francisco Diggers who their leader was; they didn't want a leader; consequently Emmett Grogan was invented." Many hippies believed that. That was cool. Emmett Grogan was a joke on the establishment perception that saw the world in terms of leaders and followers.

The truth was that Emmett Grogan *did* exist, but he instructed each Digger to tell everyone who asked for him that *he* was Emmett Grogan. It was like the scene in *Spartacus* where the slaves show their solidarity by not playing according to the Romans' rules.

Then there was the case of the psychedelic banana peel. Smoking a banana peel, rumor said, got you high. This disinformation began as a hoax. It started in March 1967 in the *Berkeley Barb*, which announced that a friend of the drummer for Country Joe and the Fish had discovered an amazing new psychedelic drug: banana peels, dried, baked, scraped, then smoked. Designed as a prank to upset straights, the banana story ripped along the grapevine, and thousands of hippies fell for it.

What a righteous put-on! United Fruit panicked. The FDA investigated bananas. And the *Mellow Yellow Cookbook*, a hippie-inspired recipe pamphlet, sincerely printed variations on the recipe, including "Frozen Baked Banana" and a medley of chewed mint gum, banana peel, and green pepper wrapped in foil, stored in a dark place for six weeks, then baked at 200 degrees and smoked.

Like the sudden celebrity of the banana, all the raciest hippie legends radiated out of the drug underworld. For formerly uptight middle-class dropouts, here was a new and thrilling dimension to life—excitement that ranged from tiny tales of personal paranoia (the time your straight neighbor borrowed the oregano jar, but it was really filled with your stash of grass) all the way to the grand epic adventure of Augustus Owsley Stanley III.

Owsley, the outlaw chemist, was the most fantastic of hippie heroes. It was he who supplied Ken Kesey with acid for his acid tests. It was he (an electronics nut) who bought the Grateful Dead their out-of-sight sound system, thus forging the crucible in which acid-rock music was born. It was he who supplied thousands of free doses to hippies at the original Be-In. The Los Angeles *Times* called him "the LSD millionaire" and depicted him with handfuls of hundred-dollar bills; *Newsweek* called him "the Henry Ford of LSD."

The LSD he made was renowned as the best in the world, allegedly manufactured during occult ceremonies in which Owsley, draped in ancient Indian turquoise, read magical incantations over the chemicals. His ability to elude the law was legendary. Owsley was known for pointing out that LSD was originally synthesized just weeks after the atom was first smashed. It was a sign! LSD was begotten for the human race to save itself from the terrible power of the atom.

Outlandish parables about Owsley saturated hippie lore between 1966, when he started tableting masses of LSD in a basement lab in Point Richmond, and early 1968, when he was sentenced to three years in jail after getting caught in Northern California with 868,000 doses (which his lawyers argued were for his private use).

The best story, told and retold by stoned hippies, was about the time he was driving a beakerful of pure, uncut LSD up to San Francisco. A policeman pulled him over. "What's in the jar?" asked the fuzz. "Taste it and see," said Owsley. The cop took a big gulp. LSD is tasteless, just like water, so Owsley was sent on his way. He sped up the road and waited around the other side of a dangerous curve. A few moments later, the fuzz's car came burning up the road; and the fuzz, his eyes dilated wide from what had been about ten thousand doses of Owsley's best acid, sailed off the side of the road into the Pacific Ocean.

Here are some of the non-Owsley drug tidings that buzzed along the lines of tribal communication:

- Some commercial tobacco companies hold acres of land in Mexico where they are perfecting dynamite strains of marijuana. They have trademarked the names Acapulco Gold, Panama Red, Lung Candy, and Thai Stick in anticipation of the day grass is legalized.
- The finest marijuana in the world is New York White, so named because the plants from which it is harvested grow in the city sewer system, where there is no light. Their leaves are colorless. The plants originally took root from seeds flushed down toilets during drug raids. The giant albino alligators in the sewers eat this grass all the time and are as mellow as doves.
- If a Hindu holy man takes LSD, nothing happens, because his consciousness is so evolved already. (Richard Alpert reported this to be true when he trekked to the Far East, met his own personal guru, and subsequently became Baba Ram Dass.)
- People stoned on acid are immune to atomic radiation.
- You can use marijuana seeds like popcorn: sauté them in hot oil until they pop; then eat the popped seeds and get stoned.
- Methedrine (speed) was invented by the Nazis in order to hone their malevolence.
- Cher Bidis, Indian cigarettes, contain rauwolfia, the powerful drug that got Mahatma Gandhi high.
- Grace Slick put LSD in the punch at Tricia Nixon's wedding. (Actually, she wasn't even there.)

By the summer of 1967, hippies had become a national and international event—a colorful story for the press to cover, and sure relief from depressing news about Vietnam and race riots. Scott McKenzie's song "San Francisco" rocketed to the top of the charts, advising visitors to the hippie capital to go there wearing flowers if they wanted to feel part of the groovy scene. June was the beginning of what was supposed to be the hippies' brightest hour, the Summer of Love.

For innovators of the hippie lifestyle, however, their summer turned into a gigantic bummer. When they had been on the fringe, back in 1965 or even '66, they were free, and enjoyed the immunity of seeming, at worst, odd. They could pull their pranks and do their own thing, and maybe freak out a few uptight squares; but no one held them to account, because they didn't really

matter. Once they became a bona-fide social phenomenon, and the core group was joined by tens of thousands who were perhaps less pure of heart and purpose, the whole scene changed. Hippie success, and the glare of publicity, was hell.

To their consternation, the hippies' relentless gaiety made them easily cooptable by the straight world they set out to reject. Despite paranoid reaction by fuddy-duddies, the hippie lifestyle was a gold mine of fun to reporters. Here was a peace-loving sect who wanted to make love and get high and wear bright clothes and dance barefoot in the park.

Early coverage focused on their picturesque zaniness—on the atavistic monikers they adopted for themselves, such as Captain Trips, Hairy Henry, or Teenie Weenie Deanie; on the confounding names of the head shops that began to sprout along Haight Street, such as the Blushing Peony, the Weed Patch, and the Drogstore *(sic);* or on those dazzling Edwardian-mod-cowboy fashions.

Hippies were written about as if they were the next-funniest thing to the Three Stooges. It was common in the Haight, *Time* reported, for a hippie to put a nickel in a parking meter, then lie down in the space for a half-hour's tan. No pictorial story was complete without nutty pictures of long hair, big beards, a painted body (preferably a girl's, in a bikini), a couple making love in public, and those rickety vans painted like rainbows with acid indigestion.

Hippies were gobbled up by stage, screen, and television. *Hair*, which opened simultaneously on Broadway and in London in April 1968, turned their struggle for world peace and long hair into a rousing commercial success billed as "an American tribal love-rock musical." It included a nude scene and an invitation to the audience to come and join in the onstage merriment: "Swing with us, turn on with us!" exulted the merry cast. It was lauded by *The Observer* in London as "a great hymn to freedom and love" and by *Newsweek* as "a vivid uproar that has more wit, feeling, and musicality than anything since *West Side Story.*"

Hippies' wacky antics provided laughs in movies such as *The President's Analyst* ("the picture dedicated to life, liberty, and the pursuit of happenings") and *I Love You, Alice B. Toklas* (featuring psychedelic brownies and Peter Sellers in hippie wig, headband, and love beads). By the time "Laugh-In" premiered as a series on NBC-TV in 1968, lewd jokes about long hair, dope, and free love made the show a prime-time hit.

A firm called Pop Publishers came out with a line of gift books with hippie themes, including *Help! My Guru Died*, and *Cooking with Grass: An Arresting Collection of Pot Dishes*. (It was all a jolly flower-power put-on: the "pot" in the title refers to a casserole; the recipes, such as "Up Up and Away Cheese Pie" and "Roach-ette of Beef" are all comfy suburban classics, made without marijuana.)

"Find Your Own Guru!" advertised the Oregonian Shops in *Seventeen* magazine, showing Nehru-collared meditation shirts and women's dresses with "potent paisley power." The same issue (September 1968) featured an ad from Campbell's soup showing the fat-cheeked Campbell Kids dressed in hippie colors, the girl with flowers in her hair, the boy wearing a mandala around his neck. They were selling "The Campbell Hang-Up," a way-out poster guaranteed to "turn your wall souper-delic!" The Patrician company exhibited Psychedelicious earrings. In the mail-order column, readers were offered their own six-inch-high fuzzy-wuzzy snuggle friend called the Hippie:

*Hippies meant big business. Even the Campbell Soup Kids got groovy.*

"Here comes himself in a pillow-pose with black straw hair and a wild-print cotton body. A cheerleader to start the ball rolling for a great new school year."

In an effort to make the hippie lifestyle palatable for readers (and readers' parents), *Teen* magazine did a phenomenal job of removing all danger from its presentation of the oh-so-trendy counterculture. It described "the new teenage rage in California—a freak out—where the revelers blow their minds to the chaos of sound, sights, smokes and smells that fill the hall." The idea of a freak-out, *Teen* explained, was

> to be as far out and nonconformist as you dare. Exaggerated makeup is a must for freakettes. Tricolored op art designs decorate Linda's fair face. Janis, in a one-piece bathing suit, is daubed head to foot in luminescent paints. Jeannie, who looks better in a leopard skin than a leopard, has painted the words "Freak Out" on her legs. Carol is wearing the new mini skirt she's too shy to wear on the street. Cam's shift was cut from a lace window curtain and Frank's slacks from a chintz couch cover.

There were, however, limits to freakiness, *Teen* warned. They claimed that California's freak-out leaders were "dead set" against drug use(!). And the article included a sorry-looking photograph of freakette Barbara Jackson, who "in a supreme effort to be different" shaved her head. "This is carrying non-conformity too far, boys declare."

Ogled by the straight world, the hippie high soured fast. *Newsweek*, which had used the January 1967 Be-In as an opportunity to profile "Dropouts with a Mission" and to conclude with the upbeat note that "they may bring with them a worthwhile residue: spontaneity, honesty, and appreciation for the wonder of life," had changed its tune by June. In an SOS called "The Hippies Are Coming" (warning about the impending "flash flood" when school lets out), hippies are described as "antagonizing the squares, frightening the authorities, and driving the cops crazy." By October, *Newsweek*'s angle was "Trouble in Hippieland"—a cover story about "murder, rape, racial clashes, and uncontrolled drug taking that have turned much of hippiedom into an urban nightmare." As the summer began, even the most charitable of the hippies, the Diggers, were worried that the pure moment of hipness had passed. They passed around a flyer warning, BY AUGUST HAIGHT STREET WILL BE A CEMETERY.

The beautiful ideal turned into a circus. Dozens of souvenir stores, head shops, and junk-food places opened on Haight Street to serve the tourists. Mellowness and good vibes grew scarce in a neighborhood ever more crowded with hustlers, sex perverts, gawking tourists, dope dealers on a violence trip, needle freaks shooting speed, too many cases of crabs, and all manner of social parasites. *Chronicle* columnist Herb Caen went to the

Haight that summer to see what was happening. He asked an "adenoidal young man" if he had come to San Francisco to protest middle-class morality. "You crazy?" the kid replied. "I came here like everybody else—to get a girl and get high."

In October 1967, Ron Thelin of the Psychedelic Shop staged what he hoped would be the conclusive media event: "The Death of Hippie—Beloved Son of Mass Media." "Where Have All the Flowers Gone?" *Time* asked in its coverage of the ritual funeral, describing how "a legion of hippies, the lads bedizened with beads and serapes, the lasses with furs and long velvet dresses," carried a "hirsute 'corpse'" through Golden Gate park, then burned a casket filled with charms, peacock feathers, orange peels, money, flags, and a marijuana cookie. "Thus last week in the mecca of mindlessness did the hippies proclaim their own demise."

The Summer of Love was over. After the ceremonial funeral, a few veteran hippies lit off for Washington to levitate the Pentagon. Many others had already left the Hashbury, transplanting hippie ideals into communes, where they intended to continue the great group grope towards higher consciousness by growing their own soybeans.

It was inevitable that hippie values would lead true believers back to nature. Hippies believed that natural was good. Being natural equaled being free. Bare feet, for example, were free feet, and therefore better than ones in shoes. Letting hair grow long and wild, unrepressed by barber or Brylcreem, was natural, and the sign of a head that did its own thing.

It hadn't been easy for hippie pilgrims to feel natural in the Hashbury, especially in the summer of 1967, when the fog made the nights so cold that sleeping in Golden Gate Park was an impossible bummer. The hassles of city life were compounded by a rumor that spread through the hippie community in July with the kind of urgency that only the underground grapevine could muster: California was about to get swallowed by the Giant Earthquake. If hippies wanted to be natural and free, it was time to go someplace else where they could do it in peace.

The goals of those who split were these: to groove on nature; to grow their own grass; to bake their own bread; to seize cosmic truth by getting *real*, slopping hogs, planting beans, and throwing clay pots. The more primitive, the better.

The main thing country hippies sought was innocence. Hippie logic presumed that innocence was good. From the beginning, acid trips were marketed as great ways to sweep your mind clean in order to rediscover the glory of being simple. The hippie fascination with beads, bright colors, and flashing lights had a lot to do with their earnest attempt to become simpleminded. Their favorite phrase—"Oh, wow!" said with awe and naive stupefaction—perfectly conveyed the newborn sensitivity with which hippies wanted to meet all of life.

In *The Alternative,* a 1970 book about "Communal Life in New America,"

William Hedgepeth rhapsodized that after the Haight experience of "feeling, seeing, hearing, smelling, soaking up, and grokking" (a term for total sensory absorption that hippies borrowed from *Stranger in a Strange Land*), as well as rediscovering the "perfect wholeness of their own bodies," it was time to create "not just something so simple as a totally different order of social reality, but an entire new heaven and new earth."

The only way to do that was to begin naked. Nakedness, being natural, was very big among country hippies: it was good to farm naked; swim naked; lie naked in fields of flowers. Naked (i.e., completely free) children were inspirational beings to have around the commune. And naked breasts were very popular, with or without suckling babies attached. The story of New Buffalo, one of the first and most famous hippie communes in New Mexico, includes this account of Ishmael, a former Hell's Angel recently arrived: "Oh, wow," he gulped as he watched a hippie girl bare her breasts in a tribal dance around the campfire at night. "This is a real return to earth. Really savage." With awe and admiration, visitors to the commune observed that hippie girls who worked in the fields were even-tanned above the waist.

Although not as strong a political statement as being naked, loincloths were approved commune attire because they were what Indians wore; and Indians, being spiritual and close to the earth and even being into peyote, were the supreme role models for the hippie in search of nature's truth.

Indians were the country hippie's favorite fashion guide. Headbands, moc-

casins, and even turquoise jewelry were all adopted as symbols of one's close-
ness to North America's original tribes. Bare feet and body paint were shared,
too. Wearing beads became "a symbolic rejection of a corrupt society and a
return to the communal values of American Indians," announced Columbia
University student rebel Ted Kaptchuk in an *Eye* magazine article that said,
"From the East Village to the Cote d'Azur, men are wearing beads, bells, and
amulets." (Jim Robins, a Columbia varsity diver, disagreed, saying, "They're
artificial and feminine. I wouldn't wear them if it were the last day on earth.")

Love beads, mandalas, serapes, peasant blouses, monks' tunics, feathered
headgear, bells, and biblical robes were all emblems of primitive cultures and
therefore perfectly in tune with the country hippie's ideals. To wear such
native symbols was to reject the uptight aesthetic of the Western world. Similarly, hippie parents often chose names for children that defied Judeo-Chris-
tian tradition. They didn't want to raise a Tom, Dick, or Harry, a Jane or
Nancy. So they gave birth to Moonbows, Rainbows, godz, Neons, Sunshines,
and Moon Units.

Although virtually all of them were Caucasian, hippies relished their romantic self-image as nouveau red men, living in harmony with the universe,
fighting against the white man's perverted society of pollution, war, and
greed. Country paradise, hippie style, was like a vision of Indian life from
some old Hollywood movie, in which long-haired tribesmen in buckskin
fringe sit around their tepees smoking pipes, beating tom-toms, and speaking
in portentous homilies, while the squaws (bare-breasted, natch) tend the babies and make dinner in elegantly primitive huts.

When possible, they actually allied themselves with real Native Americans.
"The Indians of the Taos Pueblo helped the New Buffaloers by being friends
and teachers," exulted former communalist Lisa Law in her book *Flashing
on the Sixties*, "and the young Indians in turn gained self-respect when they
saw other men with long hair." At a conference of the Underground Press
Syndicate in 1967, Chief Rolling Thunder of the Shoshone Nation declared
hippies the fulfillment of an Indian prophecy: after great tribulations, the
Shoshone tribe would be reincarnated as white men.

Not all American Indians were so pleased about being adopted as the
hippies' favorite groovy people. "The way of the hippie is completely at vari-
ance to that of the Indian," wrote Rupert Costo, president of the American
Indian Historical Society. "It is disgusting. It is demeaning. It is the way of
the bum."

To kids freshly dropped out of their coddled middle-class lives, the self-
sufficiency trip was very romantic. Living in tepees north of Taos as part of a
big, sprawling family of babies and dudes and chicks and chickens and dogs,
getting high on homegrown grass or on the mystic beauty of a macraméd
God's-eye mandala, draped with pounds of turquoise jewelry, delivering your
own baby: here, it seemed, was the Utopia of gentle people, peace, and love
from which the Haight had been diverted.

Because hippies disdained earning money, the communes were created on land bought with rich kids' trust funds or given by wealthy patrons such as Lew Gottlieb, former member of the folk-singing Limeliters, who used his profits to found the Morningstar commune along the Russian River in California. As for how they would manage once they got there, that did not seem to be a problem. Eventually, robots would do all the work, as described in Richard Brautigan's "All Watched Over by Machines of Loving Grace." For the time being, a Digger named Noel told Burton Wolfe, "We have many skilled people dropping out, and they will contribute the structure, engineering, irrigation. . . . We are now able to create strong vibrations to move things and people. If we create these vibrations and get to know them well, get to the point where we can get down inside them, then we can do anything."

Powerful vibrations were nice, but for most of the rapt dudes intent on getting natural, rediscovering oneness with nature meant ridding fields of rocks, irrigating, mulching, planting, fertilizing, weeding, hoeing, hewing, harvesting, making adobe bricks, constructing outhouse facilities, and gathering firewood. Being self-sufficient was mighty hard work.

As for hippie women, they, too, had plenty to do. Their communal duties were dictated with the rigidity of an Amish sect. They included "sewing, cooking, cleaning, or child-tending," according to William Hedgepeth's paean to the new life, "but also freely voicing their views and mystical visions."

Chicks, mystical chicks: being witchy and spiritual was the main contribution women were supposed to make to commune life. That and dinner. "A girl just becomes so . . . so *womanly* when she's doing something like baking her own bread in a wood stove," a New Buffalonian observed. "I can't explain it. It just turns me on." Hippie chicks were also supposed to have lots of babies (the natural way, of course) and to nurse them freely in public, showing how uninhibited they were. In the communal world of extended families, to be a hippie chick was to be not only barefoot and pregnant but barebreasted, too.

The most important culinary skill of a country hippie chick was baking bread. Righteous bread was swarthy, weighted with oatmeal and honey and unsprouted things, or with zucchini or pumpkin from the communal garden. It was all-natural, organic, and crusty. It had a lumpy contour that no machine could fabricate. Slice it by hand, please, extra thick.

Ita Jones, author of "The Grub Bag," a counterculture cooking column syndicated by the Liberation News Service, recalls how such a loaf changed her life: "It was dark bread, like the earth and birds' shadows. Thick, browncrusted, with a taste I remembered for days. Standing in the wind, I slowly chewed while watching nothing happen in the huge air above the valley." The charismatic loaf was made by her Chinese art prof's "beautiful, dark, large-boned, long-skirted wife [who] makes it twice a week before the dawn."

Note the motif *dark* in Ms. Jones's yeasty epiphany: dark bread, dark earth,

and dark bird shadows (and a dark wife, too). If there was one quality shared by all hippie food, it was darkness. On the country hippie's table, brown rice is always preferable to white rice; lentils are favored over mashed potatoes; honey is healthier than sugar, and of course whole-wheat flour trumps the chalky white stuff. Here is a recipe for a righteously dark, leaden loaf from *Feast: A Tribal Cookbook by the True Light Beavers*:

### OATMEAL HONEY LOAF

1 cup steel-cut oats
1 cup boiling water
2 1/4 cups unsifted flour (whole wheat, natch)
2 1/2 teaspoons baking powder
1 teaspoon salt
1/4 cup melted butter
3 tablespoons honey
1 egg
2/3 cup milk

In large bowl, combine oats and water. Stir well. Let stand until cool, about 2 hours.

Preheat oven to 350 degrees. Grease a 9 × 5 × 3–inch loaf pan.

Sift flour, baking powder, and salt.

Add butter and honey to oatmeal. Mix well.

Beat egg with milk.

Add flour mixture to oatmeal, then add egg mixture, stirring until combined. *Do Not Overmix.* Turn into loaf pan. Bake 70 minutes.

Country hippies who weren't so zealously self-sufficient, such as the residents of Drop City, Colorado (a community of geodesic domes built from discarded auto parts), got their bread from nearby supermarkets by means of creative scrounging (which they declared "a new art form")—begging stale Wonder Bread that would otherwise have to be thrown away. Food stamps helped, too.

It wasn't always easy for children of uptight city ways to get into the creative-scrounging, back-to-nature bag. "I'll confess," wrote Paul and Meredith, last-name-less co-authors of the hilarious ode to hippie naturalism *Chamisa Road: Doin' the Dog in Taos* (actually, they wrote "i'll confess," uppercase letters being too much of a power trip), "i'll confess . . . sometimes we spend days/nights stumbling in the loveliness, trying to find something to DO. sometimes we watch every show, one after another, eating tv dinners and feeling ashamed. wavering admidst cityconsciousness. missing the nightly nod-outs on st. marx [Paul and Meredith's spelling for St. Marks Place in New York City]." Fortunately, such boredom never lasts too long for Paul and Meredith, because something natural always comes along to relieve them: "trippy and lee come & maybe we get stoned or talk about silk-screening or making jam & maybe do it."

# REBELS

Our tactic is to send niggers and longhair scum invading
white middle class homes, fucking on the living room floor,
crashing on the chandeliers, spewing sperm on the Jesus pictures, breaking the furniture, and smashing Sunday school
napalm-blood Amerika forever.        —JERRY RUBIN, 1970

FOR A DECADE that started so perky, the sixties turned mighty nasty.
Assassinations of the Kennedys and Martin Luther King, Jr., body counts
from a futile war in the jungles of Southeast Asia, bloody murder in the
struggle for civil rights, rioting in city ghettos and on college campuses: such
catastrophes were beginning to seem routine by 1969. The dawn of the age
of Aquarius was eclipsed by a mean and scary time.

To *make a difference* in a world where you feel helpless in the face of
capricious evil, you seek company. You enlist in a political party or an army.
Or if you aren't so gung ho about it, you may just start to feel in your gut that
you ought to stick close to your own kind, even if it means being pitted against
everybody else.

That's the way the sixties ended: people gathered into clusters, factions,
and "families," each bunch suspicious of anyone outside.

Even the crowning triumph of the love generation—the Woodstock Music
and Arts Festival of 1969—had far more partisan muscle than the kindly
love-ins of two years before. Woodstock Nation seceded from the establishment. To be part of it was to feel the delirious siege mentality that reigned
among the 400,000 utopians who were determined to show that the counterculture could come together, smoke pot, and skinny-dip in their own alternative world without cops, guns, Nixon, or napalm. Like a right-minded
militia, the pilgrims who occupied the New York farmland bivouacked in
tents, took their meals in makeshift mess halls, rallied by torchlight as their
leaders exhorted them to resist the war makers, then marched home and left
the battlefield in ruins. When it was over, the myth of *victory* was triumphant.

Woodstock Nation came to symbolize youth's righteous crusade to change the world, and the most militant kind of love.

The moral zeal of the new rebels made the sixties a golden age of vilification. Spitting noxious words became a way to steel one's resolve as well as aggravate one's enemy. Cops became "pigs" and "America" started getting spelled "Amerika" (to suggest Nazi and/or Kafkaesque repression as well as the Ku Klux Klan). The sixties' fondness for cute aphorisms—on bumper stickers or buttons—metamorphosed into truculent sloganeering as a way of life. The adrenaline rush of denunciation and obscenity was an alluring addiction that many veterans of the sixties have never kicked.

The Black Panther party railed against "avaricious, sadistic, bloodthirsty, racist, fascist pigs." With equally flamboyant rhetoric, Ronald Reagan, governor of California, condemned protesters who "dress like Tarzan, look like Jane, and smell like Cheetah." Demonstrators at the Columbia University riot in 1968 borrowed "Up against the wall, motherfucker!" from the New York City police (who used it to get criminals in position to be frisked) and made it a favorite rallying cry of the resistance.

By the end of the decade, it seemed that everybody was furious with everybody else; everybody felt threatened and therefore banded together with comrades and threatened back.

## *Freeks*

By 1968, there was a new kind of fanatic in the world: a militant mutation of the hippie. His curriculum included wanton use of drugs, raucous rock and roll, and provocation of anybody in authority.

His personality was forged as the good vibes of the Summer of Love pooped out and as the war in Vietnam dragged on. He was fed up with the ineffectiveness of the counterculture. He had learned to disdain the peace-and-love wimpiness of hippies as well as the indeterminable theorizing of the New Left. He was sick and tired of peaceful protest as a way to change the system, stop the war, end the draft, or get grown-ups off his back. Now, he no longer wanted anything to do with ordinary persuasion or demonstrations.

He looked like hell and was proud of it. He grew his hair with avenging zeal; if he was lucky enough that it was naturally curly, he let it sprout outlandishly in a homage to the Afro, whose black proponents he (invariably white) idolized. But his hair was never trimmed with the polyhedral majesty of the black brothers'. It grew wild and malevolent; subduing it in any way might make him look civilized—nothing tamed a freak!

He relished being called a freak, except he liked to write it in his own freakish way, defying even rules of spelling: *freek*.

He wore leather or denim, but without the festoonery of the Hell's Angels: he wanted to look streamlined for street fighting. Naked from the waist up was a popular freek look, perhaps with war paint, grenade belt, or army surplus bandolier. When photographed, he either scowled or grinned like a mad anarchist. Posed pictures always show him smoking a joint, banging hard on a guitar, peeing on the tire of a cop car, or doing some other thing guaranteed to annoy straight people. For candid shots, such as when he is being arrested for marijuana possession, public lewdness, or desecrating the American flag, he gives the V-for-victory sign to the camera.

We use the masculine pronoun to describe this guy because freeks were guys. Other rebel groups had their high-profile females, such as Angela Davis of the Black Panthers and Bernadine Dohrn of the Weathermen; but freeks were relentlessly macho. Their girlfriends got even less respect than hippie chicks, because ants-in-the-pants freek guys were generally too angry,

*John Sinclair, leader of the White Panthers, posed defiantly in this picture on the cover of his book,* Guitar Army.

too stoned, or too engaged in taunting authority to appreciate fresh-baked bread and other such "womanly" contributions that hippie girls used to make to the movement. (At the time, although the women's movement was gathering momentum, male chauvinism was not yet on the approved list of anti-establishment concerns.)

Being a freek was being a real man. "We're BAD," the super-freeky White Panthers of Michigan proclaimed in their newspaper, *The Fifth Estate*, in November 1968. The White Panthers were a bunch of dope-smoking, rock-and-rolling hellraisers who admired the Black Panthers (from whom they adopted their name) because they were so damn ferocious. Their position papers doted over all-male, all-black heroes from James Brown to Eldridge Cleaver, exclaiming, "These are MEN in America!"

Freeks proved their manhood by swearing a lot, giving the finger to cops, judges, businessmen, etc., or trying to rap like bad-ass jailbirds and rude, uneducated punks. They were psychedelic, pseudorevolutionary daredevils, taunting authority to come and get them.

The best-known example of these hyperbolic madmen were the Yippies, from the acronym YIP, which stood for Youth International Party.

Yippies were conceived by Abbie Hoffman, *Realist* editor Paul Krassner, and Jerry Rubin on New Year's Eve in 1967. They came up with the idea

because they wanted to devise a myth to describe what Jerry Rubin called the "new man born smoking pot while besieging the Pentagon."

He was referring to the march on the Pentagon in October 1967, two months before the creation of YIP. It was an event that set the stage for the creation of Yippies. The march was originally conceived as an opportunity to confront the war makers at the very seat of military power. Like most peace protests that preceded it, it was built upon the idea of nonviolent civil disobedience.

As it took shape, however, it was clear that there was going to be something very different about this event: a new kind of protester, with a new style of protest. Extremists and dissenters whose minds had been bent by psychedelic voyages and the hippie penchant for attention-getting pageantry planned to turn the march on the Pentagon into *street theater*. For them, this would be different from the routine agenda of waving picket signs, singing "We Shall Overcome," and listening to windy speeches; this would be an event that would freak out Pentagon generals and the public.

Hippies from San Francisco vowed to embarrass the government by panhandling at foreign embassies; the National Mobilization Committee made two-faced protest signs, with BOMB PEKING on one side. When the live TV cameras moved in, the signs were supposed to be flipped to say DOES LBJ SUCK? Many who joined the demonstration did so wearing the kind of clownish psychedelic Sgt. Pepper uniforms that hippies had been flaunting to show their defiance of normalcy.

It was a bizarre scene that would establish the freek style and the look of many confrontations in the year to follow: longhairs in Batman and Beatle outfits dancing with mischievous glee across from Eighty-second Airborne troops, who were defending the Pentagon in full riot attire. The big moment came when the Fugs, a provocateur hippie rock group from the East Village, attempted to levitate the Pentagon and exorcise its demons (hardly a tactic that the diligent New Left would have conceived!). Although nothing tangible happened when they chanted "Out, demons, out!" the demonstration, which included actual engagement with the enemy—tear gas, billy clubs, and much pissing on the Pentagon wall—set an example for a new style of counter-culture protest and for a new kind of protester, the Yippie.

The Yippie's goal was not to win votes. It was to blow people's minds. The Yippie was no do-gooder for virtuous causes. He was, in the words of Yippie founder Jerry Rubin, "a streetfighting freek, a dropout, who carries a gun at the hip. So ugly that middle-class society is frightened by how he looks. A longhaired, bearded, crazy motherfucker whose life is theater, every moment creating the new society as he destroys the old."

What many had seen only months before as a united and dignified antiwar movement got blown to smithereens in 1968 by the shenanigans of the Yippies. Consider how different they were from the young dissenters of the "Get Clean with Gene [McCarthy]" campaign, whose symbol was a daisy and whose hero was a Democratic presidential candidate. In March of 1968, at the beginning of the primary campaign, when Eugene McCarthy's antiwar supporters arrived in New Hampshire to canvass door-to-door for votes, *guys shaved their beards and combed their hair, and girls put away their miniskirts!* Those unwilling to make such sacrifices voluntarily banished themselves to the back rooms of campaign headquarters, where they worked the tele-phones. No freek would ever repress himself like that. Freeks, remember, didn't want to win friends or elect Eugene McCarthy. They wanted to blow minds.

The Yippies' kind of radicalism—insisting that the struggle was on behalf of a whole new identity composed of dope and long hair and loud music and all those other unruly symbols of psychedelic debauchery—created a huge problem for old-fashioned peaceniks who felt that effective protest had to be well mannered. Likewise, their fury was an embarrassment for old-line hip-pies, who prized gentleness above all. Hippies wanted nothing more than to groove in their own psychedelic world of flowers and mantras and love beads and good vibes. The Yippies' savage prodding of authority was a bummer. "This shocks me and alienates my spiritual sensitivities," Timothy Leary scolded.

Yippies were too agitated to hammer out manifestos and organize grass-roots campaigns. Yippies wanted ACTION! Primarily, that meant grossing people out. There was a serious political purpose to this tactic, Tom Hayden noted (but didn't endorse): "to first alienate, then challenge, and ultimately dispel the repressive attitudes of the majority culture." In service of this noble cause, English rebels joined the Yippie fun fest and considered (but rejected as "impractical") such challenges to the system as delivering ten truckloads of cow manure to 10 Downing Street, and swallowing hunks of bacon with strings attached, then pulling them up out of their stomachs in front of Prime Minister Harold Wilson.

Among the Yippies' favorite techniques for alienating the majority culture was saying "fuck." If you were serious about tearing down the pig power structure, you were required to say "fuck" as often as possible. "Linguistic therapy" is what *Liberation* magazine called it—"an essential element in the process of critical thinking." Saying "fuck" separated the new style of total lifestyle radical from the old type that wanted to work within the system. If you could say it in public, in mixed company, but especially smack into the face of the power structure (a cop, a college dean, a parent), you showed you were free of hang-ups; you were a bad-ass—a true Yippie!

Jerry Rubin explained the power of profanity by complaining that the establishment has taken all the good words and destroyed them. "Revolution," for example, has become advertisers' fodder: "Revolution in toilet paper!" "Revolution in combating mouth odor!" And "love." "How can I say 'I love you' after hearing 'Cars love Shell'?" he asked. Saying "fuck" was the solution. "It's the last word left in the English language. Amerika cannot destroy it because she dare not use it. It's illegal! Fuck is a dirty word because you have to be naked to do it. Also it's fun."

Yippies pioneered nakedness as a revolutionary stratagem. At a Democratic fund-raiser at the Hilton Hotel in New York, a band of guerrillas snuck in and dressed as waiters. When it came time for dessert, instead of apple pie and coffee, Senators Fulbright and Muskie and a banquet hall full of party

*The Hog Farm Commune, New York City*

faithfuls were served pigs' heads on platters—by stark-naked waiters shouting, "Rome wasn't destroyed in a day!"

The Yippies' moment in the sun was the Democratic Convention of 1968 in Chicago. At the beginning of the summer, they announced a "Festival of Life" to contrast to the Democrats' "Convention of Death" (so named because the war in Vietnam was considered Lyndon Johnson's war).

At first, the idea was to offer a counter-convention, a sort of be-in with free music and free dope and good vibes, showing off the power and health and high spirits of the youth culture. It was an idea that the gentle flower-power hippies of the previous summer would have relished. But a year had passed, and it was apparent to Yippie leaders that their Festival of Life, if it was going to amount to anything more than a small paragraph in the media's convention coverage, would have to go far beyond their original happy notions of everybody having a groovy time together. Yet another peaceful love-in or protest rally would have no effect whatsoever on the convention, nor would it stop the war, or legalize grass, or end the draft.

Yippies were media manipulators, and they knew the convention was their big chance to snatch the world's attention. "Nobody could pretend Chicago wasn't happening," Jerry Rubin said. And so the point of the Festival of Life became to FREAK OUT THE DEMOCRATS while the whole world watched. In the days before the convention, they threatened, among other things, to paint cars like taxicabs and spirit away unwary Democrats into the middle of the Illinois farmland, to infiltrate hotels dressed as bellboys and molest the wives of delegates, and to pollute the city water system with LSD.

With many moderate protesters scared away, with the Yippie talent for attracting attention, and with so many straight people *eager* to see peaceniks as dope-crazed outlaws, Yippies had a heyday in Chicago. Everything went according to their plan. They nominated Pigasus, a live pig, for President, spread dog-doo on rugs at the Hilton Hotel, dropped stink bombs in the Go Go Lounge at the Palmer House Hotel, and raised the flag of North Vietnam in Grant Park.

Mayor Daley and the Chicago police played their role in the Yippie sce-

*Protesters at the 1968 Democratic Convention in Chicago*

nario by acting just like the storm troopers Yippies said they were. Chicago streets around the convention reeked of tear gas. Hundreds of protesters, diligent antiwar demonstrators as well as Yippie crackpots, were chased, clubbed, and arrested. Jerry Rubin was triumphant: "The Hump's [Hubert Humphrey's] nomination took place at the precise moment the Nazi state carried out its brutal attack on the people." When it was over, he boasted that Yippies were now "more dangerous than a hundred Martin Luther Kings."

What did the Yippie's street-theater confrontation in Chicago achieve? Skeptics pointed to the fact that Hubert Humphrey was nominated as expected; and in the fall, Nixon was elected, thus beginning a dire period of repression against everything Yippies stood for. The war in Vietnam went on.

## Angry Sisters

Was the women's movement part of *the* Movement? It felt like it ought to be. The same level of fundamental dissatisfaction that generated black power, student revolt, and antiwar protest had reanimated the idea of women's rights, too. Many who joined the cause of women's liberation in the late sixties had learned how to picket and demonstrate while fighting for those other noble causes. But as their consciousness got raised, feminists found themselves in a bind.

Here was the dilemma. This thing that had started getting called the Movement (the all-encompassing movement) was so swollen by the end of the
sixties that many within it fancied they belonged to a grand popular front that
contained all the new correct ideas in righteous harmony. With chiliastic
certainty, the Movement seemed to surge ahead like a macho freight train
carrying all of Woodstock Nation, youth culture, black power, rock and roll,
long hair, marijuana, and free love. It welcomed everyone against the war,
the draft, and pollution; it flew the banners of student rights, Indian rights,
prisoner rights, Chicano rights, and . . . maybe, sometimes, if there weren't
more pressing issues and if there weren't any position papers that needed
typing . . . women's rights.

Women were the niggers of the New Left. "The girls in the movement,"
*Time* reported, began to realize that "Mark Rudd [of the SDS] was possibly
less interested in women's rights than Richard Nixon." However politically
proper a man in the Movement might be on every other issue, it was an
almost sure bet that he was a male chauvinist pig.

When women stood up to demand that the issue of sexism be addressed—
at meetings of the SDS or the Black Panthers—they were hooted down.
Among hippies, Yippies, and Diggers, and on every tribal commune, women
were *chicks*, which meant their job was to do womanly things such as bake,

clean, and be available for their
man when he was done doing the
manly things men do. "Most of the
chicks I saw [are] like the wives
of congressional candidates," one
woman said about the hippie scene
in 1967. "They're happy to sit back
and smile." A lot of New Left guys
lightheartedly called the fight for
women's rights a battle for pussy
power.

To newly alerted feminists, that
was not funny. A macho pig was
a pig, even if he called himself a
rebel. "We will not ask what is 'revolutionary' or 'reformist,' " declared
the 1968 manifesto of Redstockings,
a group that attributed society's
problems to male domination. "[We
will ask] only what is good for
women."

With an attitude like that, radical
feminists found few friends among
male radicals in the strutting and

crowing late-sixties days of the Movement. So they fought alone—which turned out to be a boon for women's liberation. Despite a separatist element that waged a brutal battle against any compromise with men, the feminist movement managed to avoid almost completely the kind of self-destructive adventurism that sapped the potency of other sixties radicals.

Although NOW, the National Organization for Women, was founded in 1966 with the levelheaded purpose of working alongside men to secure equal rights and equal pay for women, it was not until the fall of 1968 that women's liberation became a vital public issue. Its ascension into the public eye was not the result of NOW's struggle to change the laws but because a band of outlandish feminists crowned a sheep as Miss America.

On September 7, 1968, with street-theater smarts borrowed from the Yippies, two hundred women led by Robin Morgan (an actress who had played Dagmar in television's "I Remember Mama") upstaged the Miss America Pageant. Like the Democratic Convention two weeks before, Miss America was a choice opportunity for protesters to be seen and heard, an event with guaranteed television ratings. Richard Nixon, then candidate for President, told the press it was the one show he allowed his daughters, Julie and Tricia, to stay up late to watch.

The feminists put forth the sheep as a symbol because they considered the pageant a livestock auction. They snuck into the convention hall and ignited stink bombs; as the new Miss America paraded down the runway, they un-

*Protest at the Miss World Contest, London, 1970*

furled a banner—seen on television worldwide—that proclaimed a startling new phrase: WOMEN'S LIBERATION. Most viewers did not know what to make of those two words put together. "Women's liberation" was a new idea, explained to them in the next day's newspapers, which in many cases gave the protest more coverage than the Miss America contest itself.

What seized the attention of the press and public were the feminists' "freedom trashcans." Into the cans went dishcloths, steno pads, false eyelashes, copies of *Playboy* and *Vogue*, and brassieres. It was the bras that really turned people's heads. None were actually burned that day, but the ceremonial disposal of of brassieres, into trash cans or by fire, became the dominant popular symbol of the early women's movement.

Prior to this decisive gesture, radical women were admired within the movement for a kind of male-fantasy sexuality. They were considered liberated if they radiated lust (as opposed to uptight straight women) and fucked freely. Bernadine Dohrn of the Weather Underground was described in virtually every article about her, by friend and foe, as "miniskirted" Bernadine Dohrn.

Miniskirts and fishnet stockings had been the signs of a groovy, politically savvy chick. Such risqué attire, evoking the "liberated" idea of free love (i.e., whenever a man wanted it) had been one of the things about the counterculture of which even leering squares approved.

No more. The burning of bras—for freedom's sake, not to be erotically bare-breasted—marked a major change in the look of feminism in particular and of radical women in general. Go-go boots, body stockings, outrageous makeup, and tight jeans—formerly the fashion statements of free-thinking (and free-swinging) chicks—became the symbolic shackles of male oppression. Liberated women abandoned flashy mod color schemes for the sake of Mother Nature earth tones. Baggy clothes and serious shoes or militaristic boots became the look of a proper woman revolutionary. For most militant feminists, hip-hugging miniskirts gave way to shapeless unisex attire.

Hair was the place many women took their stand. Among the militants, what you did with your hair became a sign of just how serious you were about the movement. Hair cutting became a ritual declaration of feminist commitment, sometimes done in front of large groups of other feminists who cheered as converts to the cause cut their tresses down to a short, unfashionable shock. In these early days of the women's movement, at a time when everybody's hair was seen as a significant political statement, it was argued by many that long hair meant you were living your life to please men—which was treason to the cause. To the radical feminist, all such remnants of man-oriented behavior had to go.

Conversely, hair under the arms and on the legs had to stay. That was perhaps the hardest line for many to cross. *Life* magazine told about a "girl in Chicago who described the progression of giving up short skirts, then makeup, and recently, shaving her legs. 'I still look at my legs and think, oh my God, I cannot go through with this. I'll die for the revolution, but don't ask me not to shave my legs!' "

The late sixties, dazzled by so many wacky new lifestyles barreling down the pike, doted on the most eccentric and extremist aspects of the women's movement. Many of the earliest reports focus on such colorful rites as bra burning, man-hating consciousness-raising sessions, self-defense classes that teach women how to squash testicles, and attempts to de-ball the language by removing all gratuitous references to men, such as replacing the nonspecific pronoun "he" with "tey" and changing the word "history" to "herstory." Some women exchanged their fathers' or husbands' last names for their mothers' (Pat and Richard Nixon's daughter Tricia would become Tricia Patchild).

In these early years, the women's movement was cast in the same light as hippies and Yippies—a cult with strange and sometimes amusing ways. *Time*'s report on "The New Feminists" referred to consciousness-raising groups as "covens" (there was, in fact, a militant women's group that called itself WITCH—Women's International Terrorist Conspiracy from Hell). It offered a feminist glossary that explained that "Aunt Tabbies" were the female equivalent of Uncle Toms, and even found one quotable feminist who explained that women were the more daring and adventurous sex because their ova traveled alone, whereas men's sperms always went everywhere together.

The ultimate angry feminist organization was SCUM, the Society for Cutting Up Men. SCUM was the brainchild of Valerie Solanas, a playwright (author of *Up Your Ass*) and well-known denizen of the lobby of the Chelsea Hotel. Solanas *was* SCUM—its founder, theorist, and terror squad. Although having exactly one member (Valerie Solanas) made SCUM less than momentous as a social movement, no document transmits the outrageous apocalypticism of the time with more gusto than her *SCUM Manifesto*, which she wrote in 1967 and sold to Olympia Press for five hundred dollars. Olympia then peddled the movie rights to Andy Warhol (a fateful move, as we shall see). The proclamation begins thus:

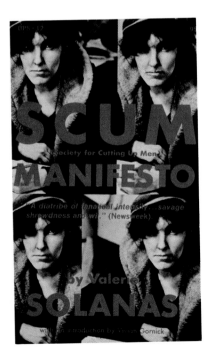

> Life in this society being, at best, an utter bore and no aspect of society being at all relevant to women, there remains to civic-minded,

responsible, thrill-seeking females only to overthrow the government, eliminate the money system, institute complete automation, and destroy the male sex.

Compromise and reconciliation were not in SCUM's vocabulary. At a time when the newly formed National Organization for Women bent over backwards to make it clear that *we do not hate men*, Solanas declared that the male of the species is:

a half dead, unresponsive lump, incapable of giving or receiving pleasure or happiness; consequently, he is at best an utter bore, an inoffensive blob . . . trapped in a twilight zone halfway between humans and apes. . . . The male is unfit even for stud service. To call a man an animal is to flatter him; he's a machine, a walking dildo.

After tallying men's flaws, the *SCUM Manifesto* describes a bright future in which babies are produced in laboratories. All are female. "Just as the deliberate production of blind people would be highly immoral, so would the deliberate production of emotional cripples (men)."

Finally, the *SCUM Manifesto* reveals its tactics:

fucking-up, looting, couple-busting, destroying, and killing. SCUM will not picket, demonstrate, march, or strike. Such tactics are for nice, genteel ladies. . . . If SCUM ever marches, it will be over LBJ's stupid, sickening face; if SCUM ever strikes, it will be in the dark with a six-inch blade.

When it did come time to strike, the SCUM weapon of choice was a pistol. Solanas—furious that Andy Warhol, the soft-spoken artist, held the movie rights to her manifesto—selected him as her symbol of masculinity. On June 3, 1968, she shot him in the stomach, seriously wounding him, then surrendered to a traffic cop (a man) in Times Square, saying, "I am a flower child. He had too much control over my life."

Ti-Grace Atkinson, president of the New York chapter of NOW, came to Solanas's defense. Atkinson was a feminist who had been widely quoted earlier that year as believing in the abolition of marriage, which she described as rape and lifelong slavery. Sex, she said, was mass psychosis; love, an illusion perpetrated by oppressive men. "It's so immature to grow babies in people's bodies," she told *Life* magazine, advocating test tubes as the wombs of the future. After the shooting, Atkinson ordained Valerie Solanas a heroine of the women's movement and began distributing mimeographed copies of the *SCUM Manifesto.*

Atkinson's position was a whopping embarrassment for NOW, which asked her to resign. She did not. Instead, she announced her intention to turn the National Organization for Women into a truly radical organization. Four months later, when Atkinson moved to radicalize NOW in the manner of the then-fashionable militant New Left (eliminate all leadership positions, declare war on the whole oppressive system), she was voted down. She exited NOW to form a more radical group called the Feminists, then allied herself with the Black Liberation Army, then with the Italian-American Civil Rights League (in which capacity she declared the Mafia "morally refreshing").

Meanwhile, Valerie Solanas was sent to the Matteawan State Hospital for the Criminally Insane.

There were many battles still to come between feminists who were radical separatists and those who wanted to work within the Movement. But NOW and the mainstream survived them and thrived, unlike so many sixties rebels who fanaticized themselves into irrelevance.

## *Hell's Angels*

Motorcycle outlaws—now there was a delicious concept! Take a large portion of freewheeling libido, a dash of old-fashioned cowboy wanderlust, and a measure of *On the Road* alienation; add the thrill of danger, the throb of unmuffled pistons, and the gleam of chrome; season with illegal drugs, then garnish with hobnail boots, black leather jackets, and bicep-revealing sleeveless denim vests. Serve it forth in California—the Bay Area in particular—and you have a dish that the thrill-hungry sixties were destined to feast upon.

Marauding motorcycle gangs were not a new idea. In 1947, a bunch of bad guys on bikes rampaged through the town of Hollister, California—an event immortalized seven years later in *The Wild One*, a movie that presented bikers as a social problem and Marlon Brando as a misunderstood leather boy with the soul of a poet. *The Wild One* came and went, and nobody thought much about Harley-Davidsons and the men who loved them. Then suddenly in the mid-sixties, Hell's Angels became folk heroes.

What made the Angels so bewitching in 1964 and '65, when their various depredations (rape, riot, drugs, drink) began getting national attention, was their ability to generate outrage. They were living symbols of everything a well-behaved, law-abiding citizen was supposed to loathe and fear. They were dirty, unshaven, and insolent. They had no proper role in society whatsoever: they lived to ride and to defy authority. They were angry rebels with no cause other than rebellion itself.

To upholders of moral virtue, like California attorney general Thomas Lynch, who made it his business to alert the nation to the menace (and thereby give the Angels their first big public-relations boost), they were depravity incarnate. And for that exact reason, they became a seductive vision of liberation to an ever-increasing segment of the Great Society that was getting antsy about rules and angry about government hypocrisy, and generally feeling itself frustrated by the confines of polite, middle-class life.

The Angels held great appeal, but their lifestyle was available to only an exclusive few. They were a private club, not a political party or social movement. Even outsiders who got very close to them, such as Hunter Thompson and Ken Kesey, were never fully trusted by the Angel hard core. Angels were a band apart, and they really were outlaws; their exclusivity was part of their appeal.

You couldn't be an Angel in your free time. This was not a club for weekend bike boys on little scooters. It was a total lifestyle commitment. They called themselves "one percenters," a contemptuous reference to the American Motorcycle Association's denunciation of the one percent of all bikers who are lawless scum. To those Angel enthusiasts outside the fraternity of one percenters, being one of them was never a real option. Hell's Angels were simply a fashionable curiosity, an enticing symbol of irresponsibility, rather like the noble savages from whom civilized people think they can learn so much.

To understand why a bunch of smelly, antisocial thugs would suddenly become culture heroes requires a feeling for just how grievously America craved a paradigm of defiance before the hippie movement conveniently provided it in 1966–67.

The trigger was the plague of cuteness that had infiltrated popular culture. It began with perky girls and reached dizzying heights in 1964 with the Beatles' immense popularity, when the world was absolutely deluged with their precious personalities and lovable hairdos and lively songs and happy-go-lucky good fortune and all the kooky mod cheerfulness they dragged behind them in those first couple of years of unblemished success. The lads from Liverpool were unbearably adorable.

Adorability was the attitude of the hour, from the Singing Nun to the cute and cranky cartoon characters of "Peanuts" to harmless television oddities such as "The Munsters" and "The Beverly Hillbillies" to Twiggy, the big-eyed waif who dominated fashion. Despite a country that seemed to be going to hell (the escalating war in Vietnam, political assassination, race riots in the South and the North), there were daisies and smiling yellow happy faces sprouting everywhere, and the salutation "Have a nice day" had begun to rear its sunny head. *The Sound of Music*, one of the most saccharine motion pictures in history, became the box-office champ of all time in 1965.

Inundated by this tide of zest, the disaffected felt a desperate need to spew some hostility. The Rolling Stones fulfilled the requirements as icons of antisocial behavior quite well with their pose of sullen blasphemy; but the Hell's Angels did it even better, because for them it was no pose.

It is important to realize that as much as the Hell's Angels were romanticized by those who wanted to see them as the Last Free Men, their repulsiveness was always very much part of the picture. That was what gave them their fiendish glamour. To be repulsive in an age of overwhelming cuteness had terrific sex appeal.

Beyond such routine atrocities of their devil-may-care existence as fighting, looting, pillaging, and raping, all stories about the Hell's Angels focused on their odious tribal rites. Here are some of the basic eyebrow-raisers found in most early press accounts of the Hell's Angels:

- Angel men greeted other Angel men with big, wet, sloppy kisses.
- Initiation of new recruits consisted of their blue jeans and jackets being peed and shit and stomped on.
- Hell's Angel's "mamas" were considered common property, available to any Angel who wanted them for any kind of sex. ("Old ladies," on the other hand, were steady women, the property of one Angel only.)
- If an Angel's colors (his denim vest, with insignias sewn on) included red wings, it meant he performed cunnilingus on a mama when she had her period.
- At Angel funerals, they all got drunk and busted up the church or cemetery, and sometimes liberated the corpse from out of its coffin and took it for one last ride.

In San Francisco's increasingly restless intellectual bohemia, the Hell's Angels were becoming impressive exhibits at hip gatherings by the summer of 1965. "It puzzled them to be treated as symbolic heroes by people with whom they had nothing in common," Hunter Thompson observed, describing them at a fashionable East Bay party. The Angels were supposed to be conversation pieces for the amusement of "several dozen young girls looking for excitement while their husbands and varied escorts wanted to talk about 'alienation' and a 'generation in revolt.' " Kenneth Anger's movie *Scorpio Rising*, a fetishistic ode to bikers, big muscles, and black leather, had been a hit on the underground movie circuit since the year before. By the end of summer, the Angels entered the pantheon of hipness when Ken Kesey invited them to his house to drop acid and party with the Merry Pranksters.

They became nationwide heroes in 1966, when Roger Corman made a movie, *The Wild Angels*, and Hunter Thompson wrote his book *Hell's Angels*. These popular tales confirmed the Angels as genuine celebrities. (*The Wild Angels* was America's only entry in the Venice Film Festival of 1966, *by invitation*.) Neither movie nor book offered apologies or condemnation for their unruly behavior. They just presented it—with oodles of lascivious details that conveyed the kicks of the Angels' life, along with a proper balance of existential angst.

The special kick of both Thompson's book and Corman's movie was that they told the story from the inside. They were *hip;* they offered not the plodding, moralistic 1950s point of view (as in *The Wild One*) but an exciting image of the Angels seen through the eyes of a young artist who appreciated the greasers' audacious style. Thompson was formulating gonzo journalism, a reportorial technique in which the writer affects the barbarous persona of his subject, by hanging out with the Angels, partying with them, riding with them, even getting stomped by them. Corman used the real Hell's Angels of Venice, California, in his movie (riding behind the picture's stars, Peter Fonda and Nancy Sinatra).

Angels came into vogue about the time leadership of the club passed from the San Bernardino chapter to the Oakland chapter, lead by Sonny Barger. "San Berdoo" had been the first Hell's Angels club, in 1950; but in 1965, local authorities in the south started laying down some heavy heat, so a lot of guys went north to the Bay Area. It was there the Hell's Angels emerged as the fashionable rebels of the moment, first among the hip literary set; then for a short while they became the hippies' favorite outlaws, too.

It was a hippie dream that the Angels ought to join them in their rejection of straight society. Hippie logic reasoned that Angels—like hippies—wanted only to do their own thing, which meant get high, have sex, and grow their hair long. Logic also said that Hell's Angels, being mean sons-of-bitches, made good guardian angels for street hippies, who were wimps. From the Angels' point of view as well, it was initially a righteous alliance. It meant they got access to powerful hippie drugs and plenty of fine young hippie pussy. For a short while in 1966, motorcycle hoods from the mean streets of Oakland partied with the gentle people of Hashbury. Allen Ginsberg took to calling them the Angelic Barbarians.

Belligerent bikers and love children: it was a strange collusion, doomed to fail. Pardon us for sounding like Marxists, but the issue that broke them up was class conflict. Angels were low-class dudes—grease monkeys, day laborers, the chronically unemployable—who had been rejected by society. Hippies were children of privilege who voluntarily dropped out to follow a romantic ideal. To an Angel, alienation wasn't something you read about in French-lit class. More likely, you learned about it doing two-to-five in Soledad for armed robbery. For a moment, the odd couple of the East Bay fancied they could be partners in their shared contempt for the law-abiding citizenry that hated them both. But it wasn't long before the Angels began to see the hippies as spineless spoiled brats and the hippies saw the Angels as fascistic gorillas.

The thing that broke them up was Vietnam. On October 16, 1966, fifteen thousand Berkeley antiwar students and assorted hippies began a march from the campus down Telegraph Avenue towards the Oakland Army Terminal, from which troops disembarked for Vietnam. At the Oakland border, they ran into a phalanx of police, who began swinging billy clubs. Into the fray charged a dozen Oakland Hell's Angels . . . *fighting on the side of the police!* Angels tore up the protesters' sound system and pummeled the demonstrators, howling, "America first! America for Americans! Go back to Russia, you commie traitors!"

The antiwar people didn't know what hit them. How could the Angels, who had shared grass and acid and good vibes with them all summer, suddenly turn into goons fighting on the side of law and order?

Another, even bigger march against the Oakland Army Terminal was planned for the next month. Head Angel Sonny Barger promised he would marshal a huge force of bikers to whip the tar out of the chickenshit antiwar hippies. Allen Ginsberg wrote a long poem, "To the Angels," published in the *Berkeley Barb*, that asked,

If you dig POT why don't you dig that the whole generation who don't dig the heat war also dig pot and consciousness & spontaneity & hair & they are your natural brothers . . . WHITMAN's free soul, camarado, also of Open Road! I asking you to be Camarado, friend, kind, lover, because vast majority of peace marchers actually respect & venerate your lonesomeness. . . .

Apparently, few Hell's Angels subscribed to the *Berkeley Barb*, or at least Sonny Barger did not concur with Ginsberg's impassioned analysis, because on November 19, the day before the peace march, Barger called a press conference to read a telegram he had just sent to President Lyndon Johnson:

"On behalf of myself and my associates I volunteer a group of loyal Americans for behind-the-lines duty in Vietnam." Barger announced that the Angels would not storm the peace marchers . . . but only because such an attack might create sympathy for "this despicable, un-American activity . . . this mob of traitors." The Angels, he declared, would spend the day patriotically, getting drunk. It was the end of the Hell's Angels' brief tenure as the noble-savage heroes of the counterculture.

The Angels had blown it, and were pretty much passé in the peace-and-love year of 1967; but as the flower-power dream evaporated, and violence became fashionable in the street-fighting years of 1968 and '69, they had another brief moment of fame and a final ugly burnout.

By December 1969, the Rolling Stones had stropped their particular brand of insolence into a musical expression of anger, menace, and brutality. They paraded this stylishly hostile mood across America, singing "Sympathy for the Devil" (Mick Jagger swirling a satanic red-satin cape) in a concert tour that ended with a free performance at the Altamont Speedway, thirty miles east of Berkeley. To authenticate their pose as *bad* motherfuckers, the Stones hired the Hell's Angels as security guards, giving them five hundred dollars' worth of beer for their services.

What a bummer Altamont turned out to be! Bad acid, distributed free in large amounts among the audience, sent hundreds of people into paranoid conniption fits and spasms of uncontrollable vomiting. Carried away with their power, the Angels beat and raped concertgoers willy-nilly as the warm-up bands played; at one point, they climbed onstage and knocked Marty Balin of the Jefferson Airplane unconscious as he was about to sing "We Can Be Together." With Mick Jagger incanting "Sympathy for the Devil" only a few yards away, they stabbed an eighteen-year-old black member of the audience to death because they didn't like him being at the concert with a white girl. Altamont was a hideous disaster, an event that was bemoaned as the symbolic expiration of the Woodstock Nation, the death of innocence, and the end of the sixties.

After that, the Hell's Angels went back to being what they had been before they were discovered: born losers, without a friend in the world. They did, however, manage to parlay the Altamont debacle into a nice little money-making scheme. Four months later, at a rock festival in Orlando, Florida, a local Hell's Angels chapter extorted twenty thousand dollars from the promoter based on their promise to *not* show up.

## Black Panthers

Black Panthers were the leading warrior tribe of the sixties. They popularized belligerency as a style and cultivated a paramilitary pose that set the fashion for nearly all the angry rebels of the decade. To express their utter contempt

*Black Panther party headquarters,
Chicago, 1969*

for the Oakland, California, police, they started calling them "pigs" in 1966, an epithet that was soon gleefully and universally employed by all sixties rebels. They were the first of the New Left to get guns and threaten armed insurrection. Their determination and military bearing were so enthralling that the Panthers made violent words and violence itself fashionable. Police killed them in droves.

The idea of the Black Panthers was born when nonviolence began to lose its appeal in the South. Martin Luther King, Jr.'s "peaceful" march in Selma, Alabama, in 1965 ended with marchers getting beaten and murdered. In 1966, civil-rights worker James Meredith got shot. That summer, Stokely Carmichael and John Hulett of the Student Non-Violent Coordinating Committee (SNCC) created the Black Panther party in Lowndes County, Alabama. They had had enough of passive resistance. Their stated goal was *black power.*

Inspired by the SNCC's aggressive stance, the Black Student Union of Merritt College in Oakland, California, organized its own Black Panther party in October 1966. Bobby Seale was chairman. Huey Newton was minister of defense. Newton was described in *The Black Panthers Speak,* a collection of position papers, as "a meticulous student of every legal aspect of the right of citizens to arm themselves." He envisioned the Black Panther party as "an armed association for community protection against the police." Party members, armed with rifles and law books, rode in patrol cars through the ghetto, trailing police cruisers to make sure the pigs did not harass the brothers. The police were outraged; the people were impressed. News of the armed and disciplined Black Panther party, keeping pigs in line, spread quickly.

The Panthers were a charismatic idea. By 1970, there were party branches in thirty-seven cities.

It was impossible to encounter the Oakland leadership and not *feel* black power, affirmed by their walk, talk, and clothes, and especially their guns. Everyone who saw them or met them or even saw pictures or heard about them reacted with awe or fear. The dazzling image of Huey Newton sitting cool and noble in his rattan chair, wearing a rakish beret and black leather jacket, spear and carbine at the ready, a no-bullshit glower on his face, became a poster that was nearly as popular on walls in right-thinking apartments as Milton Glaser's rainbow-hued psychedelic portrait of Bob Dylan from *Blonde on Blonde.* Bobby Seale was fond of calling Huey "the baddest nigger ever."

Eldridge Cleaver recalled his first exposure to the Black Panthers as "literally love at first sight." It was February 1967, and Cleaver was attending yet another talky meeting about coordinating activities for an upcoming memorial on the anniversary of Malcolm X's assassination.

> I spun around in my seat and saw the most beautiful sight I had ever seen: four black men wearing black berets, powder blue shirts, black leather jackets, black trousers, shiny black shoes—and each with a gun! In front was Huey P. Newton with a riot pump shotgun in his right hand, barrel pointed down to the floor. Beside him was Bobby Seale, the handle of a .45 caliber automatic showing from its holster on his right hip, just below the hem of his jacket. A few steps behind Seale was Bobby Hutton, the barrel of his shotgun at his feet. Next to him was Sherwin Forte, an M1 carbine with a banana clip cradled in his arms. . . . Every eye on the room was riveted upon them. . . . Where was my mind at? Blown!

Three months later, Panthers grabbed national attention again when twenty-six of them marched into the California state legislature during a debate on gun control. They were outfitted with pistols, shotguns, carbines, and bandoliers with live ammunition. No shots were fired; nobody was even arrested (the weapons were legally carried). But after that astounding piece of theater, *everybody* knew about the Black Panthers, and everybody knew they meant business.

The Black Panthers' appeal can be understood by looking at their taste in hats. Berets were the headgear of choice for the most disciplined and most feared warrior tribe in the U.S. Army, the Green Berets. Black Panthers, like Green Berets, presented themselves as an elite, well-drilled fighting force. They prided themselves on unflappable military demeanor. The Oakland headquarters issued codes of behavior, points of attention, and rules of discipline galore, including the following:

- No party member can have narcotics or weed in his possession while doing party work.
- No party member can be DRUNK while doing daily party work.
- No party member will USE, POINT, or FIRE a weapon of any kind unnecessarily or accidentally at anyone.
- No party member will commit any crimes against other party members or

*A Black Panther leader addresses high school students in a church, Chicago, 1969.*

BLACK people at all, and cannot steal or take from the people, not even a needle or a piece of thread.
- When arrested, BLACK PANTHER MEMBERS will give only name, address, and will sign nothing.
- Each person will submit a report of daily work.
- All Panthers must learn to operate and service weapons correctly.
- Political education classes are mandatory for general membership.
- Everyone in a leadership position must read no less than two hours per day to keep abreast of the changing political situation.
- Speak politely.
- Pay fairly for what you buy.
- Return everything you borrow.
- Pay for anything you damage.
- Do not hit or swear at people.
- Do not damage property or crops of the poor, oppressed masses.
- Do not take liberties with women.
- If we ever have to take captives, do not ill-treat them.

To this military regimen, add a large measure of daredeviltry and you have sure allure for people disheartened by the ineffectiveness of nonviolent action within the system. To ghetto blacks and white activists, both of whom felt an enervating futility when they tried to combat the establishment in the usual peaceful way, the Panther program of armed "self-defense" carried the irresistible temptation of potency.

To the Panthers, Martin Luther King, Jr., was beginning to look passé even before he was killed in April 1968. His refusal to take up arms was, in the words of Eldridge Cleaver, "a stubborn and persistent stumbling block in the path of the methods that had to be implemented to bring about a revolution. . . . In the last few months [before his death] he already resembled something of a dead man. Of a dead symbol, one might say more correctly." Cleaver's article, for *Ramparts*, was called "Requiem for Nonviolence."

The Black Panthers broke out of the cycle of frustration by making it clear —in their bearing and style, as well as by the points of their program—that they didn't want the fair share of white society that Dr. King had tried to get. They aimed to create a system of their own. They were going to define a new life for black people.

The Panthers had their own national anthem, about a mysterious people's redeemer who speaks in a voice that is centuries old (". . . His full lips of night / Spoke about our people's plight . . ."); they had their own pledge of allegiance for children ("I will train myself never to hurt or allow others to harm my Black brothers and sisters . . ."); they had a ten-point program, including freedom for all black men held in prison, military exemption for all black men, and self-determination for America's "Black colonials"; and they instituted a children's breakfast program, Liberation Schools, and People's Medical Care Centers, independent of the American government.

They insisted you call them "black" instead of "Negro." "Blacks now realize that 'Negro' is an American invention which shut them off from those of the same color in Africa," wrote Julius Lester in *Look Out, Whitey! Black Power's Gon' Get Your Mama.* To be black was to be your own man, connected not to the oppressive culture but to Africa.

To be black was to take a stand against white people's cultural imperialism and celebrate the black things of the world. "The twist, watusi, boogaloo, and monkey have come from the black community and have been appropriated by whites who have no idea that these are, in essence, religious dances, rich with sexual adumbrations," Lester fumed, also noting that "men's fashions invariably come from the ghetto and generally there is a two-year lag before they enter white America."

To express pride in color, many blacks discovered flowing African gowns (dashikis) and kaleidoscopic turbans (shashoks) to express Afro-Americanism. But for the Panthers, such happy reveling in racial pride was not appropriate. It was more important that they appear combat-ready. Dashikis were festive garments; Panthers preferred to dress for action: in black leather, gun belt, sunglasses (so your enemy cannot see your eyes), and combat boots.

Nor did Black Panther hairdos strive towards the majestic heights of those brothers and sisters for whom the Afro became an emblem of racial solidarity (Angela Davis, for example). Most of them wore their hair natural but relatively short: really big hair only made a bigger target for the pigs, and besides, it didn't fit very well beneath a beret. As warriors, Panthers needed to look lean and mean, not ornate.

The Black Panthers meant business. Their battle-ready air was so persuasive that authorities were terrified. "We should kill President Nixon," David Hilliard, Panther chief of staff, suggested at a Moratorium Day rally on November 15, 1969. The government took him at his word and indicted him. The next month, police in Chicago and Los Angeles staged surprise middle-of-the-night raids on Black Panthers' apartments, killing two and wounding seven. By mid-1970, more than a hundred Black Panther leaders were in jail; four hundred more were under indictment; many others had gone underground or into exile; dozens had been killed in shootouts and police raids. "The campaign has taken a fearful toll of the Panthers," *Newsweek* reported in 1970. "They have probably never been so fearsome as the ferocity of the drive against them suggests."

Because of the campaign against them by unpopular authorities, and because of the magnetic appeal of their battle-ready posture (in contrast to the apparent impotence of liberalism), Panthers were chic. Radicals disheartened by hippielike laxity in their ranks began to appropriate their regimented mien. Bandoliers and berets became standard-issue campus revolutionary attire. The Black Panther's stirring battle cry, *"Right on!,"* was adopted by other radicals (and gradually trickled down into ordinary speech, where it has become an exclamation with no more potency than "Hurrah!").

To believe, as the Black Panthers believed, in the inevitability of violent struggle was to be at the vanguard of trendy thought. Street fighting and rioting were in vogue. On August 24, 1967, after devastating battles between the National Guard and neighborhood blacks in Newark, New Jersey, *The New York Review of Books* used a how-to diagram of a Molotov cocktail as its cover. After Leonard Bernstein's notorious fund-raising party for the Black Panthers in January 1970 (described in withering detail by Tom Wolfe in "Radical Chic"), *The New York Times* called them "the romanticized darlings of the politico-cultural jet set."

The Panthers were dropped like hot potatoes by most of their fashionable supporters when the press began to harp on the irony of rich, privileged people supporting self-proclaimed Marxist revolutionaries. Within the black community, too, they began to lose their grip on the people's imagination when the allure of their bold black-beret-and-leather-jacket revolutionary style was gradually eroded by the labyrinthine twists of ever more abstract political separatism.

Although they became passé by the early seventies, the effect of the Black Panthers on the look, sound, and strategy of radical style was immense. Thanks to them, counterculture sloganeering entered its baroque epoch, as pedantic Marxism gave way to incendiary bluster. New Leftists loved quoting H. Rapp Brown, who said, "Violence is as American as cherry pie," and Marvin Jackmon, who coined "Burn, baby, burn" after the riots in Watts. The Panther salute, the raised, clenched fist, became a symbol of all re-sistance. The credo they exhumed from Marxism-Leninism, "All power to the people," became the rallying cry of angry rebels with no interest in doctrine, for whom Marx was Groucho and Lenin one of the Beatles. The Black Panthers had created an image of radicalism cool enough to transcend the tedium of politics.

## The Weather Underground

Half a million citizens marched on Washington to protest the war in Vietnam in November 1969, but President Nixon said he didn't see the demonstration because he was busy watching football on television. That made people mad!

It had begun to seem that no protest, however big and strong, and no confrontation, however principled, affected what the protesters considered to be the utterly wicked

*By 1970, marches on Washington were commonplace.*

ways of the U.S. government. Some dissenters were convinced that they had to take the next step.

Incited by the kick of street fighting at the Chicago Democratic Convention in 1968 (where many were hurt, but nobody got killed or maimed), they decided that violent revolution was the only way to go. To beat the system they would have to blow it up. Literally.

The most conspicuous of the terrorists called themselves the Weather Underground. They were not interested in moralistic encounters with authorities, and they did not want to stage little street-theater exercises to embarrass the system. They had none of the Yippies' sense of absurdity and play, nor did they fantasize about a freeky new world of drugs, rock and roll, and free love. Ultimately, they grew to have nothing but contempt for hippies and Yippies and freeks, whom they viewed as bourgeois kids playing pranks while on an extended vacation from their loathesome, counterrevolutionary lives.

The Weather Underground hated just about everything and everybody except Marx and Mao and Ché and Ho Chi Minh; they were so mad that they didn't want to waste time talking about some forthcoming utopia they might want to create after their hoped-for revolution. They simply wanted to blow up buildings and kill people *now*.

They began as a faction of the Students for a Democratic Society. In June 1969, a group of SDSers fed up with what they saw as a gutless leadership came to the national SDS convention in Chicago with a position paper titled "You Don't Need a Weatherman to Know Which Way the Wind Blows." Its title was borrowed from Bob Dylan's apocalyptic song "Subterranean Homesick Blues." Their main point was that it was time for true believers to *bring the war home*, which meant carrying out guerrilla actions against the United States, within the United States.

The SDS was already in the hands of the faction known as "wreckers"— those who favored armed revolution rather than trying to work within the system. The convention in 1969 was the showdown. It was a rowdy scene: delegates were frisked at the door, politically incorrect speakers were overwhelmed with cries of "Bullshit!" "Shame!" and "Motherfucker!" Rufus Walls of the Illinois Black Panthers announced that "the way women can contribute to the movement is by getting laid." Women delegates drowned him out, yelling, "Fight male chauvinism!" Eventually, in a strong-arm coup, the convention minority expelled the majority; and for months after, each claimed to be the real SDS. The bunch who came away with the bank account and membership roster called themselves the Weathermen.

The Weathermen (soon to become the Weather Underground, when they discovered the sin of male chauvinism and excised "men" from their name) were proud of being more radical than anybody else. This was a peculiar form of pride that infected the New Left like a virulent plague. As other tactics failed, and a sense of futility clouded over sane efforts to change the system in any normal way, activist radicals began to develop a dare-and-double-dare mentality, everybody striving to be the most revolutionary and the most dangerous, with the least anxiety about such bourgeois hang-ups as fair play, mercy, and not murdering innocent people. "It became a matter of whether or not you were a man," Tom Hayden explained. Being a man was measured, in Hayden's words, "by how outrageously subversive you were willing to be."

Because virtually all members of the Weather Underground began as middle-class American kids—the worst thing to be in the eyes of a movement that glorified the oppressed people of the third world—they spent a lot of effort proving they had shed all vestiges of middle-class morality. They took psychedelic drugs to annihilate their polite, properly educated personalities; they slept together in polygamous groups to squelch conventional tendencies towards family and man-woman coupling; they purged intellectuals and weakling theoreticians from their ranks (*action* was the only thing that mattered); and they divested themselves of prosaic sentimentality about human life.

When Charles Manson and his family of psychopaths were indicted in December 1969 for murdering actress Sharon Tate and her friends, then disemboweling Tate (who was pregnant) with a fork, the Weather Underground lauded the massacre as a heroic deed. "First they killed those pigs," exulted Bernadine Dohrn, head of the Weather Underground, "then they ate dinner in the same room with them, and they even shoved a fork into the victim's stomach! Wild!" Dohrn adopted a raised-fist salute with her fingers pointed like the tines of a fork—to honor the Manson family's weapon, and to suggest the Mansonesque brutality the Weather Underground intended to inflict on all the unborn honky babies with whom they did battle.

The frightening thing about it was that they meant what they said. Callous sadism was not just intended as a pose. They really saw themselves as terrorists fighting a take-no-prisoners war—a war of such momentous bearing that it demanded its partisans become, in André Malraux's term, "doomed executioners," stripped of their humanity. Their intent became clear in February 1970, when Weather Undergrounders Terry Robbins, Diana Oughton, and Ted Gold blew themselves to pieces while trying to manufacture bombs in a Greenwich Village townhouse (a posh hideout owned by the dad of fellow insurrectionist Cathy Wilkerson).

Weather people fantasized they were the kernel of a new revolutionary army. Like the Black Panthers, they favored fearsome leather duds, combat boots, and berets (or riot helmets and ski masks); they printed pictures in their publication *New Left Notes* that purported to show recruits doing calisthenics and learning weaponry. They prepared for the inevitable revolution by studying such guerrilla street-fighting fashion hints as these, issued in a pamphlet by Linda Borenstein, John Johansson, and Richard Winklestern (date unknown):

The following should be worn: Protective clothing: High buttoned shirts, buttoned sleeves, laced heavy shoes, a belt, jock, bra, a helmet (or at least a helmet liner), tight-fitting goggles to protect your eyes. You should not wear contact lenses. Do not wear earrings—they can be pulled off by the police. Wear nothing around the neck (beads, etc.) which can be pulled and choke you. Wear no hanging straps that can be grabbed. If you can see without glasses, don't wear them. Do not wear false teeth; you can choke on them if unconscious.

Weather Undergrounders spent hours reading Mao's Little Red Book, then engaging in a process called "criticism, self-criticism," the point of which was to determine whether one was revolutionary enough. Nobody ever was, and so to prove devotion to the cause, good Weather Undergrounders committed themselves to ever more daring and preposterous positions. The Weather Underground's goal was to be even more brutal than the pigs.

They craved to be outlaws; they wanted desperately to see themselves like their hero Ché Guevara, who was assassinated while holed up in the jungles of Bolivia. They wanted to lead a righteous battle against an evil enemy. They even wanted to be martyred, like Ché, if the cause demanded it. What a romantic self-image, full of fire and bravery and self-sacrifice! The only problem was that they couldn't get anyone to enlist in their cause. They made headlines and carried the gauntlet as the ne-plus-ultra revolutionaries in 1969 and 1970, and they caused a considerable amount of inconvenience to many people, but they remained leaders of a revolution nobody wanted to join.

They planned for their uprising to begin in earnest in the fall of 1969. Believing themselves battle-hardened by the street fighting of the Chicago Democratic Convention, the Weather Underground plotted a ruinous "Days of Rage" engagement for October. They promised that the streets of Chicago would run red with blood, making the Democratic Convention of the year before look like a picnic. Their plan was to enlist fellow radicals and hordes of rootless, disaffected kids from around the country and wage a frontal assault on the Chicago police.

To gather troops for the revolution, they staged recruiting raids on high schools. Weather Undergrounder Jeff Jones recalled how five of them drove to Milwaukee and entered a school while classes were in session, chanting "Jail break!" and imploring the kids ("prisoners of the Amerikan school system") to join them outside for a rally, then in Chicago for the Days of Rage. "Most people thought we were nuts," he recalled.

The Days of Rage were a flop. Instead of tens of thousands of battle-ready guerrillas, six hundred people showed up—mostly just Weather Underground organizers and leftover SDSers who had planned the event. They bombed a statue dedicated to policemen who had been killed by anarchists; then, on the night of October 8, armed with Viet Cong flags and two-by-fours, they began their putsch. They invaded the nice part of town and broke the windows of stores and cars; they charged headlong into police barricades; they ululated as they ran through the streets of Chicago (imitating the Algerian women they admired in the movie *Battle of Algiers*). A half-dozen of them were shot, and three hundred were arrested (but released when bail was posted, in most cases by exasperated parents); the only casualty on the other side was one man who was paralyzed from the neck down when he stumbled while trying to tackle a Weather Undergrounder.

In February 1970, the Weather Underground went underground to stay. Bernadine Dohrn made it onto the FBI's Ten Most Wanted list but wasn't found until she gave herself up in 1980. Despite their best intentions, they never did kill anybody, except themselves, in the accidental explosion in Greenwich Village. Their activities while underground included the occasional nuisance-bomb explosion and sneaking antiwar banners onto college buildings.

Lift out TABS to remove dolls.

STAND
ASSEMBLY

BRIDE

GROOM

# MR. AND MRS. AVERAGE

BY THE END of the sixties, the weirdest thing a person could be was average. At a time when it seemed that everyone was possessed by an unquenchable thirst to be extravagant, exaggerated, way out, hairy, and revolutionary, acting normal started to look like the freakiest lifestyle of all.

The way Mr. and Mrs. Average saw things, they used to be citizens of a patriotic race whose men proudly wore enameled flag pins on the lapels of their suit jackets. They lived in an orderly land of shined shoes, pressed handkerchiefs, and weekly trips to the barbershop for a trim and a chat. Children sat at school desks with folded hands and called their elders "ma'am" and "sir." On Sunday everybody went to church, ate Mom's chicken dinner, then settled into their wood-paneled dens, where they were entertained by acrobats, jugglers, and Señor Wences and his talking fist on "The Ed Sullivan Show."

They lived in a happy community of happy people just like themselves: hardworking, meat-eating, Chevrolet-driving, God-fearing, flag-waving, law-abiding, polite-speaking taxpayers who all shared the same idea of what was right and good. It was swell; then the sixties came along and ruined everything.

For Mr. and Mrs. Average, life during the sixties was like a trip to the planet Bizarro, the perplexing contrary world in the universe of "Superman" comics. On Bizarro, normal values are inverted. Women flaunt jewelry made of coal instead of diamonds; kids eat broccoli and hate chocolate; men root for their favorite baseball player to strike out.

Was life for Mr. and Mrs. Average in the sixties any less abstruse? Instead of being lauded for their patriotism, they suddenly found themselves regarded by everyone under thirty as fascist subjects of a wicked imperialist nation. Their friend Joe, the neighborhood cop, was labeled a billy-club-wielding pig. The radio that used to play them pretty love songs by handsome, manly crooners like Dean and Frank and Tony was now the province of fruity boys with long hair screaming raucous songs about dope and sex. Their big, beautiful American car was condemned as an ecological nightmare: friends of the earth rolled their eyes in disgust when an Averagemobile pulled up to a red light, belching fumes.

Even Mr. and Mrs. Average's own children flipped their wigs. Junior wore a flag shirt instead of a flag lapel pin, and he regularly told his teacher to fuck off. Little Sis refused to eat anything that wasn't organic and left a note on the kitchen table announcing she had run away to a commune in San Francisco and changed her name from Mary Ann to Cheyenne Sunshine.

As the people that the groovy world loved to hate, Mr. and Mrs. Average found themselves blamed for everything from the Vietnam War to sexual frigidity. The happy, wholesome life that made them so proud was ridiculed as uptight, sterile, and repressive; they were scorned as lumpish blockheads clad in polyester leisure suits, lurching through a phony world cluttered with lowbrow drek. The image of the Averages was lampooned on British television in "Till Death Us Do Part" (1965), about a vulgar, loudmouthed, ignorant bigot; then in its American imitation, "All in the Family" (1971), about a narrow-minded nincompoop who lives his life in an armchair, drinking beer in front of the television set. Movies made the caricature even worse: in *Joe* (1970), Peter Boyle played a doltish Mr. Average driven to murder and pillage because his daughter becomes a hippie.

In a popular culture that seemed ever more dominated by disrespectful Beatles and Smothers Brothers and irreverent movies like *The Graduate* and boys who look like girls and girls who dress like boys, Mr. and Mrs. Average saw themselves branded the unbalanced ones. By trying hard to assert the dominion of normalcy, they became yet another freaky group of outspoken sixties people struggling to define and defend their lifestyle. Just like all the peaceniks and hippies they disdained, they found themselves gluing bumper stickers on their car (theirs said LOVE IT OR LEAVE IT) and wearing buttons with provocative slogans (theirs showed the triple-toed peace symbol, but surrounded by a novel caption of their own: FOOTPRINT OF THE AMERICAN CHICKEN). They even found their own exaggerated anthem on the radio: Merle Haggard's "Okie from Muskogee," which told all who cared to listen that they did not smoke marijuana and that they flew the American flag with as much bravado as the soldiers who hoisted it above the beach at Iwo Jima.

It seemed like only yesterday that their taste and values ruled the land, but now Mr. and Mrs. Average's most hallowed idols were being upstaged by oddballs. In July 1969, *Life* magazine's cover story offered "Dusty and the Duke: A Choice of Heroes." It was a double profile that weighed the six-foot-four, two-hundred-forty-pound, all-American masculinity of John Wayne against Hollywood's newest star, Dustin Hoffman. The very idea of the comparison was insane to Mr. and Mrs. Average, who could remember when homely half-pints like Hoffman were, at best, character actors like Peter Lorre or Elisha Cook, Jr.

In the Bizarro Hollywood of the sixties, five-foot-eight Dustin Hoffman, a nervous nonconformist with acne-scarred skin, was a sex symbol—right up there with the man who won the west! Inside the magazine, on the left-hand page, there's a photograph of the little fellow and his wife, captioned, "Dustin browses in a Greenwich Village shop with Anne and later kisses her in a taxi. A movie fan, his recent favorites are *Stolen Kisses* and *Battle of Algiers*." Dustin is carrying flowers and Anne, her bandanna tied Comanche-style around her forehead, holds a single rose.

On the right is the Duke with his youngest son, Ethan, who cradles a bazooka in his arms. The caption: "Ethan Wayne aims toy gun under practiced eye on their way to the family yacht, *Wild Goose II*, a 130-foot minesweeper which Wayne keeps at anchor near his home."

Big Duke, with his big gun and big boat, and little Dustin, with his flowers and low-budget art films, disagree about everything. Dustin says: "The youth outburst in this country is a good thing. The kids are angry because the American leaders

*Mr. and Mrs. Average's heroes: John Wayne at top, and, clockwise from upper left, Phyllis Diller, Ann-Margret, Lucille Ball, Red Skelton, Bing Crosby, Bob Hope, and Dean Martin*

have made mistakes and refuse to admit it." That's not what John Wayne thinks: "The disorders in the schools are caused by immature professors who have encouraged activists. I was a socialist when I was a sophomore at the University of Southern California, but not when I graduated."

John Wayne and Dustin Hoffman both made movies that seemed to express their views of where the world was at. In *Midnight Cowboy*, (1969) Hoffman played Ratso Rizzo, a tubercular street hustler befriended by male prostitute Jon Voight. Nothing much goes right for the two outcasts, and at the end of the picture, Rizzo dies on a Greyhound bus. This was a story about people that Mr. and Mrs. Average would just as soon not know about. And if you *did* have to make a movie about bums and such, couldn't there at least be a nice inspirational ending, like in a Frank Capra picture? Weren't movies supposed to be uplifting and about noble things?

For example, *The Green Berets* (1968). John Wayne didn't just star in this one: he co-directed it with Ray Kellogg, and his son Michael Wayne produced it. It was the Duke's personal testament. His performances as soldiers in

*John Wayne starred in and co-directed*
The Green Beret *as an ode to old-fashioned, firm-jawed patriotism.*

cavalry movies and war epics such as *Sands of Iwo Jima* and *They Were Expendable* had made him a star; and he was dismayed that the young, Nehru-jacketed new Hollywood was producing no pictures in support of America's fighting men.

To tell the red-white-and-blue side of the story, he based his film on a best-selling book written in 1965 by a civilian, Robin Moore. *The Green Berets* described the Vietnam adventures of the elite army corps of antiguerrilla fighters who had been given their distinct haberdashery symbolism by John F. Kennedy in 1961 during the early, clandestine years of the conflict. The book's jacket copy makes it clear where its author stands regarding the hostilities. While researching the Green Berets, we are told, Mr. Moore "so distinguished himself that the montagnard [Vietnamese] commander offered him the rare privilege of cutting off the ear of a dead VC!"

The movie, in which John Wayne as Colonal Mike Kirby teaches a doubting-Thomas newspaper reporter (David Janssen) that the war is noble, was aimed against domestic peaceniks as much as against the foreign enemy. Warner Bros.' advertisements challenged: "So you don't believe in glory. And heroes are out of style. And they don't blow bugles anymore. So take another look—at the Special Forces in a special kind of hell." Demonstrators outside the premiere in New York waved Viet Cong flags; veteran Green Berets invited to attend had to sneak in the back door of the theater.

The movie showed heroic soldiers giving the reds a dose of their own medicine. Critics pounced on it like VC in the jungle, calling it a "ridiculous 'Terry and the Pirates'–type adventure." *Newsweek* said, "You don't know whether to howl or weep or both." *Time* lambasted the Duke as "full of booze and passion for justice. . . . His politics are symbolized by the itchy trigger finger." Everyone made fun of the ending, which, because it was filmed in Southern California rather than Vietnam, made it appear that the sun was setting in the East. The movie made money but few converts. By 1968, there was no way to popularize the war in Vietnam.

The most conspicuous Green Berets success off the battlefield had happened on the *Billboard* Hot 100 chart back in 1966, in the wake of Robin

Moore's book. "The Ballad of the Green Beret," a song written and per-formed by real-life Green Beret sergeant Barry Sadler, became *the top-selling song of 1966.* That's right—one red-blooded American fighting man did what Mr. and Mrs. Average desperately needed someone to do for them. He kicked ass! He whipped the Beatles, the Stones, the Supremes, the Troggs, the Mon-kees, the Turtles, and the Strawberry Alarm Clock! He appeared on "Ed Sullivan!" He was banned in East Germany, where young commie rebels loved hearing his voice of freedom! The song was such a big hit that Sergeant Sadler's portrait became the cover of the paperback edition of the novel *The Green Berets.*

The ode to "fighting soldiers from the sky, fearless men who jump and die" remained number one on the charts for five weeks in the spring of 1966. Its triumph gave righteous chills to Mr. and Mrs. Average. Here was a sign that all the old values could still prevail. Sergeant Sadler slugged it out on the record charts toe-to-toe with the repulsive rock-and-roll oddballs . . . *and won!* Maybe, just maybe, America wasn't going to hell in a handbasket.

Two hundred thousand people sported Barry Sadler Fan Club buttons, and Sadler found himself busy negotiating options and licensing agreements for combat toys such as a Barry Sadler toy gun and a Barry Sadler field-ration kit. One item *not* licensed was a Barry Sadler green beret: he rejected every one as not being of high enough quality. Nevertheless, *Newsweek* reported that women in Times Square were buying "unofficial green berets" and wearing them to honor America's fighting men.

As Mr. and Mrs. Average would be ever so happy to tell you, the liberal-leaning press was vicious in its assessment of the Singing Sergeant. They sneered at him, just like at the Duke. "Banal and ridden with sentimentality," *Time* called his song. "If Vietnam has produced a true war poet he is no doubt too busy fighting to write."

Bad reviews didn't stop other record producers from climbing on the Green Berets bandwagon. MGM issued an album with the hefty title *The Green Berets: The Story and Heritage of the United States Army Special Forces.* It is a pastiche of songs about the Green Berets' A team slapped together with a blabby narration explaining their historical precedents in Teddy Roosevelt's Rough Riders and Andrew Jackson's Kentucky Backwoodsmen. Pickwick issued an album with a life-size cover picture of a green beret hat that looked like an emerald pancake, and featuring somebody named Roger Dewey crooning Sadler's song. If anyone bought this album looking for pro-Vietnam diatribes, they had a shock waiting for them. To fill out the other nine tracks, Roger Dewey includes such antiwar laments as "Ain't Gonna Study War No More" and "When This Cruel War Is Over."

In the spirit of Sadler's song came the "Green Berets" comic strip, starring Sergeant Champ Benton, battling archenemy Luana, "treacherous secret agent of the Viet Cong." The Philadelphia Chewing Gum Company, manu-facturers of Swell Gum, marketed Green Beret Bubble Gum, a flat pink sheet wrapped neatly in a wax-paper wrapper containing five cardboard trading cards. On one side of the cards were pieces of a jigsaw puzzle that when put together showed the Green Berets blasting away at the business of war. On the other side were Green Beret facts. For example, card 25 shows a helicopter dropping its payload on a ship, with the caption: "This test demonstrates the effectiveness of using a copter to put napalm bombs right on a target. A new use for big choppers!"

Let the peaceniks decorate their Volkswagen vans with stickers saying WAR IS NOT HEALTHY FOR CHILDREN AND OTHER LIVING THINGS. When it came to children, Mr. and Mrs. Average knew that war toys

**Fight with the Famous Green Berets**

$3.99
5-Piece Set

Now You Can Lead Your Forces Into Action as a member of the World-famous fighting team. Beret is type worn by the best of the U.S. Army's fighting men—complete with insignia. "Burp" gun has exciting trigger sound action, sparking muzzle. .45 pistol shoots plastic bullets, also fires cops.* Fits in Army-type belt and holster. 2 cap-firing* grenades. "Burp" gun about 18 in. long; .45 pistol about 7 in.; both made of sturdy plastic. 8 plastic bullets included.
48 HT 19606—Ship. wt. 2 lbs. 8 oz. Set $3.99

and games were extremely healthy; and there was no better role model for little tykes than a Green Beret soldier. The 1966 Montgomery Ward holiday catalog merchandised Special Forces combat toys by the truckload, promising "everything for the little company commander to hide under the Christmas tree."

For $3.99 you could buy a play set that featured a replica felt green beret with insignia, an eighteen-inch-long burp gun with "exciting trigger sound action and sparking muzzle," a .45-caliber pistol that shot plastic bullets, an army belt and holster, and two grenades. For an additional few dollars the outfit could be supplemented with a plastic M-16 bolt-action rifle, a pistol belt with ammo pouch, riflery medals, infantry badges, a compass, dog tags, and a camouflage helmet covered with netting and guaranteed by Montgomery Ward "to last through many campaigns."

It wasn't hard to support the war in Vietnam if you could see it like WWII, or even Korea, where there were good guys and bad guys and no question who was who. All the talk of Vietnam being different made Mr. and Mrs. Average most uncomfortable. That is why they relished any sign that it was just another battle between right and wrong.

The sure symbol that Vietnam was simply business-as-usual was Bob Hope. As in all previous wars, Bob was there bringing good clean sunshine to the front and, by doing so, reassuring the folks at home that the war in Vietnam really was a good one.

"A week before Christmas, while Santa is checking his south-only maps, Bob Hope, the knight before Christmas (and a few days after) rises from a Southern California airstrip, dips his wings in tribute to the USO and the

Pentagon brass and flies west." So exults the dust jacket of Bob Hope's own Vietnam story, *Five Women I Love*, a book about how Bob, along with Janis Paige, Anita Bryant, Joey Heatherton, Carroll Baker, and Kaye Stevens, toured Vietnam and Thailand and showed the boys in uniform a good time.

Mr. and Mrs. Average had to be thrilled picturing American boys being entertained by an institution as revered as Bob Hope (never mind that the boys were probably puffing on joints the size of torpedoes). It had to be worth risking injury and death if you had the chance to hear Bob Hope's famous witticisms in person. "Vietnam has me a little nervous," he began his show. "This morning my Rice Krispies popped, and I surrendered to the maid." When the troops' laughter died down, he followed with this side-splitter: "This ship really is a beauty. I understand half the whales in the Pacific are trying to get her to go upstream."

After the warm-up, Hope, along with comic Jerry Colonna and singer Jack Jones, showed they dug the youth scene by performing a musical parody called "England Swings," for which they donned Beatle wigs and called themselves the Happy Rolling Rockheads, wiggling geriatrically and yelling out cornball jokes punctuated by "yeah, yeah, yeah."

After the rock-and-roll hilarity, it was time to bring out the girls. The queen of the Vietnam USO shows was Joey Heatherton, daughter of Ray Heatherton, kiddie TV's Merry Mailman. Joey had an act that probably wouldn't have gone far outside the service, but the boys in uniform loved it. Her specialty was to dance a wild go-go number clad in a sequined black bathing suit and tights. Her bleached-blond hair was cut boyishly short, her lips painted pink-white in startling contrast to a thick line of slutty black eyeliner and inch-long false eyelashes. As she shimmied and jerked, her mouth formed a perpetual "ooh," reminding the lads in uniform that girls say yes to boys who go KA-POW.

To get the G.I.s' minds back on a

*Show-business veterans Jerry Colonna, Anita Bryant, and Bob Hope campaigned tirelessly in Vietnam.*

higher plane, Bob Hope introduced born-again-Christian song stylist (and Miss America runner-up) Anita Bryant, who belted out "The Battle Hymn of the Republic" and gave away bottles of Coca-Cola. Then, to prove that there is indeed Humor in Uniform, a male officer bounced onstage dressed in one of sexpot Carroll Baker's evening gowns, stuffed with Kleenex at the bust. After each show, the five women Bob loved whipped the camouflage hats and insignia vests off love-struck soldiers and kissed them on the cheeks for the sake of the cameras and Uncle Sam.

Bob Hope and his traveling troop of cuties and comics had not cornered the market on third-world vaudeville. Borscht-belt cutup Joey Adams also hit the road as a self-described "goodwill ambassador in greasepaint." Along with his wife, Cindy, and the rest of the Joey Adams Yankee Doodle Dandies, Joey carried forth America's banner into Southeast Asia and other underprivileged places in need of uplifting. Nightclub performer Buddy Rich showed various natives how to play the Afghan drums. John and Bonnie Shirley made balloon creations for war waifs. And the Four Step Brothers, while visiting the Beggars' Home in Chembur, India, taught the lepers how to tap-dance.

As for Martha Raye, the big-mouth comedienne from musicals such as *Artists and Models* and *Four Jills in a Jeep*, she did everything but challenge Ho Chi Minh to a wrestling match. Nicknamed "Maggie of the Boondocks" for all the hours she spent entertaining troops in remote locations at the front, she was wounded once ("Humph!" she told reporters. "I've had worse hangovers") and got a special citation from General William Westmoreland for giving forty-eight straight hours of assistance to medics near the Demilitarized Zone (DMZ) in Vietnam. She named her Bel-Air home "Maggie's Team House" in honor of the Green Beret teams with whom she served, and

*Comedienne Martha Raye snaps off a salute at the 1967 Loyalty Day Parade in New York City.*

announced that all returning Vietnam veterans were welcome. As thanks for her service, Lyndon Johnson named her the only woman in America entitled to wear the uniform of the Green Berets.

When she stood up at the August 1968 military pageant in Bridgeport, Connecticut, and declared herself proud to be an American woman, some people in the audience must have been puzzled. Ms. Raye's sex was in no way apparent to the casual observer. Decked out in her colonel's regalia, including man-tailored shirt and necktie, her chest festooned with ribbons, spit-shined boots on her feet and the exalted green military beret on her head, she had become an exact replica of an American fighting man.

The occasion for her appearance was the convention of an outfit called the Young Marines, a corps of juvenile soldiers aged eight to fifteen. The youngsters were a kiddie-league ROTC who attended "Leadership Laboratory" classes in junior high school where they learned to respect their elders, memorize all verses of the national anthem, make their bed each day, and (according to the Marine Corps guidelines) "not associate with persons who disregard authority." The Young Marines made Colonel Raye proud by marching with wooden rifles and saluting her and their parents in the reviewing stands. But even some of the most conservative members of the Danbury, Connecticut, school board expressed their unease over the resemblance of the Young Marines to the Hitler Youth corps.

Louder than Martha Raye, more militant than the Young Marines, the most bellicose uniform-wearer of the late sixties was comedian George Jessel, self-described in his show-biz autobiography, *So Help Me*, as "master showman, raconteur, movie producer, TV and radio personality, speechmaker, and Toastmaster General of the United States." Once a prominent fixture at Friars Club roasts, George Jessel appeared to go quite wacko during the war in Vietnam.

He appeared at events in a military outfit of his own design, its gold braid and campaign bars so grand it would have embarrassed Mussolini. Always a staunch patriot, Jessel grew increasingly paranoid during the sixties. He took all opportunities to mount any rostrum and, instead of telling jokes, engage in fierce harangues about those he perceived as America's enemies.

Foremost among the foes were *The New York Times* and the Washington *Post*, which he was convinced were willing stooges of the far left. His climactic donnybrook came during a "Today" show interview with Edwin Newman. When asked about the morale of American troops, Jessel replied, "Very high, but of course, when you pick up a copy of *Pravda*—excuse me, *The New York Times*, you generally see negative reporting. . . . The *Times*, and the Washington *Post*—excuse me, *Pravda* number two—take a very anti-American, negative attitude." Newman cut the interview short and asked Jessel to leave the studio.

His attacks on the *Times*, the *Post*, as well as on private citizens such as boxer Muhammad Ali, whom he loathed for refusing to be drafted in the

*George Jessel, once a comedian, often appeared on television in a paramilitary uniform to rail against antiwar protesters.*

army, resulted in his being shut out of the major media, which only added more fuel to Jessel's fire. He spent his later years appearing at VFW halls and other like-minded places, rambling on about the red menace, long-haired hippies, and the pinko press, as well as touting his work-in-progress, a book called *The Crucifixion of Richard Nixon.*

Vietnam was far away, but Jessel was a combatant in another war that was raging at home. This war was even more difficult to see in nice old-fashioned terms of good guys (us) against bad (them). It was a war fought mostly on campus, beginning with the Free Speech Movement of Berkeley in 1964, climaxing in the late sixties with full-blown rioting at Columbia, armed student insurrection at Cornell, and the shooting of four student protesters by the National Guard at Kent State in 1970. The problem with this war for Mr. and Mrs. Average was that the bad guys seemed to be the entire younger generation, in many cases *their own children.*

Ben Garris of the Denham Springs (Louisiana) *News* expressed the hostility felt by many confounded Averages when he complained that "patriotism is out and protesting is the 'in' thing." Garris grieved about " 'students,' bless their ignorant, yellow little souls, who mouth four letter words at any square who speaks well of God or country. They gather together in motley little crews called 'SDS' and curse the establishment, which pays for their food, clothes, schools, and foolishness."

This was a terrible state of affairs, but Mr. and Mrs. Average, ever resourceful, found a way to explain it. They pointed out that not all students were bad eggs; that it was the press who blew out of proportion the depredations of the few. (In 1969, as a gesture of support for the Averages' point of view, the Chicago *Tribune* declared a one-day moratorium on all news about campus protest.) Even Jerry Rubin, arch-Yippie, wrote that he was amazed at the extent to which "we freaks dominate the consciousness of middle-class America. They turn on the TV news and all they see are riots, student demonstrations, and revolution." Mr. and Mrs. Average wanted to politely raise their hands and ask, "But what about all the good students who don't riot and don't pee in the dean's wastebasket?"

Standing in opposition to radical youth groups, the Young Americans for

Freedom, founded in 1960 under the guidance of William F. Buckley, Jr., pledged "victory, not co-existence with the Communist world." They were applauded by conservative senators Barry Goldwater, John Tower, and Strom Thurmond; and they were a glimmer of hope for Mr. and Mrs. Average when television's evening news showed night after night of bad students making trouble.

Some of the greatest battles in the campus war were fought over the issue of ROTC, the Reserve Officers' Training Corps. In response to student (and faculty) protest, Harvard, Yale, Stanford, Dartmouth, Cornell, and Columbia all revoked ROTC's academic standing on campus. ROTC headquarters were pillaged and fire-bombed by angry radicals. The SDS forcibly ejected college deans from their offices as a tactic to strong-arm them into banishing the offending military presence from the campus.

You might think ROTC was on the skids, but as usual, Mr. and Mrs. Average believed the news media were showing a skewed picture of what was really going on. And the fact is, they were right. Protesters made an irresistible news story, but in 1970 Kenneth Keniston concluded in an *Educational Record* report that it was primarily the "visible, selective, and prestigious" institutions that were racked with protests. Student-opinion surveys from the 1968–69 academic year showed that a majority of students on all campuses were unwilling to participate in protests, were basically satisfied with their education, and supported "the system." In other words, not all campuses wanted to kick ROTC's butt. Small colleges throughout the land still glorified their soldiers-in-training.

Tarleton State College in Stephenville, Texas, was a fine example. Substantial pages of the 1966 *Grassburr*, Tarleton's yearbook, are devoted to such collegiate militaria as ROTC, the Wainwright Rifles (a precision drill team which performed at the Fiesta Flambeau and the Battle of the Flowers), cadet corps, and color guard. Pictures of the homecoming parade show it led by boys in uniform. And as patriotism knows no sex, so Tarleton had its Wainwright Debutantes, the distaff version of the drill team, who performed at the Fat Stock Show in Fort Worth. The year's biggest formal dance was December's Military Ball, for which huge murals were painted to cover the walls of "the Cave," where the white-gloved students danced. The murals set the mood for the evening's festivities by depicting the Japanese bombing of Pearl Harbor.

To eyes accustomed to seeing sixties students with freak-out hair, in jeans and T-shirts, giving the finger to the camera, perhaps the most shocking picture in *Grassburr* is that of senior Janice Sullivan—Tarleton's Beauty Queen in 1966, with the distinguished title "ROTC Little Colonel." She rates a full-page photograph, posed in a formal lamé gown, above-the-elbow white gloves, and queenly sash, topped by an immovable hairdo. It was Little Colonel Janice, dressed in ball gown and wrapped in her sash, who had the privilege of the first waltz at Tarleton's Military Ball.

*Janice Sullivan, ROTC Little Colonel at Tarleton State College, Stephenville, Texas, 1966*

If it was troubling to see America's college students getting stereotyped as revolutionaries, it was even worse to see Jesus suddenly stage a comeback in the late sixties . . . as a hippie! Mr. and Mrs. Average did not appreciate the comparison of the long-haired, sandal-shod, white-robed Savior with the long-haired, sandal-shod, white-robed acidhead standing on the street corner panhandling spare change. Their Jesus was no granola-eating love child with dirty feet. He was good-smelling and pink-cheeked, and would no doubt eat red meat and drive a Chevrolet if he were alive today. Sure, he had long hair; but Mr. and Mrs. Average's Jesus glowed with all the moral purity of the girls in the Breck shampoo ads.

The Reverend David Wilkerson, who previously wrote *The Cross and the Switchblade* about his tribulations among New York street gangs, came to Jesus's rescue in 1969 with a book called *Purple Violet Squish.* "When you accuse the young hippie of dropping out on life and forgetting his responsibilities, he will likely tell you that the first century prophet, Jesus Christ, was also a 'groovy cat' who dropped out," writes Wilkerson. "He will try to sell you on the idea that Buddha and St. Francis of Assisi were also dropouts who left their families to live in poverty." Don't you believe it, Wilkerson assures Mr. and Mrs. Average, labeling those who saw Jesus as a hippie "freakniks."

"Hold on to your mind," *Purple Violet Squish* cautions. "Here come the freakniks—suspended in a spirit world of oblivion! They search for God in the surrealistic cosmos [and their] religious freak-out begins with the study of Yoga, Hinduism, and Oriental Mysticism!"

Bob Larson confirmed Wilkerson's findings in his own book about false religion, provocatively titled *Hindus, Hippies and Rock and Roll*, also published in 1969. Larson traveled to India to report back to Mr. and Mrs. Average "the truth concerning the Hippies, the Beatles and Maharishi Mahesh Yogi." He concluded that "rock music is an insidious obsession which threatens the moral fiber of this country." But music was just part of the picture. As a preacher and born-again Christian, Larson explained how all the pieces fit together.

The Hindus are trying to take over the world with their Godless (or, more accurately, multigodded) religion. They use mantras to brainwash the masses into performing such unholy activities as chanting, dope smoking, and Tantric sex. In a chapter called "Calcutta—Seat of Meditation," Larson wrings his hands: "If The Beatles are going to pray to Hindu gods, invite demon spirits to enter and control their bodies, and encourge America's youth to do likewise, where might it all lead? . . . If Satan were going to introduce the youth of America to Hinduism he has chosen his prophets well."

Finally, consider *The Marxist Minstrels*, subtitled "A Handbook On Communist Subversion of Music," by Dr. David A. Noebel. Dr. Noebel, whose previous writing credits include *Communism, Hypnotism, and the Beatles*, had a real academic flair for linking rock and roll to the calamities of the sixties. Citing such erudite sources as *The American Journal of Psychiatry, Saturday Review*, Santayana, and Thoreau, he came to the same conclusion as Wilkerson and Larson: "Christians should have been alerted to the British foursome in August, 1964 when Derek Taylor [the Beatles' PR man] admitted they were the antichrist."

If Derek Taylor's declaration of satanic intent somehow slipped past Mr. and Mrs. Average, John Lennon's comment that the BEATLES ARE BIGGER THAN JESUS CHRIST did not go unnoticed. That is how an article in the American teen magazine *Datebook* was headlined, preceding the Beatles' American tour in August 1966. In fact, what John had said back in February to an interviewer from the London *Evening Standard* was even more scandalous than the headline: "Christianity will go. It will vanish and shrink," he explained. "We're more popular than Jesus now." Benevolently, John said he had nothing against Jesus personally; it was just Jesus's followers—i.e., Christians—that he found "thick."

In England, no one paid much attention to his remarks. But when *Datebook* reprinted the interview in America—well, that just about did it for Mr. and Mrs. Average! If there was any doubt in their minds about rock and roll, it was gone. Fanatical preachers such as Wilkerson and Larson had never had much success among the Averages because their prophecies of doom were just too darn frightening, and did not fit into the placid, average world in which Averages wanted to live. But John Lennon's arrogance could not go unchallenged.

The Reverend Thurmond Babbs, a Baptist preacher in Cleveland, warned his congregation: "I will tell you now that any member of this Church who agrees with Lennon's statement—or who even goes to see the Beatles when they appear here—will be recommended by me for revocation of membership in this church." (*L'Osservatore Romano*, the official Vatican newspaper, printed a terse Beatles scolding from the Pope himself: "Some subjects must not be dealt with profanely, even in the world of beatniks.")

In Georgia, one community gathered around a cluster of garbage cans labeled PLACE BEATLE TRASH HERE, into which angry citizens tossed their records. In Texas, a town rented a wood chipper for the albums. WAQY in Birmingham, Alabama, banned all Beatles music from the air, and thirty-five radio stations in the South's Bible Belt followed suit. Tommy Charles, WAQY's station manager, staged a Beatles record-burning bonfire. And as the angry Averages threw Beatles souvenir hankies and wallets and wigs and records into the roaring bonfires in small towns around the land, they felt cleansed again.

If anyone wanted confirmation of the depravity rampant in the land, they found it in August 1969, when a band of Yippies assaulted yet another icon of goodness, not quite in Jesus's league but high-ranking nonetheless. Two hundred and fifty Yippies, yelling obscenities, invaded Disneyland!

They rioted on Main Street and occupied Tom Sawyer Island. Guards were forced to evacuate all visitors. "Get out of here and leave Disneyland alone!" shouted one elderly woman, shaking her fists in the air at the longhairs as guards herded her out the gate. "Four hundred bucks blown! That's how much it cost me to bring my family out here," cried a dad in frustration. Many guests joined with police in trying to rout the invaders. The Los Angeles *Herald-Examiner* reported: "One man grabbed the hair of one youth and it turned out to be a wig."

From that ignominious day on, all men with long hair were banned from the Magic Kingdom. Marketing director Jack Lindquist said that the ban

would be accompanied by "really tough" grooming standards, thus ensuring that Disneyland would remain "the happiest place on earth."

With Yippies rampaging at Disneyland and antichrists infiltrating rock and roll, and the press doting over every minute of it, Mr. and Mrs. Average desperately needed to feel they weren't alone. It went against the essential inertia of their nature to march or demonstrate, but many gathered up their nerve, took the flag out of the attic and brought it to the patriotic dry cleaner who boasted WE CLEAN AMERICAN FLAGS FREE, and marched into the streets, waving Old Glory to declare their solidarity.

"This is not a protest rally," explained Julie James, an eighteeen-year-old participant in the teenage Rally for Decency in Miami. "We're not against something. We're for something." Julie and her friend Mike Levesque were outraged after Jim Morrison of the Doors exposed himself during a Miami concert; so they organized a rally in the Orange Bowl to support a "teenage crusade for decency in entertainment." The rally featured three-minute speeches by young people about such subjects as God, parents, and patriotism. Jackie Gleason, Anita Bryant, and the singing quartet the Lettermen cheered them on. The American Legion supplied ten thousand small American flags for everyone to wave.

Decency rallies were fine, as were efforts such as those of private citizen Nancy Palm (known to friends as "Napalm"), who personally collected eight thousand signatures in support of Nixon's war policies. But such accomplishments seemed puny compared with the great engine of protest mustered by the other side. What Mr. and Mrs. Average needed were tough heroes to lead the fight against encroaching anarchy.

Enter Ronald Reagan, who got elected governor of California in 1966 by talking tough about University of California protesters: "You don't negotiate with student groups," he announced. "If they don't abide by the rules, they can pack their bags, get out, and seek their education elsewhere." As governor, he became a hero to Mr. and Mrs. Average by squashing protest with righteous vindictiveness. After one student was killed and several wounded in a pitched battle over a "People's Park" in Berkeley in 1969, Reagan was told that the blood was on his hands. "Fine," he is reported to have replied. "I'll wash it off with Boraxo." Reagan's subsequent triumph in the eighties has been seen by some as a repudiation of the sixties. In fact, the Reagan presidency was a triumph of what Mr. and Mrs. Average, the forgotten sixties people, believed all along.

Spiro T. Agnew took upon himself the mantle of Average leadership, speaking for a conceptual constituency developed by Republicans during the 1968 presidential campaign: the Silent Majority. A national unknown when he was picked as Nixon's running mate, Agnew made himself the great mouthpiece of all the Averages who felt they weren't being treated with respect. With the help of speech writer William Safire, Agnew spoke in flurries of alliteration, fuming against antiwar protesters as an "effete corps of impudent snobs," against the press as "nattering nabobs of negativity," and against the Scranton Commission's report on Kent State—which called the killing of the four students "inexcusable"—as "pablum for permissiveness."

During the 1968 campaign, Hawthorn Books published a volume of Mr. Agnew's beliefs, with the portentous title *Where He Stands: The Life and Convictions of Spiro T. Agnew.* In a manifesto that surely cheered the soul of every Average voter who read it, the about-to-be vice-president comes out foursquare in favor of what he believes is the true bedrock of American character: dullness.

> When we win, we're just liable to bring back into American life a lot of the things that the devotees of the so-called "new politics" consider dull. Dull things like patriotism. Dull things like incentive. Dull things like the respect for law and a concern for a greater justice for all Americans. In fact things could get so dull that some of the little old ladies who wear sneakers to get a fast start on criminals might go back to wearing high heels.

Agnew posed for the press with his wife, Judy, and his daughters, Pam and Susan, whose matching hairdos and pert frocks made them Lennon Sister look-alikes. Mrs. Agnew is a perfect citizen of her husband's dull new world. The book's introduction says:

> Childbearing and the years have added a few pounds to Judy Agnew, but she accepts them with a wry equanimity. At 5′4″ she weights 140 pounds and finds dieting a bore. She eats sparingly at lunch, perhaps a chicken sandwich, and when there were fewer demands on her time she belonged to the Swim-and-Slim class at the Y.M.C.A. Dieting would probably be a lot easier if the Governor didn't enjoy her excellent spaghetti and if they didn't mark celebrations with spicy pizza.

On Veterans Day in November 1969, a month after the biggest antiwar moratorium yet, *Time* reported: "Once again, on main streets and Broadway, in village halls, statehouses and the national capital, at coliseums, campuses and churches, Americans turned out to march, argue and declaim over Vietnam." The difference was that these marchers were the Silent Majority—silent no more—sick of protest and ready to support Nixon and the Vietnam War to victory or death.

The idea behind the "protest against protest" was to cancel out the antiwar activity of the month before. But it was no contest. The Silent Majority attracted nowhere near the numbers of people who had come out for the moratorium. "Nixon's Americans seem to lack the verve, organization—and spare time—of his critics," *Time* explained. Bob Hope, honorary chairman of what was supposed to have been National Unity Week, grumbled, "It's pretty hard for good, nice people to demonstrate."

Mr. Hope knew his constituency: Mr. and Mrs. Average hated demonstrating, even on behalf of what they believed in. The truth is, they were as uncomfortable around wild-eyed hawks as they were around peacenik doves. What they really craved was for life to simply return to normal. They wanted a world expunged of not only hippies, drugs, and free love but also of crazed right-wing comedians and rallies of any kind that forced them out of their easy chairs. They wanted to be average again!

One place where they had once been certain that the world's prob-

*Lying back in a slack-jawed stupor on a plush recliner was a pleasure especially suited to sixties people who weren't inclined to march or protest.*

lems would never encroach upon the placid Eden they desired was deep down inside the safety of a good, solid fallout shelter. Before the decade's social chaos overwhelmed them, many Averages believed their bomb shelters were impregnable security.

Encouraged by leaders from Ann Landers (whom *Time* called "an all-out advocate of home shelters") to John F. Kennedy (who declared it "every citizen's duty to protect his family in case of attack," and who brought nuclear brinkmanship to its most excruciating moment in the Cuban missile crisis of 1962), Mr. and Mrs. Average were easy to convince that a concrete bunker, topped with twenty-eight inches of pit-run gravel, was the only way to ensure the continuance of Average life. Companies that sold fallout shelters and survival supplies marketed the idea as the only polite alternative to living in a public shelter on a dingy cot next to perfect strangers. In the early sixties, having a shelter at home protected you and yours from everybody else.

Properly stocked, the family fallout shelter could make World War III a mere annoyance in the comfy Average family routine. The 1960 Office of Civil and Defense Mobilization's shelter supply checklist included a two-week supply of paper plates, cups, and napkins (just like a picnic!); a battery-operated radio with the CONELRAD frequencies marked; flashlights and electric lanterns; a ten-gallon, lidded garbage pail to serve as a toilet; lots of reading material; and educational games for the children. "To break the monotony," the Civil Defense Office notes, "it may be necessary to invent tasks that will keep the family busy."

In a 1961 *Time* cover story called "The Sheltered Life," Nobel prize–winning physicist Willard Libby said that his shelter contained a vat of sleeping pills so he and his family could snooze till the radiation went away. *Time* warned readers against bogus supplies such as radiation salve (designed to make fallout ricochet off the body), antiradiation pills, and a $21.95 "fallout suit" (for quick trips outside the shelter) that "provides no more protection against radiation than a raincoat." The big issue when stocking the shelter was guns: do you keep one on hand to kill your neighbor if he tries to get into the shelter when the bombs start to fall? The Reverend L. C. McHugh, editor of the Jesuit magazine *America*, said yes—shoot him just like you would any trespasser.

*The Family Fallout Shelter*, published by the Office of Civil and Defense Mobilization, contains detailed plans for five shelters, from the inexpensive Basement Concrete Block to the elaborate six-person Underground Concrete Shelter with baffle walls, centrifugal blower, termite shield, and twelve-gauge corrugated metal door to keep out intruders. The whole book, including plans, is a mere thirty-one pages long, suggesting that a fallout shelter is hardly more complicated to build than a backyard barbecue pit—a pleasant do-it-yourself project for the weekend hobbyist.

*In this well-stocked bomb shelter, the Rosenfelds of Mount Vernon, New York, were prepared for a nuclear holocaust.*

If the homeowner wasn't handy with tools, he could buy a prefab modular shelter from the Armco Steel Corporation of San Francisco for $2,800. Lone Star Steel of Dallas offered a deluxe model for $2,550, which featured a trompe l'oeil picture window on the wall, revealing a two-dimensional verdant landscape. Top-of-the-line shelters were available with pool tables and wine cellars.

Chuck West, author of *The Fall-Out Shelter Handbook*, had a way of making nuclear war seem a lot like a camping expedition. He suggests that holocaust survivors will have bales of fun learning how to make bread "Indian style" on a hot rock, how to tell one's bearings by looking at the constellations, and how to make medicinal teas from herbs and roots like catnip and sassafras.

At the 1961 Texas State Fair, the fallout-shelter exhibition drew bigger crowds than the prize-cattle exhibit. Home economists gave out cheerful recipe booklets with lists of foods appropriate for life beneath the surface of the earth. Margaret Moore, nutritionist for the Louisiana Board of Health, offered some surprising advice: "Pickles will help ease thirst, and canned vegetables are an extra source of liquid." *The Fall-Out Shelter Handbook* oddly suggested these flatulent dishes to the close-quartered post–World War III underground gourmet: pork and beans, baked kidney beans, and chile con carne.

Fallout shelters had great appeal to Mr. and Mrs. Average because of the Averages' unswerving trustful nature. If they were properly prepared, nuclear war might not be so bad. Creating a cozy temporary home that would withstand a five-megaton blast was not out of character for people whose lives were devoted to the pursuit of normalcy. If they could keep their family together, even in a concrete crockpot, they were happy. Being a family always made them happy.

The old-fashioned family was a vital touchstone for the Averages, especially when other people in the sixties started talking about new-style families, like tribal hippies and Hell's Angels. No thanks! To Mr. and Mrs. Average, family meant Mom and Dad and a mess of kids.

And so to relax at home, they followed the exploits of families just like themselves on TV or in magazines. They adored the Lennon Sisters, the King Family, the Nelsons, the Cleavers, the Cartwrights, and cartoon families of the past and the future, the Flintstones and the Jetsons.

"The Flintstones" was the first all-animation show to run in prime time, from 1960 to 1966. It is about a suburban family just like Mr. and Mrs. Average, except for the twist that they live in the Stone Age. Fred and Wilma Flintstone, their baby daughter, Pebbles, along with neighbors Barney and Betty Rubble and their son, Bamm Bamm, ride in stone cars, speak on stone telephones, play "rock" music on a turntable that uses a prehistoric bird's beak for a needle, and, according to the liner notes from the record album *Songs of the Flintstones*, have "all the modern problems of suburbia, including bowling night, home swimming pools, baby sitting, dogs, etc." Fred is a construction worker; the motto of the company where he works is "Own Your Own Cave and Be Secure."

Although critics initially compared "The Flintstones" with the fifties TV series "The Honeymooners," the correlation was superficial. The Flintstones are Averageness personified. The Cramdens were way below that. Ralph and Alice had no kids; they didn't own a home; they lived not in the suburbs but in Brooklyn, on the edge of poverty; and they enjoyed none of the middle-class amenities that make the Flintstones' life so amusing. Fred has no Ralph Cramden dreams of glory; he just wants to enjoy his leisure time. He is emotionally cruder than Cramden (as befits a Neanderthal); and his comfortable wife, Wilma, is a lot more like Donna Reed than like long-suffering Alice Cramden.

Based on the popularity of "The Flintstones," Hanna-Barbera launched "The Jetsons" in 1962. The Jetsons are just like the Flintstones, except they live in the twenty-first century. Instead of a Flintstonian backdrop of dinosaurs and caves, the Jetsons lived out their commonplace days amidst rocket ships, boomerang-shaped coffee tables, and self-propelled vacuum cleaners.

The "gimmick" of both "The Flintstones" and "The Jetsons" is that both families are absolutely average! Each of the characters is a dull, predictable cliché; the joy of the shows, for Mr. and Mrs. Average, is seeing Fred and Wilma Flintstone or George and Jane Jetson make a bizarre world into a completely familiar, middle-class one. Thus, the Averages could bask in the monotony of their own lives playing out in centuries past and future, the implication being that civilization as they knew it, in all its comfortable mediocrity, would never end.

The TV western best-loved by Mr. and Mrs. Average was a family show, too. On the air from 1959 through 1973, "Bonanza" was the top-rated television program of the sixties, number one between 1964 and 1967. Viewers tuned in each Sunday night to watch the tribulations of the Cartwright family, who lived in Virginia City, Nevada, on a thousand-square-mile ranch called the Ponderosa. Lorne Greene starred as Ben Cartwright, a widower; Pernell Roberts as his oldest son, Adam; Dan Blocker as the robust Hoss; and Michael Landon as the youngest and cutest son, Little Joe. The Cartwright boys were half brothers (Ben had been married a number of times to women who kept getting themselves killed by Indians or rampaging horses), but the family glue was strong.

When it started its run in September 1959, "Bonanza" was not an immediate hit, despite its being the first western to be televised in color. Nor were the Cartwrights a particularly happy family. The boys feuded furiously among themselves in the first two seasons, mostly over the fact that Adam's mother was a Yankee, Little Joe's a southern lady, and Hoss's a Swede. In 1961, the quarrels began to die down (eventually to be forgotten), and "Bonanza" moved to Sunday—family night—as a replacement for "The Dinah Shore Chevy Show." Ratings soared.

Of all TV families—real, western, or cartoon—none was more beloved by Mr. and Mrs. Average than the Lennon Sisters, the four beauties who got their start singing on "The Lawrence Welk Show" in 1955. The lovely Peggy, Kathy, Janet, and Dianne were not the only stars of the show (there were accordionist Myron Floren, tenor Jim Roberts, and Artistic Aladdin, a violinist, among others), but no one else had the Average appeal of the four Lennon girls. Their charm was that although they were celebrities, their lives were utterly plebeian, uninteresting, and devoid of glamour.

While movie and TV gossip magazines played fast and loose with the high-flown intrigues of Liz Taylor and Mia Farrow, cover stories on the Lennon Sisters bore titles like "When We Get Pregnant." In 1966, *Screenland* ran an exclusive story describing just how much all the Lennons loved having babies. Peggy Lennon reveals, "I have a very easy time when I'm carrying my babies.

*The Lennon Sisters sing as their little brother prays on "The Lawrence Welk Show."*

I'm a little morning sick the first couple of months, but after that I'm fine." Dianne divulges, "My first three months I'm sick, but my delivery is very easy."

Staunch Catholics, the Lennons posed kneeling in prayer at Sunday Mass, their neatly pouffed hairdos covered with lace mantillas. They smiled holding their newborn infants aloft, or cooking Impossible Cheeseburger Pie for hubby after rushing home from a hard day with Lawrence Welk. Among the gossip-magazine ads for U.S. Savings Bonds and Sit-and-Soak toilet seats for hemorrhoid sufferers, the Lennons enthralled their fans with the modest dramas of their days. Readers learned that a Lennon baby was almost born with the umbilical cord wrapped around its neck; that Dianne Lennon, although a big star, married Dick Gass, who worked for the telephone company; and that sister Kathy had an ovarian cyst.

In 1965, the King Family, a sprawling clan of thirty-six, made a bid for capturing a piece of the Lennons' turf. The Kings were catapulted to fame after a smash performance at Brigham Young University, which led to an appearance on other variety shows, and then to their own TV show. The most

*The S & H Green Stamp Catalogue offered stamp-savers all the wonderful things in this living room.*

remarkable aspect of the King Family was that none of them was named King. They were all relatives of William King Driggs, who had organized a family chorale in the twenties. "The King Family Show" featured massive group singing, Alvino Rey and his talking guitar, a "Family Circle" segment in which family happiness was celebrated in poetry and songs, and a sign-off each week by the whole family, from seven months to seventy-nine years old, singing "Love at Home." Despite a massive letter-writing campaign from viewers who loved it, "The King Family Show" was canceled after one season: it got licked in the ratings by "I Dream of Jeannie."

If families were so great, it follows that marriages were the high points of the Averages' lives. They went in for the biggest affairs they could afford, with multitiered cakes such as "The Faithful Love," described thusly in a contemporary book of cake decoration: "richly formal, joyfully reverent, a tribute to love and religious devotion. The bride and groom pledge their lives to one another beneath a golden crucifix, while cherubs frolic and angels play their heavenly harps in celebration. 200 servings."

The great gladness of a wedding for the newlywed Averages was that it signified that they could begin stocking their homes with all the things that made them happy. An American Solid Maple Living Room from the S&H Green Stamp catalog, for example: "ever popular because warmth and comfort never go out of style! Homey-ness in every detail. Just looking at it makes you comfortable!" Comfort was what every Mr. Average sought.

As for Mrs. Average, she dreamed of the day when she could put a Montgomery Ward Learn-to-Play Airline Electric Chord Organ in the corner of the living room, next to the matching Kroehler Mr. & Mrs. Lounge Chairs and the five-piece Imperial Converta-Cart ensemble featuring four spacious TV tray tables fashioned in Leatherette vinyl and accented with Golden Decorator design.

Mr. and Mrs. Average loved knickknacks because they gave the home personality. Be it a paint-by-number set, a pair of Ceramastone Lincoln bookends featuring replicas of the famous President sitting in his Lincoln Memorial chair, or a statue of *Bold Cat* (an elongated Giacometti-like tabby), artistic touches were the mark of Average people who were proud to call their house a home. The best knickknacks were the ones that did something. Like the Yosemite. Offered by the Sears catalog, the Yosemite is a forty-inch-high indoor waterfall that promised "cascades of tumbling water rushing down five levels. It duplicates nature in both sight and sound like no other man-made rock creation we've ever seen."

"Man-made rock creation": there you have a sense of what made Mr. and Mrs. Average truly proud. *Man-made rock.* Unlike nature-loving hippies, the Averages of the world relished synthetic things. They were signs of progress, of man's triumph over nature. Yosemite was better than real rocks in the same way Tang breakfast drink was better than ordinary orange juice. You see, orange juice came from an orange, which anyone could simply pick from a tree or buy at the grocery store for a dime. Tang breakfast drink, a dehydrated powder that was mixed with water to create an orange-colored liquid, had been formulated for the *astronauts* by the *space-program scientists* and cost *millions of dollars* to develop! There was no question which one a proud citizen of the forward-looking sixties would prefer.

Unnatural products made their purchasers happy to be modern. Why buy a dirt-caked, asymmetrical Christmas tree when the Montgomery Ward catalog offered four different artificial ones, from the $8.99 Aluminum Frosty Pine with crinkle finish and embossed foil needles to the top-of-the-line $19.95 lifelike Polyethylene Scotch Pine with white needles for snow-tip effect and plastic pinecones? For homeowners completely fed up with the inadequacies of nature, Montgomery Ward also offered Natural Look Instant Shrubbery for the yard, thus eliminating boring jobs like pruning and watering.

Nowhere was the infatuation with better-than-natural products more dramatically reflected than in the clothes that Mr. and Mrs. Average began to wear in the sixties. The 1969 Sears catalog offered ladies' shorts made from "double-knit Dacron polyester perma-press" material, a worthy coordinate for a poncho made of "white modacrylic pile on a polyester back." Men's clothing was equally not-of-this-earth, available in eerie shimmering shades of chartreuse, rust, coral, and oxblood. The S&H Green Stamp catalog features one page crowded with a mesh Dacron and polyester sport shirt, a "drizzler ram jet" winter jacket guaranteed to be wash-and-wearable, a storm coat with full acrylic liner and nylon hood, and golf slacks made of Dacron polyester with a tuckaway towel loop.

Do you see why Mr. and Mrs. Average were confounded by the upside-down sixties counterculture? Malcontents like the hippies wanted to reject good modern things like perma-press fabrics, polyethylene Christmas trees, and Cheez Whiz cheese food product; and they espoused such obsolescent notions as weaving, growing one's own soybeans, and wearing leather sandals instead of Corfam brogues. Mr. and Mrs. Average were the up-to-the-minute ones! They loved TV dinners and remote-control devices to make life easier. They gobbled up deluxe garage-door openers, ridable lawn mowers, laundry detergents with miraculous powers, and fabrics that practically ironed themselves.

Because they believed in progress, Mr. and Mrs. Average fell in love with the astronauts and embraced outer-space exploration with all the boosterism they brought to each week's episode of "Bonanza." Space was a lot like the Ponderosa: a place where good, moral men still did heroic deeds. As so much that the Averages believed in began to unravel in the sixties, the space program seemed like one legacy of better times that had not gone sour.

For patriotic Americans, it was a dramatic, come-from-behind story. In 1961, when John Kennedy had pledged to put a man on the moon, the U.S.A. was far behind the Russians in the "space race." After Alan Shepard's quick ride into the stratosphere in May 1961 (well behind the Russians, who had already orbited the earth), *Time* patriotically saluted the first free man in space by hoping that "as long as the U.S. produces such explorers . . . the architects of man's expansion may well be Americans."

Sure enough, Americans began to pull ahead. After John Glenn orbited in 1962, he and fellow astronauts were welcomed in New York with a ticker-tape parade, bands playing, church bells pealing, and cheering that *Life* said "approached the decibel force of a rocket at liftoff." Awed by the sight, Glenn declared, "It gives me a kick to see so many of the schoolchildren on the street waving the flag and being proud of it."

It wasn't just chauvinistic patriotism that made the Averages so enamored of outer space. It was the idea that the sky was the last frontier; and just like the old frontier in the west, it was a place where all the solid values of bravery and courage were still unquestioned. America's trajectory towards the moon in the sixties confirmed Mr. and Mrs. Average's unshakable faith that human life was a march of progress towards an inevitably better future. "With each success, the universe will grow smaller," *Time* predicted in 1961. "But man's life will grow larger, expanding with infinite promise."

The astronauts would have been heroes for no reason other than their fantastically good grooming. Short of a Big Ten football team or a platoon of Marines, it would have been hard to find sixties men who looked so square. Quiet, soft-spoken, bland as butter, WASP men with short hair: they were Mickey Mantles in silver suits. Like the Green Berets, they were disciplined to a fare-thee-well and they were fearless, but they had none of the Green Berets' troublesome aspect of being trained killers.

There wasn't an oddball to be found among the seven men NASA introduced as the first team of astronauts on April 9, 1959 (unless you count the fact that Wally Schirra, alone among the seven, did not have a crew cut). "Ordinary supermen" is how one Air Force general described them. The semiofficial propaganda put out by *Life* magazine (to which they sold their exclusive story) dotes endlessly on the astronauts' character—not only on the qualities they shared but on their healthy, wholesome individuality. According to the editor of *We Seven*, a book written by the astronauts with the help of *Life* in 1962, Alan Shepard had "sharp wit." Gus Grissom was "a little bear of a man." John Glenn was "sternly self-disciplined." Deke Slayton was "taciturn." Scott Carpenter was "graceful as a gazelle (though he is bashful about doing a dance like the Twist in public because he feels it might not conform to the proper image of the Astronauts)" Wally Schirra (with the long—inch-and-a-half-long—hair) was "the most naturally jovial and outgoing." And Gordon Cooper, Gordo to his friends, had a "sardonic sense of humor."

"What makes an astronaut?" asked *Man in Space*, a children's book published in 1965:

> At first [people thought] that unsophisticated Eskimos, or other-worldly Buddhist monks might make the best crew members—mentally speaking, that is. Or midgets, because they take up less space. One researcher even nominated people with schizophrenia, a mental disorder, because he felt that anyone who wants to fly off into space must be a strange bird indeed.

*Man in Space* reassures the young reader that in fact, astronauts are as normal a group as could be found: Marine officers, military test pilots, clean-cut white men who are "well balanced, not supermen, just a cut above average."

The important thing about them, the trait stressed in every story about the magnificent seven in the early sixties, was that despite their individual personalities, these guys were team players. Back in 1959, Dr. T. Keith Glennan of NASA somewhat smugly described the unveiling of the astronauts as a "disillusionment" for American youth, because all seven were "mature men, all happily married, family men, serious, studious, and highly trained. . . . There was not a daredevil jet jockey—a Buck Rogers type—in the group. They are men of vision but with a practical, hard-headed approach to the difficult job ahead." These were heroes Mr. and Mrs. Average could truly love!

It was easy for the Averages to like outer space. But many of the sixties' other signs of modernity had to get filtered through a safety screen before they were suitable for Average consumption. For instance, Arthur Murray's album *Music for Dancing: The Twist* presented the elder statesman of dance himself ("As seen by 40,000,000 people on TV!") explaining the twist in his familiar step-by-step manner, providing nice, safe versions he called the Huckle-buck and Honeysuckle Rose.

Another album, *Organ Freakout!*, offered an utterly nerdish musical happening: "The Swinginest Hammond Organ Album Since the Birth of Psychedelia," with selections including "Tennessee Waltz Frug" and "Old Time Religion Gone New." The album cover warns that when "the amps start cookin—look out, baby—it's an organ freakout!"

Mr. and Mrs. Average even found a modern rebel they could like. Bursting into national consciousness in 1966 with his husky voice reciting the forlorn words to "Stanyon Street," Rod McKuen was the maverick poet of a middle class who saw themselves becoming underdogs in a world too rapidly changing. "Poignant, lonely, somewhat the worse for wear, but filled with the triumph of the human spirit" is how his work is described on the liner notes of an album called *Very Warm*. Unlike the Averages themselves, McKuen was a drifter, and he traveled a hard gravel road through the offbeat side of life. But Mr. and Mrs. Average could appreciate his brand of independence. He was like a good old-fashioned lonesome cowboy, not some spoiled, raving hippie. He was a good guy: "You can't build anything by tearing it down," he said about campus radicals. As for long hair, "It covers up our eyes and makes us unable to see the world." McKuen sold 50 million records of his poetry and songs between 1966 and 1969.

The Averages also liked some of the Beatles' songs—the pretty ones, anyway, like "Michelle," when they heard it on the elevator in the department store, or when the band at the wedding reception played it, nice and slow. And perhaps a few deep thinkers among the Averages appreciated what is surely one of the strangest albums of all time, *Sebastian Cabot, Actor, Reads Bob Dylan, Poet*. Accompanied by quiet harps and strings in the background, the avuncular star of television's "A Family Affair" recites the lyrics to Dylan songs such as "The Times They Are A-Changin' " and "Like a Rolling Stone." Mr. Cabot's evaluation of Dylan in the liner notes includes this thought-provoking reflection about "Quit Your Lowdown Ways": "If Emmet Kelly could speak in his act, he'd love to do it, I'm sure."

Mr. and Mrs. Average were hep to the folk-music craze, too, but their folk music was not exactly Pete Seeger or Bob Dylan or even Theodore Bikel or Harry Belafonte. They preferred the Up With People singers, a troupe of peppy youngsters who sang ballads with titles like "The Happy Song" and "Freedom Isn't Free." Up With People was folk singing the way Mr. and Mrs. Average liked it: big, blaring, and endorsed by John Wayne, who declared, "There is a power in it which makes you want to get to your feet and start doing something for your country."

Up With People was like a musical Olympic team, one hundred strong in each of several touring companies that roamed the land from the New York World's Fair to the Moral Re-Armament Demonstration for Modernizing America, broadcasting their message of good cheer at mega-audiences of tens of thousands. Their well-scrubbed faces were of all creeds and colors. Happy white American boys stood arm in arm with pretty brown Mexican girls, who linked hands with wholesome African boys and smiling Asian lasses, who sang to the strum of guitars played by magnificent handsome Danes. The Up With People singers were of such good cheer that they opened *both* the Democratic and the Republican conventions in 1964.

It made Mr. and Mrs. Average feel good to see such nice kids riding on floats in the presidential inaugural parade and performing "Life Is Getting

Better Every Day," dressed in wrinkle-free blazers (boys) and flannel jumpers (girls). It assured them that they were "with it"; that the average future they wanted was in safe, average hands; and that they were free of prejudice and tolerated all peoples, just so long as they dressed neatly and behaved themselves and sang songs with a cheerful message and didn't rock the boat.

Rousing as the Up With People singers were, they didn't quite tap into the basic inertia at the soul of Mr. and Mrs. Average.

Pleasant music was fine, moon landings were inspiring, that war in Southeast Asia should be won; but the one thing in the world that most noticeably motivated Mr. and Mrs. Average was the pursuit of relaxation. Hippies were looking for a high, Yippies fomented revolution, and folkniks wanted everyone to be free; all Mr. and Mrs. Average really wanted was a two-week vacation. Just like generations of Averages before them, they liked to see the world and bring back souvenirs. In the sixties, for the first time, they could do it in their Winnebago motor home.

*The Driftwood Book*, published in 1960 and reissued in 1966, suggested that the hunt for the perfect piece of driftwood was itself a reason to vacation. Of course, it was too taxing to go to the beach to look for one's objet trouvé. The ideal place to go hunting was a driftwood store, as described by author Mary E. Thompson: "The answer to a driftwood lover's dream is to suddenly come upon a shop with a huge pile of beautiful grey driftwood pieces gleaming in the sun. I shall never forget the thrill when I saw such a collection on the ground outside a little shop in Miami Beach."

The joy of traveling for Mr. and Mrs. Average was to replicate their beloved home environment everywhere they went. A motor home or trailer was the perfect vehicle, as it could be decorated just like home, with cute net curtains in the john and knickknacks safely affixed to the walls. The outside of the trailer had room for reams of bumper stickers announcing that the Averages had been to Raoul's Reptileland, Petrified Creatures Park, and Ruby Falls and had seen for themselves the blind albino shrimp at the Luray Caverns in Virginia. Driving a one-piece recreational vehicle was even better than hauling a trailer, because it did not separate the car from the living quarters: you drove from inside your living quarters: you drove from inside your living room, looking out a windshield that was a lot like a bay window.

One reassuring thing about trailering was that there was no need to eat disturbing food in strange restaurants, as home-style meals could be made in the tiny galley of the trailer. Arlene Strom explained how to do it in *Cooking on Wheels*, published in 1970. Mrs. Strom, a clergyman's wife and a veteran of over one hundred thousand miles of trailering in the sixties, collected her menus at "trailer wives' coffee klatches," where favorite dishes are exchanged. Trailer cuisine was just the kind of cooking food Mr. and Mrs. Average liked best: bland, fast, and convenient. *Cooking on Wheels* is filled with recipes for Quick Instant Party Potatoes, Jell-O Cake, Chow Mein Noodle Cookies, and Busy-Day Cheesecake. Mrs. Strom's Trailer Stew practically cooks itself:

### TRAILER STEW

2 tablespoons butter
2 pounds ground beef
½ package onion soup mix
4 medium carrots
4 medium potatoes
½ package frozen green beans
½ package frozen corn
salt and pepper to taste

Heat butter in a heavy skillet or kettle over your campfire or stove in the trailer and brown the meat. Add soup mix. Add raw vegetables first, covering with water and cooking covered until vegetables are almost tender. Then add frozen vegetables and cook until all are tender. Serve in bowls.

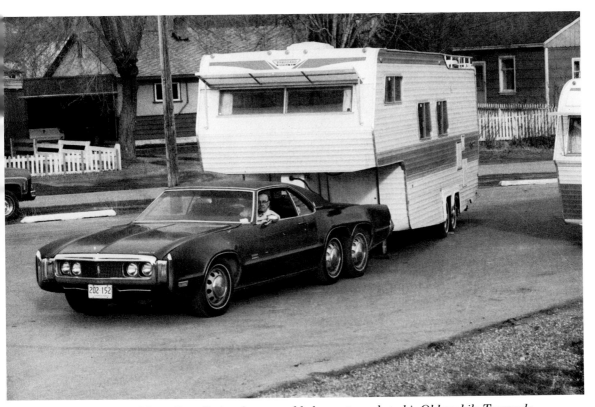

*Cecil Poston of Moose Jaw, Saskatchewan, added an extra axle to his Oldsmobile Toronado so it could pull his trailer with less sway in side winds.*

"Adventure" and "car travel" were synonyms to the Averages, and even fun excursions near home were seldom done on foot. Strenuous physical activity was not suited to Mr. and Mrs. Average, whose life full of modern conveniences was designed to avoid all expenditure of unnecessary energy. Anyway, walking anywhere would have made them unbearably sweaty in their claustrophobic synthetic-fiber clothes; it would make Mrs. Average's hairdo go limp, and Mr. Average's bunion-ridden feet ache. Steering the car was the one rewarding physical activity. Everybody piled in, with Dad in the driver's seat piloting the family in kingly fashion down the road.

One of the great places for a short car trip and a family adventure was McDonald's, which by 1965 was ten years old and had sold its first billion hamburgers. Mr. and Mrs. Average had to admire such corporate might. That number *one billion* rolled as deliciously on their tongues as the milk shakes. By purchasing a burger and fries, they became part of an all-American success story.

In celebration of its tenth anniversary, McDonald's published a book for children called *Let's Eat Out!*, the story of a happy Average family: Mom, Dad, and their two kids, plus a visiting friend—little Hans from Germany. "Each weekend," *Let's Eat Out!* explains, Tom and Sue (the kids) take turns "choosing one good thing of many that the family could do together." It's Tom's turn; and being a patriotic young boy, he chooses to show Hans "an American treat." The family hops in its "little black car" (which is drawn as a monstrous tail-finned thing that looks like a whale) and, with Tom giving directions, drives clean past zoos, museums, Sung Lu's Chinese restaurant, Tony's Italian restaurant, Pierre's French restaurant; and just as Mom, Dad, and Sue are getting awfully cranky about where Tom is leading them, they see McDonald's glowing in the distance underneath its golden arches.

Hans is mesmerized by the sight of the food being prepared. His eyes pop to see twenty-four hamburgers cooked all at once. "That's pretty American," Tom explains. "It's called mass-production."

After the happy family has eaten its fill of hamburgers and french fries, the author of *Let's Eat Out!*, listed as John Jones, breaks free of the story in a fit of hamburger-induced ecstasy. As Hans and the family head home, Mr. Jones addresses the reader directly: "A billion hamburgers have been served. That's a lot of hamburgers. Just how many is it?" he asks the reader. "It's a hundred thousand head of cattle," he answers back. "If these hamburgers were laid end to end they would measure 68,428 miles. Shot into orbit they would form two complete rings around the earth. And if they settled in one place they would fill Yankee Stadium." Enthusiasm unchecked, John Jones unleashes a corker: "It's enough flour for buns to cover the state of Pennsylvania."

That night, Tom and Sue and little Hans and Mom and Dad, their bellies full of burgers, drift off to sleep in their chenille-covered beds, happy to be average in a land where people of all races dress as neatly as the Up With People singers, happy about the brave astronauts and the billion burgers sold and the bomb shelter in the basement that will save their way of life.

No sixties people were more optimistic than they. Despite longhairs who laughed at them, and news reports of crazy malcontents rioting in the streets, they carried on being absolutely average. They endured the chaos of the decade with their eyes to the sky, inspired by their flag waving high on its aluminum pole with the replica colonial eagle and by rocket ships blazing trails into the future above their split-level home. And they dreamed of their next vacation to that little driftwood shop in Miami Beach, and their car trip through a state as big as Pennsylvania covered border to border with hamburger buns.

# INDEX

Numbers in *italics* indicate illustrations.

# PHOTOGRAPHIC CREDITS

A NOTE ON THE TYPE

The text of this book was set in Walbaum, a typeface designed by Justus Erich Walbaum in 1810. Walbaum was active as a type founder in Goslar and Weimar from 1799 to 1836. Though letterforms in this face are patterned closely on the "modern" cuts then being made by Giambattista Bodoni and the Didot family, they are of a far less rigid cut. Indeed, it is the slight but pleasing irregularities in the cut that give this face its human quality and account for its wide appeal. Even in appearance, Walbaum jumps boundaries, having a more French than German look.

Composed by Dix Type, Inc., Syracuse, New York
Printed and bound by Kingsport Press, Inc., Kingsport, Tennessee
Designed by Iris Weinstein